So

The Life and Passions of Aggie O'Hara

To Mable & Walter Grasley — Love Aggie O'Hara

Janice Brown

Smiles & thanks
Janice Brown.

Published by Seaforth Management Ltd.

Copyright © 2013 Janice Brown

All rights reserved.

ISBN-10: 1490377190
ISBN-13: 978-1490377193

Someday House
The Life and Passions of Aggie O'Hara

Author's Notes and Acknowledgements:

On a sun-shining day when everything seemed easy, Aggie and I gabbed on the phone about the missing eighteen years, the gap between when I first met her and when we saw each other again, when I married her son.

Stories of her early life tumbled out and it struck me—if I do not record the amusing, inspiring, and sometimes horrifying stories—who will? They are perfect examples of the often-difficult climb towards an inner dream, and staying true to your own vision of perfection, not someone else's.

Aggie is an attractive woman with a mind as quick as a spring-loaded trap and she quickly learned what all smart girls know. To become adept at intricate jobs or in real estate, she only took the advice of those who were successful.

In this collection of stories, we share her desire to tell the truth regarding the character-building events that include violence, laughter, determination, and a lot of dancing.

As news spread that Aggie was having a book written about her life, some family members included details previously unknown to others and they were usually surprised and delighted to learn of them. As if striking oil once a gusher breaches, my pen flew over my notepad during lengthy phone calls and most characters desired identification, but some did not, and I respect their privacy.

This book, a creative biography based on the recollections of Aggie and her family, illustrates Aggie's struggles, passions, and loves along the way. Her never-failing focus to achieve a goal, and to grab the best life has to offer while she is doing that, has inspired three generations.

I gratefully acknowledge the guidance from writer and editor, Joyce Gram, at Gram Editing Services, the first brave soul to have a go at the book in its raw entirety. I appreciate Maple Ridge Writers whose combined skills, companionship, and generosity did their best to keep me on track along the way; the creative critique at Port Moody Kyle Center with Eileen Kernaghan, and Golden Ears Writers at "the ACT" in Maple Ridge.

I thank my daughter, Arlene Hansen, for reading with savvy eyes, and foremost is my husband, Ron Lauria, without whose contribution the project would have been impossible.

Janice Brown

Someday House

The Life and Passions of Aggie O'Hara

Chapter	Title	Page
1	O'Hara—O'Hell	5
2	This Day	17
3	Rosie the Riveter	30
4	Someday House	41
5	Boy in a Box	54
6	Small Mercies	58
7	A Man's Man	66
8	Broken	80
9	Hello Suburbia	85
10	No Surrender	92
11	The Wire Snapped	97
12	Real Trouble	102
13	It Ain't Easy	109
14	Panic	119
15	Shopping USA	128
16	Mr. Hyde	143
17	Some Fun Tonight	162
18	Hooked	167
19	Legs on Rye	173
20	Little Blue Pills	179
21	Aggie and Me	184
22	Like Father	192

Continued....

Continued from previous page:

Chapter	Title	Page
23	Elvis & the Clock	200
24	Girl Talk	206
25	What If?	212
26	Take a Chance	219
27	The Real Thing	227
28	In the Stars, Wild Love	234
29	Girls' Day Out	240
30	Lunch at Davidson's	249
31	Throw It All Away	255
32	Fit for a Queen	262
33	Love Me Tender	270
34	Uh, Oh	277
35	One Life	283
36	Lovin' USA	289
37	Finding Normal	300
38	BBQ Spaghetti	312
39	Living Legend: One More Time	318
40	Inside Story	326
41	Making Sense of It All	333
42	Everything I am	339
43	Buying Paradise	343
44	Salute	352

O'Hara—O'Hell

1937

Chapter 1

"Bastard!" Mother cursed her absent husband, consumed with jealousy, as she always was whenever Dad was out of sight, and mumbled passionately behind her unkempt hair, "Whoremaster!"

Aggie glanced sideways; she knew how to sneak a peek and how to duck a blow.

Mother did not see her, Aggie, the oldest daughter— her slight and pretty girl with the same blond hair, blue eyes, fair skin and freckles splashed across her nose— that everyone else saw. Mother saw the birth of all her problems, the root of her misery, the first of four children in nine years that had ruined her forever.

She recognized her Mother's revulsion, she saw it on her face every day, and felt it as a force of wind pushing her away. She had learned when to shut up ages ago, to stop talking and listen for rising voices, but still her rapid heartbeat knocked against her ribs. She was wary of Mother's movements while her own small hands plunged a breakfast bowl into the quickly cooling water in the basin and then scrubbed a washrag over it. Balanced to dry, the bowl leaned against an upside-down teacup on a flat metal pan.

Now Mother sat hunched over, on a sturdy chair beside the wooden kitchen table, her thin, fine-boned face buried in her hands, while dry sobs and guttural moans escaped from behind her shaggy curtain of fair hair. She was not dressed for the day although it was almost noon, and her hand clutched a woolen shawl to her throat, the shawl Granny knit before she fled back to Scotland at the start of the war. It almost covered her long, gray nightdress that hid the bump of Mother's belly on her slender frame.

Mother thought she was pregnant again, she had cried out—she was sure now—and her blue eyes filled with anguish that burned into Aggie as if it was her daughter's fault that she was firstborn and started it all. Now another abortion was certain, by doctor's orders, as she had no meat on her bones; her face was skeletal, deathly ashen, and a fifth child would kill her.

"I'm sick of the whole lot of you!" Mother moaned, and with a loud wrenching groan, she jumped up, kicked the creaky wooden chair aside and stumbled away from Aggie. Up the stairs she staggered, her shawl clutched in one hand, her other hand reaching for the door with both hands outstretched as if leaving the place would change things. Mother yanked open the door of the basement quarters in their unfinished house and fled, a tall wraith clad in gown and slippers with long blond hair streaming behind her.

"So, it will be this again," Aggie murmured quietly to herself, and hung her hands into the murky water that distorted their shape into pale fish and let them float for a few moments, embracing the weightless feeling, thinking it must be how freedom felt. At least Mother had gone without calling her a whore or beating her, or breaking the broom on her back again.

Aggie's pensive expression changed.

She slumped against the table. Darn! Now she was disappointed. She was supposed to babysit for the O'Toole's tomorrow night: the pleasant Irish people down the road that always had a smile for her, their house filled with the wonderful aroma of cooked meat and fresh, sweet baking when Aggie opened their door.

Maybe a late-season fruit pie with leftovers from the meal would be waiting on the table for her. They said it did not taste quite right the next day and she might as well finish it, do them the favor, so to speak.

Their three black-haired and rosy-lipped children, all under eight years old, had the palest skin she had ever seen, and they knew their "please and thank yous," and their mother smiled at them, and they smiled back, then they all smiled at Aggie and she liked that very much.

She would have taken her school clothes and stayed the night snug in a warm bed with two blankets and no need to share with anyone else, and those 25 cents were gone now.

In the stagnant silence, the loudly ticking clock reminded Aggie of her younger sisters and little brother, consumed in their own world at school now.

Beatrice would huddle at recess with her grade four girlfriends and chatter their private language, while little Nancy tagged along clutching her fabric-scrap Raggedy Ann doll securely to her chest.

The boisterous boy, in the lowest grade this year and now not underfoot every moment of every day, would race ahead at lunchtime and lead the girls pounding down the stairs any minute now. He would be hungry, hoping for a bit of bread and bacon grease and being loudly disappointed that there was nothing to give him.

Dad received his layoff notice and now the only income left was their Government pittance of pogey, spent for the month, and Dad away on a four-day job doing under-the-table metalwork, he told them, so no food remained, not a crumb.

"One more day's work and I will hitch a ride back," Aggie muttered his promise to her, and then maybe he would bring a treat like jam...but that was just a daydream. Maybe at Christmas that would happen, but she had to think about food for them tonight, and again tomorrow.

"Maybe," she grumbled, "I won't go to school ever again."

The Principal sat behind his enormous desk at the end of the last school year, when Aggie answered the summons to attend at 3:30 p.m., and he leaned over on his thick arms and twined his sausage fingers together as if he was going to pray. He peered over the top of his thin glasses with gold rims and said clearly, "You are supposed to come to school, Agnes. You are only twelve years old and rules are rules, so there is nothing more to say about the subject, and tell that to your mother if she is too ill to come and hear it for herself."

The rotund man held her gaze as if daring her to object, while she watched his moustache twitch in his beefy face with the red streaks on his cheeks, growing brighter as they talked.

"I'll be thirteen soon," she offered.

The principal's opinion did not matter, actually, as he did not live at their house where each week was worse than the one before and one way or another, Mother could not cope without her. Mother staggered from chair to bed, bed to chair, feeling sick and throwing up even the weak tea that was almost as colorless as she was.

All Aggie seemed to do was carry things back and

forth, back and forth, with Mother shrieking or crying, and Dad coming or going to work, or looking for work. Unoccupied meant lazy in her house and if she was not busy she had to pretend, or someone would say, "Don't you have anything to do—I'll find you something to do!"

"But, I truly want to go!" she grumbled aloud to the tepid water in the pan, reminiscing about the school baseball team, when the sun burned down on her arms in her short-sleeved red and white school jersey and the wind cool on her face, free to smile, whoop and laugh. It seemed like she had waited years and years to be old enough to be on a real team and Aggie could not, would not, give it up. Her stubborn desire turned into firm resolution.

Even if she had to take her troublesome little brother with her—a real nuisance when he chased behind Aggie and screamed as she ran the bases, and then usually fell and skinned his nose or knee and bawled his eyes out like a wounded wildcat—it was worth it. Somehow, she was going to play baseball.

When Dad got a better job, a steady job, he would buy a car again and take all the kids for a drive and each would get an ice-cream cone, for a special treat. All would be better when Dad got home. Dad never came empty handed. He would stop by the butcher on the way and buy some bacon, the very idea making her mouth moist in anticipation, and bread from the bakery. Maybe butter. It was her favorite: bread still warm from the baker's oven with butter.

Her dark spirit lifted. Determinedly, she picked up the bowl of water, with a film of grease-shine afloat from the last of the bacon fat, and climbed up the basement stairs with care.

Opening the creaky outer door, she slung the oil-topped liquid into space in a practiced arc, as far from the half-finished house as she could, careful that it would not be on her pathway when she returned from her chores. She reached back in to pick up an empty pail just inside the door and stepped outside, thrusting the door closed with her foot.

Aiming for clumps of grass or a useful flat stone amidst the suburban mud, Aggie made her way to the rain barrel. Each step placed with care, like a dance for one, the pail hung from one hand and metal bowl dangled from the other.

She swished fresh barrel water in the bowl to freshen it, filled the pail for cooking or bathing, and grunted at the effort for her skinny young arms to lift the full weight.

Soon that barrel full of water would freeze solid and be useless until spring melt. Then a family expedition had to hunt snow and ice, chop it, and take it home to store it in chunks behind the house that could melt in a pot on the back of the iron stove when needed.

Last year they desperately chipped ice from the culvert at the back of their lot where overflow sewage often ran.

She raised her head to look around and sniff the chilly air before the trek back to the door. A shiver raised goose flesh on her thin young arms, under her hand-knit woolen sweater, a thoughtful gift from Granny. The trees were mostly bare, their last leaves surrendering to the season.

Feeling the sting in her nostrils that predicts freezing, probably snow, she knew it would be cold inside when the precious heat from the breakfast fire wore off. Her head swiveled to the woodpile; it was low. What we need is coal, Aggie thought, and Dad might buy some when he comes back home, but what we really need is money.

"We need money," she told the black crow on the clothesline that watched her every move, as she was the only active body in sight. Even though he curiously cocked his head at the sound, he would not be any help, and the clothesline reminded her of the laundry waiting in the box in their bedroom.

Her mother was a stickler for fresh clothes and clean socks. Even when she ran away, Mother expected spotless underwear on the children or Aggie would feel her wrath, her hatred, curling into her dreams.

None of it is my fault, she insisted to herself, even though Mother often complained that she was the reason she had married a poor Irish workingman, but Dad said this Depression made almost everyone without a job poor.

Mother had come to Canada at seventeen years old, she told everyone, a visitor fresh off the boat from an advantaged life in Scotland. Fate found her when she turned her blond head the wrong way and fixed her gaze on Melville and they fell in love, a mad jealous love that drove them apart and together like erratically reversing magnets. Their wedding picture on the mantel betrayed her rounded belly; it was Aggie in her womb, and Mother never let her forget it.

"I hate you, you little bitch!" Mother shrieked, "I never wanted you!" especially when expecting another child, and now three girls crowded the bed in the tiny second bedroom like sardines in a can with one growing boy across the bottom, and hissed complaints filled the night.

"Don't be such a bed-hog!" or "You little brat, you take up so much room!" then "Daddy! The girls are kicking me!"

Father's fed-up voice boomed a stern warning from the other concrete bedroom—a threat always honored with a belt if not obeyed. The vocal fussing stopped, pushing and silent punches continued, but four in a bed was not so bad in winter, Aggie considered, when chill seeped to the bone and only the bodies spooned together cast an aura of animal comfort.

No matter what patching or stuffing of cracks they tried, the concrete block cellar was frigid in winter, except for the black iron stove in the area they called the kitchen with their table and four chairs, where they spent the majority of their time.

Dank with earthy smell in spring and fall when wet marks seeped through the blocks, and silent spiders nested in imperfect plaster in between, it remained coolly damp in summer.

Until their house was finished with a proper first floor above their basement, it would always be drafty and cold and it seemed that none of it, including the children, was good enough for her mother. Aggie shrugged; her Dad loved them and that comfort had always been her saving grace.

Her focus snapped back to attention as the first breaths of winter wind circled her neck, seeking her warmth and a steely determination pushed her lips together tightly. She could not wait for Mother. When would she return this time? A few days? Forever?

"So go!" she muttered to the fading image of her mother's contorted face, "I've got things to do."

She felt strange after that thought, perhaps a little frightened. There would be no more school for Aggie, only be the same day as this, looking after the children over, and over again. If Mother came back with the new baby, a baby needed to be warm and winter's only heat came from the greedy stove! Her mind seemed to be circling, spinning, always returning to the same place: Mother, prodding her to take the majority of the responsibility because she was the first child.

Granny told Aggie that she was important and money was important, and talked to her about getting it and holding on to it, and now Aggie had plans. If an adult gave her a coin, she kept it to herself, carefully wrapped up and hidden it so she would not have to share it—it was hers. She would buy a candy for her sisters and brother on their birthday, but that was that.

Money and staying active were Granny's secrets to living well. Her smiling little Granny taught her many things when she visited from Scotland, many shared confidences on long walks with their heads together. Granny did not care about rain or cold.

In any weather, Granny Agnes wanted to walk with their hands locked, as similar as two blue-eyed, blond-headed peas in a pod, sisters of the soul, separated by two generations.

Amazing to Aggie, Granny loved her best, and she made special parties for her birthday, with little candles from the drugstore on the cake she baked especially. Granny combed Aggie's long hair, twisted the long hanks into braids and then tied it with pretty ribbons, talking all the while of taking her home to Scotland when Granny went back home.

Oh, she wanted to go, and Dad thought it was a good idea, as she would receive a full education, but Mother had said no, glaring with her words. Like the stab of a knife into Aggie's heart, Mother had cruelly pushed her own mother's hands away from her first daughter's head.

The hint of possibility ended when political unrest in Europe caused rumors of war, and her dear Granny found passage on a ship back to Scotland before it was too dangerous to cross the Atlantic Ocean at all.

The coldness of the breeze passing through her thin

knit sweater woke her from the old daydream. The temperature was dropping quickly and she shivered throughout her body, blew warm air on her hands and rubbed them together for friction warmth. Dad taught her that.

"Pap!" Aggie said aloud. She would make pap for supper and it would stretch out to breakfast if she made it thin—it would just have to last. She had seen Dad make pap hundreds of times, when Mother ran away, and there was enough wood for the stove. The one quart of milk for the week had run out yesterday but there was water now. Pap would stick to their ribs.

"And tea," Aggie muttered, thinking of the few flakes of tea in the bottom of the red tin with the oriental woman on it. At least the hot water would have tea flavor.

Lost in thought, she pulled open the heavy door to the big grey box of a basement that they called home.

Dad said this depression would not last forever and they would have money to build their house properly with three bedrooms, a living room, a kitchen, and a nice bathroom. It would be built over the cellar they lived in that was half-underground, like the old country little people Granny spoke about.

Dad kept telling them about some bricks left over from "Casa Loma" that an Englishman built right here in Toronto. The castle had an elevator for his crippled wife, but it took so long to build the house that she died soon after they moved in.

Dad could get a good deal because his best friend works for the manufacturer and he will treat us right, she thought. Best of all, the house will have a furnace; it was good to think about that.

She felt hopeful, negotiating the steep steps, one at a time, down into their hobbit domain. It seemed so gloomy without sunshine coming through the ground level windows. Maybe she could improve it, with Mom gone. There was an old piece of lace shawl that would look nice over their sleeping-area window.

Her mind entertained soft, shining fabrics she had seen in a magazine, and pictures of women's hats with high brims, and skirts with kick-pleats, and blouses with a row of frills, and a neat little jacket, or a dress belted at the waist, on skinny models. When she grew up, she would save her money and wear nice clothes, too. She was not sure how—but someday she would.

Now that Mother was gone, she could paint the trim on the window, and maybe Dad had a bit of stain left from his last job that would look nice on the wooden window frame. She would not miss her mother's swift hands, her sound slaps, her hateful hisses.

She felt her neck stiffen with the physical effort of heaving the pail filled with fresh water onto the still warm black iron stove. Now she needed the broom. If she worked fast enough, there would be time to roller skate down the road before the girls came home, before those lowering clouds turned into falling snow.

Dad bought the metal roller skates for all the girls, and Aggie kept them hidden in her secret spot, wrapped with care, safe from prying eyes.

She would wear the thick sweater that Granny knit for her specially; then take joyous long glides on the asphalt road, maybe try going backwards, her mind open to possibilities.

"Ha!" Aggie exclaimed, arms outstretched and skate-wheels spinning, cheeks aglow and her hair flying in the wind as she swooped and dived like the birds.

"I'm not afraid of you!" she said to the image of her mother's face contorted into the hatred of Aggie's very being.

Her father loved her and her grandmother loved her. Let Mother slap and curse. The stings would go away.

Aggie would make her own plans and she shouted to the wind, "So go, Mother! So go!"

This Day

1942

Chapter 2

Aggie was too contented to move. This large bedroom was heaven compared with the dank basement they used to call home, and all due to Dad's supervising job at the airplane factory.

The room was big enough for one double bed, one single, a double door closet and a big airy window. It was so easy to find cheap paint on sale and change the room to whatever caught her eye, like this one that matched a soft butter-yellow silky scarf she found at the Sally Ann last month.

She did not want to wake her sister, sound asleep beside her in their bed. She had hardly slept at all, giddy from the possibilities that chased in endless circles around her mind; today could change her life.

Aggie's nose crinkled remembering the stinky canneries where she started working underage and the putrid dying fish smells that clung forever to her clothes, but she liked the fine-tooled shop with intricate machinery where she now worked. The complex machinery suited her small and fast hands and time flew when she focused.

Dad always told them to follow the paycheck. If another job paid more money, he figured out how to do it, and Aggie had watched, followed his example and improved her skill level. Now she had money to spend and money to tuck away, just the way she liked it, but she would always welcome an increase.

She yawned luxuriously, still sleepy, closed her eyes and let herself slip into reverie that felt like the distant past but was only two years ago; an event, a moment in time that cast the dice, as fate does so well, and she was a different person after the toss.

Aggie heard three short rings from the telephone exchange, their number on the party line, and scrambled to pick up the phone. Hunched over to absorb the noise, she answered it just before mother hollered at her, "Get off the phone. It's not for your social calls!"

She tried to explain to Jane, on the other end of the line, "I can't talk now—you know my mother."

"Meet me at the Chinaman's if you can sneak away," Jane offered in a rush, "I'm so bored! It's Friday night!"

Aggie envisioned a long, dreary evening stretching out ahead if she stayed at home, with her mother inventing tedious chores. "I'm coming, save me a seat!" She hung up the receiver noiselessly and melted from the room.

Jane said be there by seven-thirty, but Mother insisted Aggie take the laundry off the line, fold it, and distribute the stack of towels around the house—three in the girls' room, one to each wooden rack. Although she flew around the house to comply, it seemed ages before she could bend over the bathroom sink to wash her face and change her clothes behind the closet door, then apply her brand new Devil Red lipstick and sneak away, shoes in hand. She smiled to herself at the deception and kept close to the brick wall of their bungalow until she was out of sight of the front room windows.

Tap, tap, tap, tap! The sound of her freshly polished white, high-heeled shoes echoed in the high entrance as she scurried up two floors of broad marble steps to the local hangout. Anticipating adventure, the reverberation of lively jukebox tunes lured her forward while her light floral perfume trailed delicately behind.

The joint was in full swing from the ring of tinkling cutlery and glasses, and the familiar smell of Chinese food wafted from the doorway—fried noodles and cheap meats simmered too long in the pan.

She stood at the door, a tiny purse clutched in her hands, and she scanned the jammed restaurant for her friend Jane—no, not at their usual table. The light was dim inside and the air emanating from the cavernous room was warm on her face, like a sauna of bright eyes and romantic expectations sheltered from the glare of the overly bright stairway behind her.

The restaurant was busy, the tables jammed together, and it buzzed with the noise of conversations between the boys and the girls that filled the chairs, and that was good. The old Chinaman would not care if the girls nursed a Coke all night. The young girls brought in the ever-hungry boys, who shoveled in cheap platters of fatty meat and starchy, greasy mountains of noodles.

He turned a blind-eye to paper bags that tipped into over-priced Coca-Cola but would call the cops at any hint of roughhousing. Everyone knew the rules and played the game or left the premises swiftly and rudely, down the steep stairway.

Oh, boy! This was exciting! As she turned her head to survey the room, her heart pounded against her ribs, surely Jane was here somewhere in the heat waves palpating the darkened room. Bright red lipstick and a body-hugging scarlet dress felt sinfully outrageous, but maybe nothing disguised the youth of her pretty face, the eager look in her searching eyes. She felt ready to play, so ready to flirt, laugh and tease, hidden away from parental eyes and tattletale, troublemaker sisters.

Several men turned to look at her, including young soldiers, scarcely older, freshened up from training at the base, chests puffed out in creaseless new uniforms, but she knew to avoid them. They were volunteers for a war in a foreign land, and who knew if they would return?

Something flashed through her mind and made her eager heart beat faster; maybe tonight she would meet the one man to love forever.

Aggie's cornflower blue eyes widened, locked onto a smoldering stare she would never forget, that boldly demanded her attention.

It came from confident eyes in a handsome face, under wavy, curling black hair and she stepped back in surprise, amazed at how the look held her when every rule said to look away. It seemed amused and teasing, daring her with a romantic net of suspense, fully understanding the effect on the feminine heart.

Suddenly shy, and buoyant at the same time, her heartbeat quickened and she hoped he would ask her to dance, played the image in her mind and felt his body pressed tightly to hers, imagining they swayed in a mist of perfume and boy-sweat on the crowded dance floor.

Mother would be angry if she found out and she would instantly despise the boy's obviously Italian swarthy skin and his black hair puffed up too high for Mother's liking.

The boy's casual swagger would outrage Father. His face would tighten up and he would stand rigid, then he would demand that she forget about those dark eyes and not trust the boy as far as she could throw him, because everyone knew that foreign boys were never content with just one girl.

With a sharp intake of breath, she broke the handsome boy's magnetic spell and she swung her head to the right as her blond curls flounced, creating sweet reward for spending the day in pin curls. She scanned the restaurant for her friend, Jane. Jane must be in the half-light somewhere dressed to show off her enormous bazooms to full advantage, and yes there she was, half way between the spot where Aggie stood at the door and the busy kitchen—grinning and waving madly to her—a couple of tables beyond Mr. Bedroom Eyes!

Causing a stir among young males jammed around crowded tables, Aggie squeezed and wiggled into the tight space, sneaked a peek at the young animal with hungry eyes roaming languidly over her slight and curvy female shape, and she wondered. Who was he really, and would he ask her to dance?

She draped herself across the chair and crossed one leg over the other, the dangling foot bobbing in a restless rhythm until the beat caught her fluid body, moved it in waves, flowing with the music. Keeping time, her agile fingers tapped the table while she chitchatted with her friend about their day, and asked if Jane had spotted any cute guys. She was not really showing off—she loved the tricky beat of the latest song from jukebox, but it would be all right if Mr. Wavy-Hair noticed, and she hoped he liked to dance.

A fair-haired boy she had known in school called out, "Hey, Aggie! Come dance!"

She grabbed his hand and the eager twosome started the fast stepping intricate dance of Big Band sound, instantly grinning, dipping and jiving, off her feet then back on the floor, spin and rock, blocking out the world and the war.

She remembered the tempting boy with the black hair, the bedroom eyes, and she scanned the floor, checked the gang by the door, but Bedroom Eyes had gone.

The unholy racket of the alarm clock at four forty-five a.m. disintegrated Aggie's memories. She yawned involuntarily and threw back the confining sheet, this was going to be a long day and the east-facing room was stuffy already from the breaching sun.

Ten seconds later, Dad's feet hit the floorboards with a resounding thud in her parent's room on the other side of the wall from the girls.

Her sister Bea threw her arm over her eyes when Aggie arose and flicked up the window blind with the blazing sun barely crowning the horizon and aiming for their bed.

The youngest girl, Nancy, struggled towards consciousness, moaning from the skinny single bed, "No, no! It can't be morning already. I don't want to get up."

"Oh yes you do." Aggie yanked her arm. "Get going and wake up Chucky too."

"Why-y-y?" Nancy whined, thrashing her halo of fair hair back and forth on the pillow in useless protest, although she knew the answer.

Aggie overheard their mother telling Nancy last night that she was in charge of the boy today, the brat of the ages they called him, and it was Nancy's job to get him up, fed, and out the door to summer camp. Operated by the Salvation Army, the camp cost nothing. The counselors seemed blessed with eternal patience, kept Chucky busy and out of trouble, but Nancy had to get him there before they filled up for the day.

Everyone understood Chuck was a holy terror and if they were late, and the camp was full, she had to take him with her to babysit the undisciplined brats down the street. They drove her nuts by dinnertime, but she was blissfully happy come Friday with a dollar and a quarter in her hand.

She was the only fourteen-year-old she knew with a bank account, she often bragged, saying it was nice to have money. Five dollars a month added up fast and Nancy dearly loved her money, but hated the work that went hand in hand.

Nancy sat up dramatically, shook her head to chase the cobweb of dreams back where they came from and slid her legs out from under the cozy covers, then sighed like a bereaved movie star losing a lover.

Aggie turned away; she was first at the mirror on the dresser and time was moving fast. Inspired by the smell of breakfast, Aggie and Bea stepped their slim young legs into cotton skirts and pushed their arms into freshly ironed blouses retrieved from hangers hooked over their bedroom doorknob. Once in the kitchen, each girl grabbed a bowl and ladled in porridge from the pot their father had simmering on the old black stove.

Her eyes flicked to Dad's calm face. It took an extraordinary event to ruffle his feathers, but there was stiffness to his tall, wiry frame this morning and tenseness around his mouth, as if he was clenching his teeth. He got that look on his face when they talked about the hard times and she wondered if he was remembering when their house was finally completed, and the family proudly moved upstairs from the basement. He shared the same fair skin as his wife and children, but more time spent in the sun gave his lean face a more rugged, weathered look.

Dad refused to give up their old stove, the solid iron monument to the hard times that newspapers called the "Dirty 30's", before the depression waned and the job market jolted back to life with the war effort.

The youngest two children looked blankly back at him if he talked about the cold and hungry mornings when the only heat came from this stove, before this job that he proudly packed a lunch for six days a week. If there was food in the lean years, the youngest two got it. Aggie thought about it every day.

Sips of strong tea took hold in the girl's brains a few minutes later, lending fire to the table clearing. It was too hot to dream of leaving unwashed dishes. Scout-ants-of-summer quickly located leftover foodstuff and led a trail of vermin to polish it off, no matter how many times the humans tried to plug the holes.

"Keep an eye on your brother," Dad said over his shoulder to Nancy, now plunking down into her kitchen chair. "Where is he?"

The smallest sister slumped over the table with the enthusiasm of a deflated balloon. "He's such a brat, Dad, he won't listen to me." Nancy hung her head down and mumbled behind her mass of curls, "He's got to get some sense in his head. And...he's bigger than me."

Her father did not turn his lanky body around, his sinewy arms and sure hands repeating tasks he could do in his sleep. He replied evenly, "You are the oldest one at home today."

With a steady hand, he poured tea into his thermos, reached into the icebox for bologna and assembled two sandwiches, wrapped them in yesterday's newspaper and placed his customary fare into his lunchbox. "You've got to grow up now."

He commented that the block of ice would barely last until delivery day then added, "Make your beds," to no one in particular, and "Sit up straight," to Nancy.

Aggie knew he was working towards his reward. At the end of this long day, as every day, he would disappear for a few peaceful moments alone in the shed and tinker with this or that in blissful quiet and dream of the new garage he was designing. It would be equipped with heaters for comfort in his hideout in the winter, he confided, sharing secrets with her and her alone.

There was no sign of their mom yet, she noted, nodding towards mother's empty bowl and Bea shrugged her shoulders. Well, that was none of their business, but still, this was a very important morning and nothing could rain on her parade today. Her brow furrowed, "Darn," she muttered, "I'll go check."

Aggie walked quickly with a mug of tea balanced in her hand stuck her head into her brother's room on the way to fetch her mother. It looked an awful mess in there. Dirty clothes flung on the floor, his bed sheets twisted into ropes around his strong young body laying flat on his back, he looked half-wrapped like a mummy bursting out of its wrappings.

She bent down next to his ear and hollered, "Get up!" but he had disappeared into the somnolent stupor of a twelve year old boy and it was not her problem today—it belonged to Nancy.

She stuck her head tentatively into her parent's bedroom and predictably Mom was grumbling about the early hour, her long hair hanging loosely around her shoulders, but she was on her feet.

"Tea, Mom?" Aggie offered.

"Thanks," her mother murmured, their identical blue eyes communicating for the briefest of moments with less challenge today, more cohesion, as if this morning had a sharper edge than everyday chaos. Today proffered a vision, a chance of a lifetime; it seemed to be holding its breath.

Dad's aging truck swayed this way and that, as he knew every cavernous pothole personally, and Aggie held on tight to the back door handle as her father skillfully missed the biggest permanent ruts.

It was already muggy and only 5:45 a.m.

Employed at De Havilland as a supervisor for a few years, Dad heard about the hiring interviews first and she was excited when he made them hustle to leave with him this morning, headed north, and coached them the whole way on what to say, and what not to say.

"Aggie, you tell them about your factory jobs," he said, "and the machines you've run. Say how much you liked it and how careful and fast you are on the line. Do not hold back—say it straight out. Be sure to say you are never sick, which is true for you."

"Yes, Dad."

Aggie knew Bea was excited at the thought of a steady job. She had rehearsed what to say in her mirror over her bureau all the previous evening, as this would be her first job because she had stayed in school longer than Aggie had.

Dad tried to coach his yawning wife but she turned up her nose and looked out the window. It seemed he could not do anything right in her eyes but she hoped her mother listened anyway, even if her response was the usual snub.

Talk about the sticks! The long drive went on and on, as the airport spread to the north from Wilson Avenue, between Dufferin and Keele Streets, in the northwestern suburb of Downsview. Dad knew the route by heart, he drove up there six days a week as Aggie, her mother, and her sister Bea would do if they were lucky and gained employment today. They could all chip in a bit of money and take advantage of his weekly driver's bonus for gas.

Finally, she could see the buildings and her curiosity flicked her eyes back and forth, as she hoped to work among the huge metal hangers for airplanes that rested on enormous dried up fields with a network of runways that sometimes ran beside the road where they were driving.

Wherever the work was, she would do it, but still she started to feel edgy as the day heated up and the closer they got to their goal, as this day could change her future.

Jittery, giggly, and relieved at the same time, there was nothing to do but chatter together and wait for the first bus on the long trip home, but at least the trio jumped the employment line thanks to Dad's contact, they all agreed with happy head bobs.

They all secured jobs that earned more money each than they had collectively made before, and would do for as long as the war continued, until the soldiers came back to work.

The nervous excitement wore Aggie down gradually when a bus did not show up for an hour and the blanket of humid heat was so thick you could cut it with a knife, she figured, and her sister and mother nodded in agreement. Everything around them seemed to be the same brown color to her in the blazing sun, dead-weed beige. Her mother leaned on the wooden pole painted as a bus stop trying to hide in the splinter of shade and Bea sat down on the wilted scrub grass, best dress and all.

Too worn out for much enthusiasm, they were, nonetheless grateful when a dirt-coated bus eventually arrived.

Waiting between multiple connections after that, exposed to the blinding sun in the middle of nowhere, Aggie felt the constant jab of blisters rising on her heels, but she dared not take off her shoes for fear of swelling, and then not be able to get them back on. Her dress clung to her chest and back, and she could smell sweat eating at the fabric in the armpits—her powder was not dry anymore.

It was late afternoon when they staggered in the door, hungry and drained, and Aggie made a couple of peanut butter sandwiches while Bea sat at the table with a piece of ice chipped from the block in the icebox, alternately running it over her face and down her arms.

Their mother went to bed.

Two days later, when Aggie saw the exciting newspaper advertisement calling their jobs "Victory Shifts," she pulled up a kitchen chair beside the telephone on the wall and tilted it just the way she liked it. She lifted the receiver gently and listened to make sure there were no busybodies already gossiping on the line, and feeling secure she dialed the number for her best friend, Jane.

"The newspaper says, '116,000 new jobs are opened in the Canadian aeronautical industry and 30,000 are for women; jobs usually done by men that are now overseas.' 'There will be work for women,' this other article says, 'until the war is over,' soon, they figure optimistically. That is not at a man's wages, mind you, but the money is so good that girls and women are lining up in droves. Another article has a picture of smiling women waving at the camera, happy to be at the front of the lineup for an interview!"

She spoke softly and explained to Jane that some of the newly hired men came from the States just to work at the plant and workers were pouring in from everywhere, her Dad told her, but the new Supervisors were all men, so it was no use a woman applying for that job.

"Lucky we had inside information and got there first and snagged the best jobs," Aggie spoke covertly into the telephone, "we all start on Monday."

She leaned to her side, rested her head on the dining

room doorframe, then told her friend about that exhausting day waiting in the unrelenting sun and the long bus rides home and plotted her excuse to get out of the house to see her boyfriend. Jane was the cover story tonight and Jane could tell her parents she was meeting Aggie and sneak away to meet her boyfriend, too.

"I had to use my sister Bea's school grade for the job application, it's only fair, you know I had to leave school to look after the rest of them and I helped her with her homework. It is the same last name if they check, but no one ever does, I used the same grade on my last job, too."

"Well, enjoy your new job," Jane remarked coolly as the conversation wound down.

"Come on, Jane, don't be sore, I am sorry you couldn't go today, but Dad said no, family was the best he could do."

The telephone was silent for a few moments then Jane softened the edgy tone in her voice, "Well, the war is good for something. Women are earning real money without working two jobs to make a man's pay, and anyway your Dad told me he has the telephone number of someone to see."

"There, see? It will all work out." Aggie was relieved; the last thing she wanted was a rift between herself and her good friend.

"Hang up that telephone," her Mother yelled from the bedroom, "it is for important calls and you are tying up the party line!"

Rosie the Riveter

1944

Chapter 3

"Mom—you ready?" Aggie held the wooden screen door open, listened for the usual scurrying sounds of her mother in motion but heard nothing and hollered again towards the back of their house.

She had been tapping her restless foot, leaning on the house, reminded of the leftover bricks from Casa Loma that Dad's friend had stashed away. As soon as bricks arrived the girls started to squabble about the bedrooms. There was always something to make a fuss about, like now when it was getting late and she had to get her mother moving. All their jobs depended on punching a timecard—on time.

Aggie's blue eyes blazed. "C'mon, Mom, we're supposed to be outside! Dad has the car ready. Bea is in it, too. Get out here!"

"Don't feel well," her mother called out feebly from the back bedroom.

"Are you on the level?" Aggie yanked the door open and ran pell-mell down the hallway with her hands outstretched ready to strangle her mother and not for the first time.

She leaned her head into the room so darkened with

the window shades drawn she could hardly make out her mother huddled on the bed, curled in a ball, hugging her body with one arm and holding her head with the other.

"My head! My head," her mother croaked. "It's like lightning bolts up the back and everything spins when I move, and my eyes... I feel dizzy. I want to throw up!"

Aggie shouted. "Never mind that!" but her mother covered her ears.

She persisted. "You need to come now. You had your last warning about being late and if you just get to work, they will think it is the flu and maybe send you home for a couple of days, then they won't fire you. Besides, you are making us all late! Dad is red in the face, he is so mad. You don't want him to look bad too!"

Her mother moaned.

Then she mumbled, "You're right."

Her dark blue eyes squeezed down into slits to keep the stinging sunshine at bay, she edged onto her elbow. "Give me my shoes and help me up. Don't tell your father—he'll get worried—I just need some rest."

"Yeah, yeah, Ma. You must be alright; you're giving orders just fine."

She got a hint from her Dad that some women had left their jobs at the plant already; they could not tolerate the clinging heat or chocking dust, and then he told her Jane had applied for a job, so that meant it was OK to pass information about it on to her friend.

"The biggest problem is the uniform and gloves," Aggie told Jane over sodas at the counter of the drug store after work on Saturday. "The standard issue gloves are all too big for most of the girls. You can't hold on to rivets or even a broom to sweep a floor."

"So what do you do, at the factory?" Jane asked, but she was distracted and her eyes followed the soda jerk as if his every move was fascinating. She had a "thing" for him, she said, and could sit there for hours, slouched over the counter with her chin resting on her palm staring at the boy that was much too old for her. He had to be all of twenty-two, a mature man, Aggie figured, if he was a day.

His eyes fixed on Jane, he flexed his upper arm muscle even when he did not have to and the bulge was handsome in his white, short-sleeved shirt. Aggie noticed him, but she already had her man; she was not impressed.

Jane looked like she was going to melt on her bar stool, but Aggie persisted.

"I am riveting airplane parts and doing other jobs that suit my small hands. I can use our bare hands, which is easier because the gloves are all too big, but they get dirty fast, and there is always a lineup for sinks," Aggie pursued.

"Uh-huh."

She got serious. "Jane! Pay attention! This place is closing in ten minutes and I have bus to catch. If I miss it, I will be walking for an hour. Your application could be accepted any day now."

Her friend's head swiveled back to her.

"You may or may not have to wear a kerchief, depended on the job. Most hairstyles are shoulder-length and permed, you know, like yours, so we have to tuck our hair in neatly. I always wear mine to keep the dust out. I knot the kerchief in the front, on my forehead, with no hair trailing to catch in the whirling machinery of the automated line. The bosses say it would slow down production; that is how much they care. The girls say it could snatch us bald."

That got Jane's attention.

"What clothes do you wear?" Now Jane was interested, as if it was getting more real to her.

Good, she thought. I am not wasting my breath.

"At first my uniform was like a balloon around me, but a nip and tuck here and there made it fit better. We might as well look as good as possible—we live in it six days a week. The manual names the employee wearing the uniform as personally responsible for safety, so it is up to us to make sure the uniform stays free of grease. Other thing catch on it, too, like loose fluff that could put a soldier at risk if got caught in an engine part, or foul up machinery."

"I know it so well because the supervisors drill this into us every day, and it's funny, see, they don't lecture the men that much."

They were both quiet a few moments and then Aggie volunteered, "My Dad never does that."

"Yeah, I like your Dad," Jane added, nodding to prove her sincerity. "I'm ready to go, you know."

She was curious now that it seemed to be really happening. "What does your Mom do up there?"

"Mom works in the cockpits; specialty finishing on the Mosquito—you'll get to tell the planes apart. It is cramped work, sometimes with several women bent over or reaching up, spending a long time in each plane, and she is in there all day, even in this August heat! It gets hotter under the canopy glass and the air is stale, hard to breathe. The glues and paints sting her nose and make her feel sick."

She paused with her mother on her mind. "At the end of the day," she continued, "Mom is too tired to talk about it. You would be good at that job too—you are so artistic, and can take the heat better then my Mom. I'll tell Dad, but you have to take what you get and expect it to be hard work."

Jane's eyes were dancing, trying to picture it. "Do you like what you're doing? Is it hard?"

"I'm good at my job, see? I love it, it makes the time

fly." Aggie found it easy to concentrate on the small parts despite the constant bombardment of noise.

"Just remember this: there is a line up a mile long to take your job if you mess up."

They finished slurping the tasty glass of soda through the straw to the very bottom, where it made the funny squeaky sound they loved, and the soda jerk looked up with a small pout of disappointment when Jane got up to leave, and that made her very happy.

As she did every morning, Aggie headed to the safety window to pick up special job supplies and listened carefully to any new instructions. She often thought her small hands were a gift, passed down to her from her Scottish grandmother who could knit and crotchet so fast the needles seemed to spin.

She stepped promptly to her position in the center of the machines that created a clamorous ballet of organized chaos in the dome that normally housed aircraft. Perched on a high stool, she leaned forward as a moving belt slowly circled in front of her and, with intense concentration she reached for the next, and then the next object to be riveted before placing it back in precise position on the moving belt.

Large lights hung down from the high ceiling, brightened the enormous work hall but added to the heat, and her bright yellow headscarf clung to her damp forehead. It almost drained all the focus and energy she had in her, and she knew she had an exceptional capacity for work.

Huge ceiling fans slogged the muggy air around while her intense concentration melted the hours. Her ears rang from the clamor for an hour after she got home, she told her friends, but it was worth it to do something interesting that paid so well.

Aggie knew her work was vital. This unit would be

in an airplane flying Canadian aviators into battles halfway around the world; she did not need reminding.

"Rosie!" That deep male voice rang out, louder now as the lunch tables promptly filled with men and women maneuvering for a seat close to the hottest gossip or beside the most popular, just like school.

A couple of straight-backed ladies pinched their mouths in disapproval but the younger girls ducked their heads, giggled, and tittered. Most of the boys called to them when supervisors were absent, whistled and teased the girls in sometimes strange and pleasing accents from everywhere, from all the provinces, the United States, and even Europe.

Aggie smiled with contentment to be in the lively throng, and there it was again, "Rosie the Riveter," a boy called, dragging out the syllables as the Americans liked to do. He was a tease like most Southern boys, staying slouched in his chair, not coming over to see her but only calling out to annoy her, to woo her, and remind her that he was still there.

The Canadian workers had other names for the young women, like "Ronnie the Bren Gun Girl," named for the girls that worked at the munitions factory at the former John Inglis plant that used to churn out appliances, and now the highly valued Bren Guns.

The supervisors gave the women threatening looks, as all the girls had eagerly promised "No contact" at the interview—no contact with the other two thirds of employees, men. What they did once hired, feeling competent and necessary, swept away by the male smorgasbord of nations calling out to them as if they were the most beautiful thing the boys had ever seen on two legs, well, that was different.

She had learned so much here, at Downsview's De Havilland airport, one of several factories in the

Toronto area where many women, like Aggie's mother, worked on the wood Mosquito fighter-bombers flown by the RAF and RCAF squadrons in England. Often they were called the "Phantoms of the Air," the front line series, but this was information Aggie's family had learned to keep to themselves. As they heard every day—"Loose lips sink ships."

Driving to work and back, their family passed several artistic renderings of different pin-up girls wearing overalls and the ever-present kerchief, displaying their determined eyes, "can-do" smiles and ample bosoms. The posters showed up everywhere, on billboards on the highway, in newspapers, and on posters plastered to fences and the sides of buildings. Some of the younger girls at the plant practiced the poses in their mirrors at home and showed the others how to do it at lunchtime.

This annoyed the older men, no end, but the girl's were happier in their busy day with a laugh now and then, even if they did get stern looks from supervisors or older women used to being quiet when the men were around.

"Don't think you're going to keep that job, girlie."

No pictures decorated the lockers of old-boy male employees at the airport. She figured they thought it showed solidarity to give the women a tough go.

"You'll be gone when the men get back!"

A couple of old goats, and younger ones, too, with curled up bitter scowls, said worse things to the girls as they passed in the lunch hall, checking first to make sure Aggie's father was not around.

"Mistakes bring down planes!"

If they could trap the girls by the lockers, the overbearing men ranted until spittle spewed from their mouths trying to belittle the girls, to show how inconsequential they really were.

"How would you feel if a Mosquito crashed and burned in Europe or North Africa? The very planes we make here at this plant! Our own RCAF boys or the Royal Air Force lost in the desert because of your error?"

They always said, "Crashed and burned."

It always ended with, "Shouldn't you be home with babies and a husband to feed?"

Aggie was lucky her Dad was the lead hand over the crew that she and her sister worked on. He gave reprimands as necessary, without hesitation, but it was never because they were just girls.

The hounding from the old men did not work on Aggie. After all, the girls do the jobs right she figured and the men know the girls are just as productive as they are—it was male jealousy, plain and simple.

The biggest problem, Aggie knew, was that with more money comes more power.

The male workers were off-limits to the girls, their bosses stipulated firmly, but that did not stop tiny slips of paper with a name and a phone number on it passing through a few hands, or an "accidental" nudge at lunchtime. Flirting ran rampant as hopeful young men vied to sit near Aggie and the lookers. If they wanted to think the pretty, young things were pinup quality, the girls did not mind a bit. Sure, it was a come-on, but it still felt good.

Aggie (on right) with friend

"Where's the party?" was the Friday question. The appropriate information buzzed from ear to ear around crowded lunch tables, accompanied with titters, grins and pointing—that guy or this gal, his or her house.

Rowdy parties happened at the drop of a hat, no excuse needed. Most young folk were stifled with hawkish authority and were over-the-moon, giddy to be free from bosses, army, and parents with too many questions. A record player unveiled, records magically appeared, or a battered radio blared. Furniture was shoved back, carpets hurriedly rolled up; it was time to boogie.

Booze appeared, too, restricted or illegal, but that did not seem to matter; it was everywhere. The bootlegger was king.

It was all great fun! Many local boys had enlisted, but at the factory on the airforce base, men were thick as fleas.

"I'm sorry you don't like parties," Aggie told Hank when he dropped her off one night, secretly relieved that he did not want to go in and sit like a handsome but grumpy, bump on a log, and try to get fresh with her when no one was looking.

"Why don't you tell them you're engaged?" Hank suggested this, trying to sound off-hand, Aggie knew, as they sat in his parked car with the windows rolled down to enjoy a balmy spring evening. One hand was on the steering wheel and the other arm rested contentedly around her shoulders and she knew his problem—he was jealous.

"Well, I would if I had a ring to prove it," She countered, wondering if an awkward proposal was really happening or if he was teasing, holding out a carrot if she behaved. After all, they had been an item for three long years.

Darned if he did not surprise her a week later and "Oh yes!" was her answer.

Then she asked a question, "when?"

Hank looked a bit dismayed as if he had only planned on the ring, not the whole deal and she hurried to clarify.

"Well, I can't wear it, not on the job, you know, no jewelry allowed." Aggie figured it would not be wise to hoodwink him; the bargain was faithfulness for a diamond ring and she hoped Hank understood that. Finally, he nodded as if they had struck a deal.

Realizing all would change soon gave her a surging buoyancy she had never known before. This was not the brief thrill of backseat romance, lost in his passionate embrace, but a direction, a plan. It was simply delicious to think of being out of her stifling family home and into a fresh run at life for themselves.

At an independent eighteen she was beyond ready, and she could manage a respectable wedding within a couple of months. In fact, she knew a shop that often had clearance sales and tiaras with a veil, and she had seen one in a sweetheart design that followed the shape of her face.

It was funny really to think Hank had been concerned, because he did not need to worry. Not one of the boys at the parties could match the looks of her guy. He was so handsome it almost made her blush to look at his olive skin, his full head of dark curls and his bedroom eyes. Her Scottish-Irish family was upset though, and called him an "I-talian" with a sneer in their voice, like he was a darkie or a foreigner that did not speak English, or something.

"Put the wedding off," Dad said sternly, thinking that the final statement on the matter, before he disappeared into the new garage. "I won't be walking you down the aisle to marry him. And, tell him to put his collar down—he looks like a hood."

The wedding dress appeared shortly after and wedding gifts began to arrive with the big day now only two weeks away. The girls at work put money together and bought them a big, blue, and comfy blanket, softer than any Aggie had ever felt before. She was blissful when she was not abuzz with her wonderful plans and the necessary phone calls that her mother could not legitimately shout at her about. .

Yes, Dad swore he would not walk her down the aisle to give her to Hank, but he would in the end. He was like that: he did not want to disappoint his Aggie.

All Aggie really wanted to do at lunch was stand out of sight of the other workers in solid shade between two big airplane hangers to see if a breeze had sprung up. It was a relief to undo her uniform, and the top buttons of her blouse that stuck to her with sweat, and allow the refreshing breeze to breathe on her skin.

Aggie patted the chest pocket of her blue uniform overalls, as this was payday, and this hum-dinger of a wage would give them a great start when they got married, because the groom-to-be did not have a real job. The pool hall held more appeal he said, and he made good contacts there, but she was never sure what the contacts were good for because Hank's money came in globs—he had it or he did not have it, but she could not tell Dad that.

Someday House

1953

Chapter 4

Aggie yanked the chairs away from the kitchen table and bent over to reach the broom underneath, amazed at the quantity of rolling clumps of dust. She swept there yesterday, and the day before that, but she would never defeat the dirt that blew in through the gaps in the walls.

It was dustier than it had been on the factory floor at De Havilland where the sweepers had worked twenty-four hours a day to keep the floor clean enough for aeronautical standards.

She heaved a sigh as she remembered the freedom she lost, and she groaned aloud at all the fun she used to have and the money she made during the war, working on the riveting line. That was a long time ago; she had two boys to look after now, and her husband was a far cry from her romantic visions.

Her skin felt dry as a bone in this dust and she hated that. It used to be soft and moist and she had been proud of it, like it was in that fateful moment when she first saw her husband-to-be at the old Chinaman's restaurant.

Looking back, it seemed a trick of nature—the physically perfect man showed up before her eyes and she wanted to mate.

Now she had him all right and she could not change a thing. What is an innocent young girl supposed to do—it was Mother Nature's sweet trap—so why was she now haunted by her romantic memories? Maybe that is my problem, she thought: I remember everything.

Well, that was a long time ago, Aggie commiserated to the echoes of those dreams. She knew, now, that the boys had seen a delicious little red lollipop, a baby-faced toy in tight women's clothing that could not be sixteen. Even so, her full breasts had filled the neckline to overflowing. She had learned a lot about men since then—she knew they wanted to be first.

It had not taken much time for him to find her, claim her, and then wait the three years until their marriage. Blinded by gasping passion stolen in darkened corners and the back seat of cars where no one could see, she listened to her own pipe dreams and longed for the marriage bed.

She knew so much more now, all about the dark-haired stranger, Hank, his easy smile that she did not see much of any more, his kisses and his persuasive loving, his lack of ambition and the rough crowd with whom he palled around.

Ironically, two babies later, desire done to excess and both of them completely disillusioned, her husband was still always gone.

What she had not yet learned about money from her hardscrabble Irish-Scottish family who lived through the Depression, Aggie learned from the tight-fisted Italians that were now her in-laws.

Her father-in-law, Anthony, came to Canada as a young man, before World War 1, but went back to Italy when the Germans threatened his homeland. He was wounded twice, he told her, but recovered well enough to join the police force for three more years.

Then he met a girl, a young Italian girl that changed his plans forever. It was what he wanted—a traditional Italian marriage to last a lifetime. He longed for the freedom to expand that Canada had given him once before, and he figured, correctly as history proved, that the fascist politics and the vile hatred between the parties and clans was destined to never end, and he was right. He chose the better life waiting in Canada. He and his bride came over on a ship in 1919, with little more than the clothes on their backs, and Aggie's mother-in-law never let her forget it.

Those Old-Country people turned every proudly earned penny into useful property, so how their son got so lackadaisical, she would never understand, but then she would never be a favored, first-born Italian son.

"You make me so angry!" she squeezed out through gritted teeth, barely able to restrain a scream, but not wanting to wake her sleeping child.

Hank was gone again, while she remained with the boys, in this ex-garage shack covered in black tarpaper and jammed into the driveway against her Italian in-law's house. It was one narrow room with a cold-water sink on the side, a door beside it opening to a pathway beside the house next door, and a small window smack dab in the middle of the front. There was no bathroom, just a hike to the outhouse out back, through thigh-high, sharp-edged weeds. Garter snakes wiggled through the stinging rushes in the summer and the stalks honed into knife blades when it froze. The road in front was deeply pitted—a quagmire in the wet months, a dirty place where dust bolls endlessly swirled in summer, and an ice rink in winter, which made it a year-round challenge.

Last night, the heat laid them flat like unrisen bread,

lumps of sweaty dough gone sour in the afternoon sun and sweating Crisco back into the oven of a makeshift bedroom.

Aggie slammed the broom to the bare floor, partially satisfied with the resounding crack. Dreams of freedom teased and tumbled through her mind as she stared at the open door, itching to run as fast and far as her strong legs could take her. Only one thing, no, two things kept her here—her boys…and the mortgage.

Aggie sighed and picked up the broom again.

Someday she would not need to soften Sunlight soap to fill the holes when winter winds whistled through. Their house would be snug, draft free, not covered with thin strips of weather-whitened wood. Hammered on helter-skelter, they looked like scattered bones of skeleton arms reaching out to keep the tarpaper sheets from blowing off in a high wind, or curling up in Southern Ontario's steamy summer heat.

What a laugh on her! She had paid for the wedding and had been paying ever since.

To pay her share of the mortgage, insisted upon by her in-laws—an outrageous mortgage on a shack—she and Ronnie went together, to do whatever jobs she could find in this far end of Toronto. Jobs like dispatching in the drafty old taxi shed near the corner of Dufferin and Eglinton, that looked like it was falling down, and there she was with a two-year-old heavy in her arms and the only way to get there was to hitchhike.

That intersection grew busier and busier with the growth of the city and the surrounding suburbs. The speed of the traffic seemed to increase every week, too, but the faster the cars went, the less likely the drivers were to stop for them, especially in the dark nights of winter.

Aggie had worried while she ordered the cabs and

made excuses for the driver's tardiness, trying to keep her eye on the boy at the same time, as she was the only one working the slower, but safer, day shift. Ronnie played, contentedly, tethered outside on a clothesline beside the tiny office to get some fresh air and play in the dirt. If he needed to use a bathroom, he went in a poop and piddle bucket, just like at home.

For her own needs, and when the boy grew to the training stage, she ran with him in her arms to the closest restaurant and then raced back to frustrated callers wondering why there was no answer when they needed a cab.

Worry, run, grab a laugh with a friend, worry, run— the young mother's carousel.

Babysitters cost money and brought their own danger, Aggie ruminated now, washing cups and plates in a pan of tepid water. Like the time when her two boys came home with a head full of lice from sleeping over at a babysitter's house while she worked her night job on the telephone emergency line.

Aggie held their heads down and her girlfriend, Jane, picked the creatures one by one from their heads, like vile berries, and crushed them.

She had bought a used couch from the same babysitter. It was a beautiful dark blue, a real bargain, she remembered—but still—twenty-five dollars was a lot of money to her. The bugs that traveled in the couch came free. She planned for the solid couch to last forever, but afterwards Ronnie, and barely walking Melville, writhed and howled in protest, as they went through the lice-killing ritual again, their hair shampooed and rinsed, shampooed and rinsed, with freezing cold tap water. It was gruesome!

What a joke on us, she snorted, thinking about all

the money it took from her jobs, and running a booze can hidden inside a hole in her kitchen floor, to buy that old couch.

Then Aggie smiled, thinking of the intrigue when she purchased the booze on payday, bumped up the price when the bars were closed, then waited for the signal knock on her door late at night, or anytime on Sunday. It ran smoothly until Officer Raymond stopped in one night and told her it was too well known. He said he did not care, but there was a new push to close the illegal business up tight and he did not want her to get into trouble. He knew she was alone, with two little kids to feed.

"People are careless, and people are helpful," Aggie said aloud. "Sometimes it's hard to know ahead of time what they will be."

Aggie picked up the faded mat from the floor in front of the sink and shook it out the door; it was falling apart with every new shake. Someday she would get a new rug but for now, it would have to do. Everything about this place was third rate and made her feel lonely, and she was tired of lonely. She would stop for a cup of tea now, before Melville woke up, and she would drink it alone.

Her sleek-haired pampered husband was gone, always gone—shooting pool with his crony's day in, day out or coming back from "jobs" with no money left in his pockets and endless excuses. Hank had lost it, or gambled it away, like that disaster up north.

"It's going to be so good," his friend, Al, had told him, "tons of money; and nowhere to spend it. Nothing happens in Cochrane, Ontario. We just haul logs out of the bush after the other guys are finished felling."

There was only one child then.

"Come up," Hank had begged her on the phone after

a month alone. "Bring the boy. I have a place."

"But I'll lose my job at the taxi company," she answered him, thinking as fast as she talked.

"It's pretty good money, $18.00 a week. You'll have to give me back the train fare as soon as I get there. We will be out of money. There is still the mortgage to pay, you know. Your mother will have a fit if we don't."

"Come on, Aggie," he urged her. "There's nothing for me to do here but get into trouble. All the men do is drink and gamble every minute they're not working. I need you."

She had to admit it, she missed him, too, missed the body in the bed, the romping and moaning and the making up after fights. All the memories were so clear in her mind.

It had not seemed such a good idea when she had lugged squirming toddler Ronnie the length of the long and cold train station platform. She had balanced their small suitcase and food bag in her other arm, and wondered how she would dig out the tickets from her pocket. Return fare for herself cost her last sixteen dollars, so they could not buy anything else. The boy was free if he was on her lap.

From the top of the standing railway cars, wind drafts swirled snowflakes down around their heads, yet she felt sweat inside her coat from carrying the heavy boy in her arms to keep him from slowing their progress. Accustomed to the length of his tether at the taxi office, but brought up short now and held by her, he wriggled like a strangled snake to get free. Aggie could not put him down without the lead that attached to his harness or he would be gone, his silver-blond hair bobbing in and out of the crowd. As long as Ronnie knew where she was, his two-year old legs seemed determined to run and he would bolt away to explore.

On the platform, the crowd was mainly men heading north. Most acted respectful enough, as she had a kid in tow, but none missed the glance at her ample breasts, or her shapely legs stepping briskly along the station corridor. A skirt was a stupid decision, she mused, and she should have worn her warmest slacks.

One man, a colored man, stared at her bust, gaped with his mouth dropped open as if he had never seen a woman before. Aggie had noticed his great height, sloping shoulders and extra large hands. She did not like the look in his empty eyes, showing no emotion, soulless, like a rutting bull in a field. She had seen that blinded look before when a man got drunk, but she did not smell booze from his breath, just a musty scent from his clothes, as if they had been in a damp place too long.

The man edged forward until he was brushing against her as the line of passengers began to step up into the train coach. She thought she might gag from the smell as he tried to brush against her body. Her arms full, she struggled with her restless boy and their paper bag of food, and swung her suitcase slightly to get a better grip, catching the man in the shin with its sharp corner.

"Sorry, sorry!" she spluttered, automatically.

He grunted, and shot her a surprised look that quickly turned mean.

She had seen that look before, from soldiers to business men when they felt rebuffed. She needed to keep an eye on him. There was life in his eyes now. She could see that he did have a soul, but it looked damaged.

To her relief, the piercing warning whistle startled him into looking away.

She grabbed the hand bar beside the steps into the railcar, and hauled them up, relieved to board.

Aggie and Ronnie almost fell into their seat, the boy pushing away to look out the window and then jumping up to see who was behind them. She turned to apologize, or at least be friendly, only to meet the same black eyes glaring at her. He looked smug, as if he had found his reason to hate her.

As the train pulled out she peered up and down the aisle—there were no more empty double seats. She only had a single seat ticket and they would need the extra room. At least no one else wanted to share the seat that she and her boy occupied. She spread out, occupying the space.

"Sit down, Ronnie, sit down and let's have our nice sandwich," Aggie cajoled, making a fuss as she unwrapped the crinkling brown paper, trying to make peanut butter sound delicious.

"No dear, I will hold the bottle of Coke, it's safer that way. We can share."

She could feel the man's stare, watching her as she turned her head to murmur to her son. The man was probably mad at the world, she mused, but she seemed to be his target. She had not done a darn thing to him on purpose, she reasoned, going over the suitcase incident in her mind. Anyone would know that was an accident and he would not be the first to mistake her small size for opportunity. No, it would not be the first time.

She talked to distract herself, and her son, answered his "what's that...what's that..." questions and pointed out passing trains and sign posts, until there was only barren field and the fast and early sunset in a darkening winter sky.

The click-clack wheel noises and the rhythmic motion of the rail car rocked the tired little boy to sleep. Aggie pulled his winter coat up around his chin, and then tried to settle herself to pass the night in some form of comfort on the hard seats made for day travel. Feeling somehow safer in the dim twilight of the coach now, she stretched her body forward a bit to peek at the reflection of the angry man that sat directly behind her. Thankfully, he seemed out cold. Probably a worn out working-man she reasoned, and they should be safe until morning.

Steadily, in the quiet of the dimly lit coach, the rocking, click-clack, and hum of the great machine they rode in lulled her into a barely-aware sleep.

Like in a waking dream, a hand moved up her skirt toward her woman mound and Aggie almost relaxed, forgetting where she was, but the touch was wrong. It was not her husband and it began to grab and dig at her. She jerked fully awake as anger surged through her mind and body, and thrashed her left arm out with all her power into the face of the man.

The man that hated her grunted and grabbed for her flailing arm, twisted it behind her, trying to pin her to the seat with his huge and heavy body.

Her right hand balled into a fist and her arm shot out to smash her knuckles into his eye, and in shock he jerked back a bit but made no noise, and then kept advancing, trying to wedge himself between her legs.

Her hand flailed about the seat between her and the sleeping boy, and found what she sought.

She gripped the empty coke bottle hard and smashed it into his face with all her might—the only sound a muted crack. It was not enough force to break the sturdy bottle but the man pulled back cursing, releasing her left arm, and she shoved him away from her as he slid down into the aisle. Blood poured down from his eyebrow onto his sweater as he staggered backwards, falling towards his seat.

She rested her head back, exhausted, waves of disgust and rage racing through her body with the heavy beat of her heart. She rubbed her sore left arm and tender right knuckles, wondering how she would carry Ronnie in the morning, and did not close her eyes again.

The man disappeared by morning: gone before Aggie and Ronnie disembarked, stiff, grumpy and cold, into a bitter wind slicing through their clothes and her boy huddled close to her legs.

Excitedly, Hank greeted them at the station with mushy, lost-puppy kisses. He was so happy to see Aggie that he lifted Ronnie out of her arms and carried everything himself.

They walked several blocks through a simple town with mostly squat houses, on wide snow-clogged streets spreading carelessly over a depth of cold never before experienced. The snow creaked and crunched under their feet like old boards, as if it contained no moisture at all and her coat felt like a sieve, full of holes, useless against this brutal wind crossing vast fields of polar ice to find them. It swirled around her numbing legs, bare but for her only pair of stockings, quick-frozen now into paralyzing cages.

Their heads bent to the wind, they scurried to the old house they were to stay in, and climbed the interior stairs that became steeper with each floor, up, and up again.

The ceiling, in the tiny apartment in the attic, sloped down from a high point in the middle like a tent, and they huddled together with no insulation above them and no heat escaping from the floor register. They saw their breath and the chill pierced their bones. The lack of refrigeration did not matter; everything liquid became frozen solid. A tiny stove sent a feeble gas flame that valiantly wrestled the thick frost coating the window and took an hour to heat a small pan of water.

The memory of the attack lingered, and loomed

when Aggie lay down with the boy to share with him whatever warmth she had left in her body. The child shook until his teeth rattled and slept fitfully snuggled to his mother's chest as she hugged him to her on the bed, and tried to fall sleep herself, but sleep was impossible, yet she had no discernable feelings.

It was better to be emotionally flat than acknowledge the rage rising in her gullet from the train ride, at the "rights" men assume with unescorted women. It far overshadowed the disappointment in finding this miserable excuse for an apartment.

It was not her problem that her husband's hopeful expectations of sex grew dimmer, and then died, on the stone cold mattress that offered her no comfort, no warmth. Passion had evaporated, worn too thin to rise to his excitement and she did not seek out his eyes; he would not comprehend her revulsion with all things sexual.

In the morning, Aggie stood at the ticket office wicket and two days after that, she and her boy were back in Toronto.

Oh well, she had her job back at the taxi company, Aggie had told Jane on the phone when she returned. They could not find a replacement because no one else wanted that crazy job in the little cabin.

Jane had heard that Kodak was looking for girls for factory assembly jobs in their plant and Aggie was sure that her wartime riveting experience at De Havilland, qualified her. It had certainly been good training and it could count as similar experience. Now that had been excellent money! One way or another, the girls might have to wait in line to hand in their application, but it would be worth it, just to get their names in the hat.

"You cannot win if you do not enter the contest," she told Jane, parroting her father, which made them laugh.

The city emergency line had openings, too, Jane told her, and either of those jobs sounded like a step in the right direction.

Hank came home, eventually, she remembered with a wry smile, shaking her head until her pin curls loosened, with two, two-dollar bills to show for his six months away.

"It's tough up there, Aggie. There was gambling, and drinking," he told her. "I didn't mean to, but there was nothing else to do."

Still, all the trips down memory lane, all the emotions, had nothing to do with today. Now it was stinking hot, there were two boys, and she was still in this black box of a house.

She had to hustle to the butcher, feed the boys, drop them off, and get to her job on the night shift at General Electric. At least the money was better there and she could handle her share of the mortgage.

No one could say she was not clean, Aggie reflected, while dunking the little curtain from the only window into a freshened and sudsy dishpan. The boys were no exception and small pan served the purpose to warm water on the stove for the boy's nightly wash. Hands, face, feet and all in-between, her boys would be clean, and every night she vowed, as some people pray, someday this house will be done up properly or the boys and I will be gone.

Boy in a Box

Spring 1952

Chapter 5

The hazy heat of the day settled the classroom like the hush and calm of a stale funeral parlor, while outside the window a dedicated bee flew in lazy circles, buzzing outside the window, as it made its industrious journey from one clover to another. It settled into the flower's sweet spot to feed, and repeated that over, and over again under the blazing June sun.

Young legs, crossed under the children's bottoms, or hanging down, wore a veil of earthy sweat as their arms propped up their heads, leaning on their hands. Trapped humidity pressed tightly to the captive teacher and students and made it hard to breathe, while the hands on the clock seemed to push against deep water, slowly, slowly, towards the final bell of the year.

The teacher's stockings clung to her legs and her dress was soaked where it lodged against the back of her wooden chair. It was almost useless fanning her face, her legs but it felt worse when the motion stopped.

Maybe, she thought, if this weather would break on the weekend and bring a few clouds or a thunderstorm to sweeten the fetid air and shake some energy into the town and stir up this paralyzed feeling, the holidays could start with more enthusiasm.

Nonetheless, as the afternoon dragged endlessly on, duty called to make a show of interest for the pupils' sake, but pushing herself up from the desk made her head spin so she reached her hand behind her to steady herself on the strong oak chair.

Wisely, she had decided on a project to keep them busy. She handed out a large piece of craft paper to each child, and a few crayons, with instructions to draw a picture of their house.

In motion now, albeit slow, her gaze wandered over her young pupils' lackadaisical response and she noted some students attempted artistry while others were playing with the crayons or folding their paper into smaller and smaller squares. One boy had given up entirely and was using the paper as a big fan, while a few looked out the window, their heads nodding sleepily.

She made her way down between rows of wooden desks with scarred chairs, some bearing new initials, or arrows piercing ancient hearts. A few of those desks, their ages uncertain, barely noted the occupancy of another student, or another year. Year in, year out, they stood testimony to a culture determined children would read and do simple arithmetic.

With luck, now and then, a creative cord would be cultivated and blossomed into art, real art, that unique expression of humanity that lifts our hearts and minds away from the mundane to the possible. It was all possible, she hoped, and it was worth a try on a day without a goal, when the relaxed imagination was free to roam. She continued her vigil, her search for the daring, the unique, something quite capable of leaving her speechless.

Ah! There was a girl's typical picture, a pink house with fanciful red hearts decorating window shutters.

Encircling the lawn, blooms were forming under her hand into a hedge of surreal, swirling purple. Slowly the house was disappearing within an ever-expanding mass of make-believe foliage, like in a science fiction picture at the local movie theatre.

Well! That was a startling view into the mind of the little girl dressed in pink, with pink hair bows holding back her long, dark curls, feeling swallowed up by purple. The teacher made a mental note to look that up in her new psychology book. Fascinating!

Several children had drawn houses with many windows and waving children in them, or a smoking chimney and dogs in the yard. Red brick houses, grey stucco houses, and then a house with a painted barn and very green grass.

Slowly, the teacher moved down the aisle towards the boy with white-blond hair and great intensity, his hand resolutely moving back and forth clutching his black crayon. She looked at his paper with some surprise, not understanding. She had asked them to draw their house and all the other children had done so, but this small boy had drawn a clearly defined square filled with black, leaving a smaller blank square in the centre. Scattered over the solid black were a few thin white lines going every which way.

She asked, "What have you drawn, Ronald?"

The boy looked up at her, startled, his vivid blue eyes wide with surprise to see his teacher standing there.

"My house," he replied with perfect logic, his head cocked as if wondering why she would ask such a thing—it was what she had asked them to do.

"A black house?" she asked.

"Yes," he responded matter-of-factly and bent his head back down to continue his work.

The concerned teacher knew him quite well, and

throughout the school year, he had tried his best at all subjects and was not a troublemaker, beyond being a boy.

Perhaps he just liked the color black, or maybe he copied something from the comic books these tykes could not seem to get enough of, no, she corrected herself: it could not be his home.

He was clean and polite and his clothes were in good order, so perhaps the trouble was in his memory, in his mind, and she felt she should tell somebody, report that this boy thought he was living in a black square box.

She would have to look that up at the library. A strange psychology that pictured a person's house as a black box was not something she had read anywhere. There was still so much to learn if she wanted to become a professional psychologist. That was what the professor told her last week.

The clanging school bell rang, the final bell of the year, and changed the turbid energy in the room into a jubilant scream for freedom. Pictures, papers, books and pens flew through the air across the room as the sluggish amoebas sprang arms, grabbed their books and bags, and their legs unfolded in a flash to sprint for the door.

No one heard the teacher's plea to line up and the wildlings brushed past her as sweaty racing horses ignore a stray mouse. Once outside, their useless schoolbooks tossed above their heads into the open air, they kicked up the dried dirt at the side of the road into clouds of dust, onto unsuspecting passing cars.

It was not important, that no one had finished their experimental artwork. The teacher was completely satisfied that the children had found their boundless enthusiasm.

Small Mercies

1952

Chapter 6

Preparing to shop, Aggie listened as her little boy stirred behind the curtain that created a bedroom cubbyhole at the end of the room. He flopped his foot on the sheet, again, the signal that he would soon be awake. It would be any minute now.

She took the last bite of a roast lamb sliver and thought about how much she respected her father-in-law, as she put away the dried dishes and flicked a cloth over the table dislodging lunch crumbs—her everyday routine.

She appreciated his unending kindness, his day-long walks from his house on Preston Road, a few blocks south of Dufferin Street and Eglinton Avenue, to Canada Packers to buy a big loin of pork, then carry it home on his shoulders, not caring what anyone else thought about it. The meat was for his family and that was what mattered.

She understood him completely. He was an unselfish, kindhearted, family man, like her father.

Her mother-in-law was a different story—watching, frowning when she suspected handouts. Rotund and always dressed in black, her sour face was always suspicious whenever Aggie was around.

"Da English—English girls a-no good" was the

theme from her. She played little tricks like feeding the boys just before Aggie's dinner was ready on special occasions, a tight smile brightening her eyes, small revenges for a major crime. The plan had been for him to marry Italian style, to his own godmother actually.

Aggie boasted aloud, "Ha! That was before Hank saw me!"

Then she quietly pondered, for the thousandth time, how different life would be if she had not seen his handsome face at the dance hall when she was Sweet 16, and she sighed. That was a long time ago and at least she had her treasures—her boys.

The only time her irritating mother-in-law was pleased was when Aggie found a good deal like the nanny goat she got a lead on. For four dollars each, Aggie bought it and they slaughtered it together, knives sharpened to a razor edge as they sliced through the sinews and sawed through the bones. A bit for a few meals kept aside, the rest stored in carefully marked brown paper packages with name and date in the huge basement freezer.

Some meat came from Hank's favorite thing to do: tramping and hunting through the northern bush with a rifle across his arm and his good-hearted father by his side.

Some contributions came without a calling card, like in the dead of winter, when she thought she heard a scrabbling noise outside her door one morning, and opened it a crack.

A wild animal lay there cold and dead, with orange color fur, a contribution from Hank's friend, she found out later. When she asked everyone she knew what the beast was, most guesses were muskrat, perhaps trapped by a friend that expected to find something else in his snare, but meat was meat, and if it was edible, it came to Aggie and her boys. She cooked it up, but called it something else.

She never forgot kindnesses, large or small, like the day when some friends of her Mom and Dad brought her a bit of bread and butter, as a treat for the children.

Slaving away in their garden or orchard did not count with the miserable mother-in-law, Maria. Everyone in the family picked the abundant tomatoes, green peppers, and bushels of mushrooms gathered from the local graveyard. If they wanted to test for a toadstool, they put a dime into a pot of water with them and let it sit. If the dime turned black, the pot contained a poisonous toadstool and had to be ferreted out.

After that procedure, the mushrooms were fried in oil, preserved in jars, and finally stored in a cool spot in the cellar.

Fresh peaches picked from their own fruit trees turned into preserves, Aggie following her mother-in-law's directions. Together they peeled the skins and chopped the fruit, their hands red and sore, and finally at the end of the long day, a label would identify, designate, and date the bags or jars. The peelings were then returned to the soil to enrich it for next year's crop.

Although he was afraid of discovery by his wife, sometimes Hank's father surprised her with a small tap, tap on the door. There he would stand, a conspiratorial smile creasing his work-weary Italian face and a peach or plum heavy bag from the freezer, in his hand, eager for a piece of Aggie's luscious pie.

"Aggie, this-a for da boys. Maybe I come getta piece later?"

Having starched her little niece's bonnet to make it stand up firmly—pleased to have a little girl to dress up—her sister Bea had picked up her daughter and taken her home.

Now it was Aggie's turn to get ready for the day and she quickly changed into freshly washed and ironed red slacks. The pants were older now but still got a charmed reaction when she rolled them up like the new pedal pushers she had seen in pictures in the magazine at the drugstore, a perfect choice on this hot day.

Still working at T.A.S., the telephone answering service, from four to twelve, she couldn't see a reason not to wear them, no customers saw her after all, and everyone admired them. Like last week, when that truck driver passing by had whistled. Now, he was really good looking, and a man with a steady job. She had noticed him in the same truck several times before, and there was no harm in flirting; it kept her spirits up and she was sure he was on the lookout for her.

Maybe there would be empty pop bottles in the alley that she could cash in for a few extra pennies towards fresh bread. You never knew what people would throw out.

Aggie counted out some change to take to the butcher. She would be home before her bigger boy returned from his friend's, and she thought about how hard it was to know what a kid would bring home next. Like yesterday, the last day of school this year, and he brought a picture he made that looked like a black box. That was the only thing on the page, a huge black box with a tiny square in the center that looked vaguely familiar.

"What is that, Ronnie?"

He looked up at Aggie with his innocent blue eyes, so like hers, as if it should be obvious.

"That's our house. The teacher told us to draw a picture of our house, so I did."

She was embarrassed to think that the teacher at school knew what they lived in. Unless something changed, unless her semi-useless husband found a real job—that lasted for more than a month—it would be the last year at that school; the last year in the tarpaper shack. She had decided on the spot.

A dash of Woolworth's new red lipstick for a pretty face and yanked out bobby pins to create a halo of fluffy curls brought an instant smile, a rejuvenated faith. She was carrying the house now, why couldn't she carry a better one. She would figure it out as she always did. The realization relaxed her, if her husband did not want to come with her, she would do it alone.

A fresh white sleeveless blouse and those bargain red high heel shoes from the Salvation Army worked their magic, too, just in time, as her younger boy, Melville, was stirring now, listening to his mommy rustle through her things and talking to himself in bed, trying out words and settling on "shoes."

"Shoes, shoes, shoes," he cooed, quite in love with the sound, then smiled broadly, as his mother came into his sight.

Tonight, while she worked the nightshift, the boys would stay at her friend Mary's house, in a room freshened by an electric fan stirring the stifling air.

Aggie caught the boy's eye and they traded a happy-wake-up smile while she counted out some change, all she could spare in case her hitchhiking smile failed her and they had to take the bus. The small bit of money left over had to buy them supper.

A sweet-sharp smell of freshly cut sawdust arose from the butcher's floor, stronger at first than the pungent and rosy slaughtered meat behind the glass partitions.

The butcher liked her. His face lit up and he was kindest when the store was empty, a small boy hanging on Aggie's hip, and his wife gone home to cook supper. Hazel eyes, and the butcher's round, red, sweating face and Polish accent, greeted her with a warm welcome, watched her preen and turn this way and that, lower her lashes admiring his nice looking bacon, in the store empty of every other person but themselves.

"Mrs. Subrinsky gone home so soon?" she asked breezily.

"Oh, yes, yes, too bad you miss her," he responded with a sly smile. "I have such nice chops today, Missus, you should try two. I will cut them thin, the way you like them."

They both knew that he would cut them thick, and charge her for thin. If she leaned over the counter to watch him and her white blouse with the frills parted slightly with the weight of the child on her hip, a small mercy like a nice end of bacon would magically appear in her paper package to chop into a pot of macaroni with a bit of cheese.

She was truly grateful when the butcher opened his large air-cooled refrigerator and let her hold her smiling baby up to it. The contented butcher, wiping his hands on his bloodstained apron, stood back to let them enjoy it and to watch.

Aggie glanced now and then to the window, while playing the coquette, seeming not to notice the butcher's flirtations and wondering if the truck with the mysterious stranger would pass again.

Everyone was happy.

She needed to hurry now, there was no time left for socializing and the packet of meat grew warm in her hand, and the sun's heat blistered, radiating merciless glare into their eyes. Better to take the laneway separating the houses and backyards. There would be more shade for her fair-haired child reddening and growing listless as the moments passed.

Various odds-and-ends littered the narrow alley: discarded cushions, colorful but tattered; a rusted sink, useless now; a broken chair that needed a bit of glue and paint, but there was no room for it in the shack.

They stood for a moment in the shadow of a concrete garage offering solid shade. She hoisted the heavy and energy-drained child from one hip to the other, and rubbed her arm where it had grown moist and hot from his body. Looking across the grit-dusted laneway, she spotted something pleasing to the eye with muted shades of browns and gold—a carpet that seemed in decent shape.

"Here, sit here for a moment," she muttered to the child, plunked down now in the shade of the garage and too dulled by the muggy air to protest. In a few quick steps, she crossed the airless alley to the carpet and quickly unrolled it, pleased and surprised by its good condition. Dusty, yes, but it would clean, and she could do it.

As she began to roll it up, a car abruptly turned into the alley with the sun fully onto his windshield—seeing nothing.

Darting and stumbling across the lane, Aggie grabbed the boy up into her arms and flattened them both to the garage door. Oblivious, the passing driver hardly abated his speed until he spotted them and hit the screeching brakes hard with both feet in great exasperation, waving his hand in the air in the universal, "What the Hell?"

"You almost hit us! Slow down, you animal!" she spluttered at him.

"Oh, I say! So sorry!" he exclaimed wide-eyed, his long, thin face contorted with surprise at seeing the mother and her baby.

In a broad accent newly arrived from England, he called out, "What on earth are you doing here?"

"Trying to take this carpet home—down the street a couple of blocks. Will you help us?" she responded quickly, taking full advantage of his guilty moment.

The driver opened the passenger door with a congenial smile to let her quickly deposit Melville on the clean, tan, leather front seat, and she watched as the sweating man opened his trunk and stuffed the dust-puffing treasure inside, as if it was the filthiest thing he had ever seen.

Now it was hers. She would clean it up to make it look like new and make that place pretty on the inside and to hell with the outside.

When they left, they would take their magic carpet with them.

A Man's Man

1950's

Chapter 7

Hank was not exaggerating: he told Aggie the truth, just not all the truth. It really was tough trying to find a regular job out there, and a man had to trust somebody before he dared to be honest. One thing he knew for sure—he could trust her to keep quiet.

It was a rough time in Toronto in the late '40s and early '50's after the war. Guns were everywhere, and daily papers sold out in an hour, grabbed up as soon as they hit the stands, and filled with the ongoing saga of the Boyd gang, who carried out a series of well-planned bank robberies in the city.

Edwin Alonzo Boyd, Leonard "Tough Lennie" Jackson, Willie "The Clown" Jackson, and Steven Suchan—everyone knew their names. Boyd and the two Jacksons had met in Toronto's Don Jail after separate run-ins with the law. Their entourage included Alonzo's beautiful wife, Doreen, and women copied her hairstyle. Their thrilling jailbreak and subsequent bank robberies filled Canada's newspapers with shocking headlines and photos of the gang members.

Two members of the Boyd Gang, Suchan and Lennie Jackson, killed a detective and wounded another. The city locked down tight; the police had their mandate—shoot to kill. A Globe and Mail headline on September 9, 1952, declared, "Wanted, Dead or Alive, $26,000 Reward. Armed-to-Teeth Police Search for Boyd Gang."

The manhunt fascinated the frightened or titillated populace who were on high alert, eating up the latest news. For ten long months, squads of twenty or more officers, heavily armed with rifles and sub-machine guns, raided places with known criminal activity and swept the heavily wooded Don River ravines that sheltered many misfits, crooks, and the down-and-out. Someone even said there used to be a nudist colony living there.

The wanted men were captured alive and sent back to the Don Jail. They managed a second jailbreak, along with newly apprehended Boyd, and Willie Jackson. Following an all-forces search, it ended in a barn near Yonge and Sheppard with the gang members recaptured, nearly starved.

The judge demanded hanging for Suchan and Lennie Jackson and they both hung from the end of a rope until dead.

Willie Jackson and Boyd were found guilty of bank robbery and other crimes; Jackson got 31 years and Boyd got eight concurrent life sentences.

Hank still had to find his way around violent Toronto. It was where they lived, after all, but it was tough times.

Nothing had changed simply because he and Aggie were married. Married, or not, and a father, it was impossible to keep out of trouble. Employment generated from the pool hall was all he knew. Hank tried to explain that to Aggie, but that did not matter to her. She wanted him to have a regular job.

She told him, "This is it—make it or break it," and he

nodded. He vowed to try to work it out with her in the converted garage attached to the side of his parent's house.

They could settle down there, he figured. It was one large room with a sink and hydro, so they could hook up a stove. It would have to do. Someday, he vowed, the outside would be finished, so they pooled their money, coughed up the eight hundred dollars, four hundred each, which his parents demanded, as an investment in their future as a family.

She was at him all the time, her hands on her hips and a disgusted look in her eyes, just before she left for work. "I thought you said you were going to get a job?" or "Aren't you working today? I'm working today!"

"I don't have a trade, remember? I'm looking, Aggie, I'm looking!" Hank shot her a look that would turn a normal person to stone, but it did not faze her. She just glared at him, then turned around, grabbed her purse and left, slamming the door behind her.

Hank ran his hand through his dark hair in frustration, grabbed his jacket, shoved in his arms; now that she had finally left, he had business of his own to do today, business she knew nothing about and would not understand.

At the ripe age of twenty-six, a gang came up to city outskirts to hunt him down after he beat up one of the hoods in a fight. For extra persuasion, in case he needed it, Hank bought two pistols, a German Luger and a Belgian P-38, to hide in his stylish big jacket that had many deep pockets, some inside next to his body to stash things like bullets.

For several nights, Hank climbed to the roof of their home with his two guns, plus a .22 gauge automatic rifle, and a .303 army rifle. Thus armed, he awaited the battle, fitfully dozing on and off throughout the star-filled hours of darkness. Then one night it happened.

The big black Buick pulled up and parked in front of the empty lot across the street, with its engine running, brazenly glistening under the nearby streetlight as if the sight of the car, alone, would frighten their target into submission. Nobody got out but Hank knew that car. It had done the rounds downtown; it was not there to wish him a long and healthy life and was he not waiting for the occupants to make the first move. He aimed the .303 at the side of the car behind the front wheel and pulled the trigger. Immediately after the gunshot, a metallic clang rang out as the bullet penetrated the thin steel of the Buick, the sound reverberating through the still dark night. As he quickly fired another round into the car, it suddenly jerked forward, tires squealing as it sped off into the night.

Hank stayed on the roof in case they came back, watching the street and surrounding yards for any movement. A half an hour later another car pulled up in front of his parent's house next door and two men in suits got out. He watched as they came up the driveway, across the walkway, and stepped onto the porch. Hank leaned down from the roof, one hand gripping the edge of it and the other hand pointing the rifle in the general direction of the two men.

"Don't shoot! We're police!"

Hank had the message loud and clear from Aggie: this ongoing violence in his lifestyle and their own volatile relationship was tearing them apart.

"I am working!" Hank shouted. "What does that look like outside? It's a damn truck! Shut up! I'm leaving, I'm late!"

"How long is this job," Aggie countered, "two days?"

Hank slammed the shack door for emphasis and

reached the door of the truck parked in the driveway in four quick strides. As he yanked the door open, hauled himself up into the driver's seat and reached back to grab the door handle to pull the heavy door shut, it flashed through his mind—he had not seen Ronnie in a while.

"Where's Ronnie?" he mumbled. He checked the rear view mirrors for a glimpse of blond little-boy hair. Ronnie was such a quiet kid, he could be playing anywhere, but Hank had not seen him in the house for a while, so shaking his head in wonderment at what kids do, he decided to walk around the truck, just to be sure.

Slowly he re-opened the door, convinced he was being stupid, the kid could be anywhere else but there, but he climbed down, heading for the back of the vehicle. Yes, there was Ronnie on his tricycle, reaching up to the monster-sized tire with a contented smile and sending little fistfuls of sand running down through the grooves, out of the view of truck mirrors.

His heart in his mouth, Hank reached down and pulled the tricycle all the way to the side door, giving the pleased kid a ride. Hank bent down and looked into the boy's blue eyes, so like his mother's eyes.

"I'm off to work, now," he told the boy. "Stay inside until Daddy leaves, and never, ever, play behind a truck." He would be late now, but at least the kid was still in one piece.

Hank ruffled Ronnie's hair, climbed back up into the truck and slammed the door shut. Maybe he was not home as much as he should be, he reasoned, and maybe he relied too much on Aggie, but there was no one better to look after the boy; she had a way of getting things done.

He whispered to her in the pitch black of their

bedroom, after the boy had fallen asleep on the little mattress by the foot of their bed.

"I got rid of them once, but they might come back."

Aggie did not move; she did not like to talk about the gangsters and barely turned her head on the pillow towards him.

"What are you going to do?" she whispered, her eyes rounded in concern as if the hoods were hiding under the bed. Her face pinched, her eyes squinted, and she acted wary of any answer he might give.

"I have an idea," he confided. He sat up halfway, balanced on his elbow so he could look down into her worried face.

Despite her fears, Hank told her anyway. "You know I have to get away from those hoods. I think I found a way to keep out of trouble—avoid those men." He did not say that they were out to kill him.

His wife listened with skepticism; her head turned slightly aside, suspicion looming in her eyes when she flicked them in his direction, probably wondering what on earth he was going to come up with next. She picked absent-mindedly at the fluff on the blanket.

"There's a job up north," Hank said, keeping his voice down so he would not get her overexcited. "It's really cold there and they have trouble finding workers. The money is terrific and we could pay off the house."

She sat upright and stared at him, looking flabbergasted, and he could see her reasonable mood was shattered.

Her voice squeaked, "What am I supposed to do for money while you're gone? It's cold here, too."

It was more of a croak, now. "I'll have to work two jobs again!"

"Oh come on, Aggie, you know I can't stay around

here. It's too dangerous for all of us."

Hank was picturing it in his mind, a little rented apartment up north, the boy in ski boots, Aggie and Hank reunited in a bed after missing each other, happy to be together like the early days.

They would not be safe from the gangs until they forgot about him.

Aggie became quiet, dangerously quiet. Eventually she looked away and said in a low tone, "Your idea better work," and rolled away from him, taking their entire blue wedding blanket with her.

No one told Hank it was a staggering, shivering five-mile walk every morning through snowdrifts from the trailers to the jobsite six days a week, and when the tough shift finished, he slogged back to the rusty barracks.

There was a drawback to the job, one little flaw that bomb-shelled the huge check, making it possible to come home with his pay spent. There was zilch to do in the spare time, so after work and a raucous meal in the cookhouse, the men smoked cigarettes and gambled with cards or chess, hour after blank hour. The cycle was money in, money out.

He talked Aggie into coming up once, with the kid, but that blew up in his face and made it worse.

Hank came home almost broke and the couple stood, one on each side of the doorway, observing each other in mutual understanding: things had changed.

Ronnie was in school, growing taller by the day, and she had little to say to her husband. She was cool, kept him at arms length, said she was fed-up with the whole deal and needed a new start.

Their toddler, Melville, the curious boy with a big smile, (from a passionate moment when Hank came back from up north for a couple of careless weeks,) leaped forward from crawling to running, everywhere.

"I can't do it anymore," she said.

Hank got in touch with some old friends again that knew how to turn a buck.

When their miserable house sold, to pay back the parents, the long-time lovers decided on one last try without the burden of debt.

In the upstairs of a house, their apartment was closer to bus lines and near a park, within walking distance to a plaza and a small grocery store where Aggie could get another part-time job. It had a bathroom with a tub, and two bedrooms with doors, but it did not stop their battles.

"You're never home!" she hollered at his back as he pushed his way past her and headed out the door. "Where you going now? Got a new gang?"

Hank did not bother to reply.

"Who cares?" She hollered after him, not caring who heard. "You're never home anyway. And, you never had a real paycheck you didn't gamble away."

"Well, you're a bloody nag!" He was shouting now and he hated shouting. "You nag and nag...and interfere with my life. I don't know where the hell you go...going to dances and bars downtown, probably messing around!"

"Not yet, you idiot," she yelled to his back. "When am I supposed to have some fun? I have to laugh with somebody, but you wouldn't understand that."

His pal John spotted Aggie, and some creep, sauntering across the park beside the apartment building on a warm April evening.

Hank roared, "I hope you got running shoes!"

The dumb guy with her stood still, tried to act tough; doing the old "put 'em up," and gyrating his fists in the air like John Sullivan, as if he knew how to fight. Hank knocked him down a few times until the jerk did not get up again.

Aggie whaled on Hank with her spiked high-heel shoe, shrieking, "You got it all wrong! You always get it all wrong!"

Backing away, Hank spotted a pile of bricks beside the park keeper's shack and edged towards it, to put a space between them. He knew what he had seen and that was enough for him. Years of pent-up frustration almost choked him.

Strangely, his gut was suddenly full of the whole sham. There was something wrong with them trying to be together and he knew in a flash—he had enough—it was over. He stood up straight and calmly looked her in the eye.

"Shut up and go home. You've caused enough problems tonight."

Aggie answered Hank by charging him with assault and then she sued him for support. Split up—their kids farmed out to another family for care for a few months while she got organized—it was the end. Between the two of them, they had finished their marriage.

Full of glee to have a bankroll when his car sold for $1,400, Hank completed his plans to get out of town and watched the pieces fall into place, vowing on the spot, when the money for the car was in his fist, that no one else would get one dime.

Before he could leave town, he had to spend 10 days for the assault charge and to cool off in the Don Jail. He served eight days, then they let him go without a reason, and he laughed it off later with his buddies. He figured it was all his complaints about the miserable excuse for food, and no one searched him, lucky guy. The officer would have found the fourteen-hundred in his pocket, a big wad sticking out like a sore thumb, but the dumb new recruit did not even notice.

Exhilarated, Hank took off out west: now he was free, absolutely free and only 29 years old.

Gypsy longing filled his heart and freedom whistled through his wild nest of hair as he stood up on top of a freight train laughing into the wind. The railway police had chased him down the track with flailing arms in the air motioning him to come down, and they did not see him take a big breath, jump off the other side of the railcar and roll into the underbrush.

Hank lay still, getting his bearings, checking his scratched limbs that hurt all over—nothing broken, all else would mend. Scrambling across the swamp that stretched as far as he could see, he understood, to his disgust, his body would soon stink of a coating of early-autumn slime from underbrush rotting in the water.

Within an hour he was ecstatic, spread-eagled clutching the top of another train roof, heading in the opposite direction. He would climb into a boxcar later.

Now he wanted to hang on tight, the air stream blowing his coal black Italian hair into a refreshing whirlwind. He would find an open freight car later and maybe a beer, maybe food, and then a bath; right now the black sky and a million stars were fine companions.

West! Adventure! Feeling ravenous for freedom, a trapped animal escaping with no one to demand a thing from him, he stopped off in several cities and calmly walked into a local bank to deposit part of his bankroll.

In Calgary, he looked around at the tellers and they looked better dressed than the folks at home did, so it seemed the west was doing just fine. He knew it was possible to wire money wherever he wanted and if it was not in his pocket, it could not be stolen or spent. It was just the way he liked money, either tight in his fist or safer in a vault far away from spending on frivolous things; that's what his wife spent money on, frivolous things. She had always worked, even with the kids, so he figured she could work now or get her boyfriends to help her out—he was finished with all of that.

He strode down the bustling streets of Calgary, a booming cowboy town where the industrious population had big aspirations, loved tall and wide-brimmed hats, and imposing structures sprang up right and left while the bosses screamed for more workers.

Hank turned down four job offers in one day in that city, but he did not need a job yet, and when he cast his thoughts towards the future, he acknowledged he would rather see the Pacific Ocean.

He picked apples in British Colombia, hot and hard work in the Okanogan Valley, while the sweet smell reminded him of family fruit trees at home, ripening now, in Toronto. He had never felt homesick before, but he let the feeling pass. It was adventure he was chasing now and he wanted to keep his distance from Aggie; it was better for them both that way.

When summer was gone, and when the leaves had morphed into brilliant color and the nights grew longer than the days, Florida called to Hank. It was due time to turn south and risk the border, a tricky proposition for a man with a record, freshly out of jail.

The word on the street was that border authorities remained vigilant and checked warrants, even with many of the famous Boyd gang members all dead now or in jail, and he did have unfinished business with the law, but he was in a mood to take risks.

With a new friend, tall and lanky Norm McDonald, with a twang in his speech like a cowboy, Hank thought it was worth the gamble to try the border at Vancouver, early on a sunny morning, and the lax guards believed his story of going to the States for a day.

He drove endlessly, state after American state, mesmerized by the mountains and then the flatlands, always southeast all the way to Florida. He'd see it all, he decided, and his new buddy Norm was eager to go anywhere but back home, it appeared, although he never said why, but first on the list were the car races on Daytona Beach.

"Hey, Hank. Look at the gas gauge!"

Norm's shout roused him from the eyes straight-ahead stupor of highway driving.

"Damn! A quarter tank means fill it up to me." Hank flicked his head to the right. "Did you see a turnoff?"

"Yeah, about a mile back."

They decided to risk it, took the next exit to hunt for a gas station, as there was none in sight, and Hank picked a random direction at the crossroads and kept driving until a crude sign and an arrow pointed towards "Restaurant."

"They will know where gas is." Norm nodded his head in compliance, sounding sure about that, but it was more of a track than a road, and eventually ended abruptly in a dead end.

"Damn!" Hank cursed, and he hardly ever did that, but they were obviously lost and he had one choice only, so he followed that primitive road between fields of gigantic corn until it turned into a flat savannah.

No road signs had appeared to direct Hank, baffled as the sun quickly disappeared. He figured they were either a quarter mile off the highway, going in circles, or miles away from it now; in this black muggy night it was impossible to tell.

"One last try," Hank muttered, veering to the right when the headlights picked out a crossroads in the track, and he looked at his gas gauge.

"Almost empty," he added unnecessarily to his

already spooked passenger.

Like a magic trick, they spotted a light up ahead in the darkness, a mere pinprick of rosy glow that grew into a row of lanterns as they neared, glowing red on the ground at the right side of the road. From the quiet night came live music that grew louder as they drove slowly towards it, a heavy downbeat, high keening, and then the blare of horns and a solid bass line.

Hank pulled up alongside a dilapidated building and they could hear feet stomping to the beat, and see shadows jumping in the space between where the walls ended, and the roof began. "What a joint! Darn, that music is catchy!" he shouted to Norm. "I'm going in."

Norm's arm shot out to block him, "Hey!" he said earnestly, a worried frown creasing his face. "Are you sure you want to do that?"

A big black man sauntered around the side of the rickety building and spotted them.

"We're lost, and we're looking for gas," Hank explained with a charming smile, while unfolding his legs from the front seat.

A huge grin split the big man's mouth wide open, "Well," he drawled, "Come on in!"

Hank got out of the car slowly, stretched his arms up high, then took in a big yawn of air into his lungs and bent forward holding onto his knees, while he exhaled and un-kinked his back. "Do I smell food?"

"Man, you ne'er done taste food so good befo'," the black man told him proudly, showing a row of brilliant white teeth with one missing, "an' I cook it. My lady helpers, o'course and me. I get hit on the head wif' a pot if I done forget to mention 'dat!"

Hours later, with the gas tank full, Hank, Norm, and two exceptionally big and muscle-bound men sat in the back seat escorting the travelers through the maze of roads. With the windows cranked down, to let any breeze freshen the fetid air and dilute the perspiration plastering their shirts to their backs, they passed tiny shacks and chicken coops and a couple of hard-scrabble dogs barking at their wheels until the mutts flopped down exhausted, giving up the chase.

It was hard to make out the road ahead in the pre-dawn darkness. The rough roads grew into tracks, the car bouncing in wheel ruts through dark tunnels of underbrush, in the light of a half-moon chasing the tops of tangled mangrove trees.

They passed row upon row of coconut palm plantations, and endless fields of late bare corn like ominous sentinels guarding the first shards of dawn.

The men in the back seat grew quieter as they indicated a place to stop, a fair distance from the rear of a small and likely moldy motel, showing one dim light in the office window.

"You can go in dat place," their escort told them, "it clean," he said, but pointing to it as if it had serious vibes of dark magic, and the duo seemed subdued for the first time that night.

"De's always got room and de show you du way to the highway out front in de mornin'. Stop here, here! We not 'sposed to be in your automobile. We git out now."

"How will you get back?" Hank asked.

"Ne're mind. Dat not your concern. We-all had good times tonight. Tomorrow is diff'runt. Tomorrow we is strangers."

Quietly, the pair of heavy-set saints in their Saturday night dancing pants left the car, and melted into the sun rising over the forest.

Broken

1954 era

Chapter 8

"Where is it, you stupid shit?!" his crazy uncle yelled, and stomped his black motorcycle boots around the tiny kitchen, listing sideways in his stinky white shirt and his previously slicked-back blond hair now standing on end.

He flung open the flimsy cupboard doors and slammed them shut as hard as he could and laughed when the draft knocked over neatly stacked paper serviettes that fluttered to the floor as he advanced on his trembling young nephew.

"I told you," Mel retorted with a force that sounded shaky to his own ears, "Mom took it with her."

"Oh, bullshit! Your mother always leaves her money at home—so she won't spend it!"

Uncle Chuck turned, towering over him, his voice a growl, "The rent money is around here somewhere and when I find it—I'm going to say you took it!"

Mel's widened eyes frantically and circled the sparsely furnished living room trying to remember Mom's last hiding spot. The red couch cushion? The baseboard? The inside pocket of the coat on the rack?

If he could get there first, he could grab it and run and run. Mom would never believe he stole the money.

He wished his older brother were here, too, in the

apartment but he was out playing somewhere.

His uncle smelled like puke and he always looked taller when he was plastered, and ugly, too, waving his arms around as if he owned the world. His blue eyes squeezed up into little slits of meanness, as if he did not remember that Mel was his nephew who he drove around in his car sometimes. Mel thought Uncle Chuck loved that car almost as much as he loved booze and he only loved his nephews when he was sober.

If he could just get out the door with the money, Mel figured, he could head for the hall stairs and snake his way down the stairwell so fast that Uncle Chuck would be spinning if he came after him and fall over like a top.

Mom never hid money in the same place twice so he didn't know where it was either. She learned that early, she said, because when men are drinking they forget families need things like groceries.

Mel sprinted for the bedroom and slammed the door shut.

His new lion-colored spaniel puppy jumped up to play this game, whatever it was, gamboling and trying to stand on her back legs but falling to her side, weighed down by her oversized baby tummy. The little dog started to yip, yip, joining in the noise and frolic.

As Mel reached for the pup to shush her, the bedroom door crashed open sending waves of confusing noise careening around the room.

Mel's head flashed around looking for her but did not see his puppy and he hoped she was safely under the bottom bunk of the bed. She liked to huddle there sometimes if there were loud noises. He thought she felt safer in the darkness.

Uncle Chuck lurched around the small room. "You got the money in here?" he shouted, reaching down to Mel where he cowered in front of the bed instinctively protecting his pup, the only thing he loved besides his mom and brother, and his girl cousin, Marilyn.

The tall man's face screwed up cruelly. Mel saw no light of acknowledgment shining in his eyes for his six year-old nephew as he towered over him.

He grabbed the front of Mel's shirt. "What are you hiding, you little shit?" he bellowed in his face. "Is that my money?"

Mel staggered to the floor howling, "No, no!" as his uncle pushed him away from the bed and crouched down to grab his treasure, probably hoping for his next round of drinking money, and looked closer when faint barks sounded from the darkness, back against the wall.

"Lots of money for dogs, eh?"

His uncle reached under the bed cursing, his long arm swinging back and forth, back and forth almost to the wall.

"Leave her alone! Leave her alone! She didn't cost anything!" the boy cried out.

The uncle's hand found fur and grabbed the yelping pup easily in one hand. He dragged her from the safety of darkness far under the bed into the sun streaming in the window.

Mel grabbed his arm and yanked as hard as he could, "No, no, Uncle Chuck! I'll help you look for the money, I don't know where it is, but I'll help you look!" His voice was cracking, begging, knowing from experience that Chuck was insane when he was drunk and he never remembered anything. He laughed when he heard about his own antics as if it was all a joke, as if no one got hurt.

"Please, please, Uncle Chuck! Leave my dog alone!"

The man flung the boy's hands away effortlessly with one hand, keeping a grip on the squirming, squealing pup in the other hand held high over the boy's head, and pushed past Mel into the living room.

He took a stance, winding up as if he was a pitcher at baseball practice. "So where's the goddamn money?" he growled.

Instinctively, the puppy seemed to understand what her sharp little teeth were for and sank those deeply into the brutal hand squeezing the breath from her round abdomen and immature chest.

His uncle stood still for a moment, eyes flung open wide, as if time stopped when the needle teeth punctured his hand, a look of pure amazement turning to hatred pouring down on the small dog.

"No, no, Uncle Chuck!" Mel gasped, reading his uncle's ugly expression, but the drunk did not hear or care. Without hesitation in his booze-soaked dream of power, the man hurled the puppy at the wall.

She thudded dully and slid down to the floor.

Mel's hands flew up to his mouth in protective shock, and he stood frozen in place as the pup jerked and then lay completely still, a trickle of blood oozing from her nose.

The boy heard the apartment door open as his mother, Aggie, entered in a rush, rustling paper shopping bags, but he could not move.

"What's the racket all about?" she asked, her face flushed from rushing to be home to be with him, then stopped when she looked at her brother, his greased-up hair on end, framing blood-red eyes in his rage-twisted face and his arms hanging down at his sides.

Her eyes riveted on Mel's face, a horrified picture of despair.

She looked where her son looked, down to the golden mound of puppy lifeless on the floor.

"You bastard!" Aggie shouted, flinging down her groceries and handbag. Crossing the room in an instant, she reached up and slapped Chuck soundly across the head.

This shocked Mel. In all the years of caring for his troublesome uncle, Mom always gave her brother the next chance, and the next, telling gossipy stories about him but bailing him out of jail when her own children were almost starving. Mel could see his mom was through with that and he had to help her now.

Uncle Chuck lurched to the side, flinging his arm trying to strike her back, galvanizing Mel into action. He ran at his uncle, his fists pounding air before smashing them into Chuck's belly.

His Mom gripped Chuck's jacket with one hand and slapped him even harder with the other. "If you ever touch my son, or anything else of ours, I will disown you!" she shouted as he ducked, trying to fend off her blows with one hand and fend off Mel's kicks at his shin with the other.

Mel's feet slipped out from under him on the fringe of a scatter rug that his Mom had found at the Sally Ann. His legs slammed into Uncle Chuck's shins, sending both of them crashing down winded and helpless.

Mom, half the man's size, seized the advantage, grabbed her brother's slippery yellow hair, yanked his head up, and smacked it down soundly on the hardwood floor.

She and Mel sat back, their breath ragged from their struggle, and watched the unconscious man breathe in and out. Then she did something Mel never thought she would do. Instead of dragging him out and locking the door, she crawled around his passed-out body to reach the telephone and called the police.

Panting, head pounding, feeling too numb to cry, Mel hoped that after the cops would beat Chuck up, like they usually did, and they would find a way to keep him in jail forever this time.

Hello Suburbia

1956

Chapter 9

So, now what? I'm 30 years old with two boys and I need a house. Jobs are easy to find for someone willing to work—so I'm not worried.

That house the brother-in-law told me about sounds good, at a really low price, but it needs a little fixing up. I hope the roof doesn't leak! The house is in Weston and a long way to a bus stop, but we can still get into the city. I'm going to the bank.

"Good morning, Mrs. Lauria, making a deposit today?"

Aggie recognized the bright voice and smile of the teller, Mrs. Madison, standing behind the glass wicket in the varnished, dark wood partition and looking so smart today, with white collar and cuffs accenting her navy business dress.

Aggie felt satisfied that she had chosen a simple dress of coral cotton, that fit snuggly across her ample bosom, nipped in at her small waist, gently hugged her hips and now pressed to perfection. Her white pumps trailed a faint scent of liquid shoe polish that she had not noticed on the bus.

She spoke up firmly, not wanting to distract herself

with chitchat, "No deposit today. I'd like to speak to the manager."

"I see. Do you have an appointment?"

"No, but I do need to speak to him." Aggie's voice was firm now and she waited calmly blinking, her bright blue eyes holding the steady gaze of a woman in business, ready to make a deal.

"Oh! Well!" Mrs. Madison responded, a little smile curling one side of her lip. "Let me ask about that."

When she patted her curly permed brown hair and straightened the belt of her robin's egg blue shirtwaist dress, it seemed a familiar action to Aggie when a girl was approaching the boss's office.

As if it was an afterthought, Mrs. Madison motioned to the two wooden chairs beside the manager's office and offered, "Have a seat, Mrs. Lauria," as her heels clicked across the marble tiled floor to a door with a glass window. The teller knocked twice quickly and entered, shutting the door quietly behind her.

Aggie turned gracefully on the ball of her foot like a dancer and walked towards the chairs, swallowing hard, certain that her heartbeat would echo through the high-ceilinged bank, all the way to the manager, all the way to the vaults that held the money that she desired and could be slamming shut, sensing an intruder.

Voices sounded from inside the inner office.

First, the female voice made an inquiry in a level tone of voice and the male voice politely protested.

Then Aggie heard the words "new company policy" sharply stated as the woman asked the man her question a second time, in a slightly higher tone.

He protested more firmly, the female voice continued with her request, followed by a mix of their voices speaking loudly at the same time, and then there was silence.

The door opened and Mrs. Madison calmly returned to her post behind the wicket, patted her hair-do from habit and nodded her head in accord towards Aggie, indicating she should stay seated until called into the office.

Aggie settled on the creaking wooden chair and resigned herself to whatever would happen next.

"Oh, well," she thought, "this plan will work, or not."

There were alternative ways of finding money but the bank was her best option to secure the future of her family. She had an excellent job record, had dressed appropriately, her perfume was light and floral, and that would have to do.

She was blond and knew she was pretty: the two-edged sword that opens doors and then shrinks credibility as if it proved she was not a hard worker, or did not have an adult brain. It was nothing new. She just talked faster to compensate, wore them down so to speak. She'd do that today.

Sitting with her back straight against the wooden slats, Aggie crossed her ankles to one side and placed her hands one on top of the other in her lap reminding herself to stop flapping them like a nervous hummingbird.

She picked up, put down, and turned over, the envelope of papers her brother-in-law, the lawyer, had prepared, wondering why the manager was taking so long to see her.

In hopes of distracting herself from the numbers on the papers in her envelope, Aggie tried to count the styles of matron's hats that seemed to float in and out of the bank's revolving door under their own steam and then escape outside. Flowers, birds, veils, wide brims like umbrellas and thin brims like sailor's hats drifted by. She relinquished her count at eight when the styles began repeating themselves.

The central clock on the wall next to the vault was ticking too slowly. She thought it must need repair and debated mentioning it.

Really, no matter how she tried to distract herself, the numbers that mattered were not on the clock: they were her income figures and the proposed loan payments that juggled and jumbled together like a circus act that depended on her performance inside the closed office door.

Courage chased doubt away as soon as a small bell sounded and Mrs. Madison nodded in her direction, indicating the invitation to follow her to the manager's office.

"Thank you for seeing me, Mr. Brewster. You see, I sold a house a few years ago and I want to buy another one, but this time I'm buying it on my own, with my own money, for myself and my boys, no partners. We've been living in apartments since then but I want my own house, and I've been waiting for a deal like this, and I know I can rent out most of it, we can live in the basement and that will get us started..."

The portly bank manager, complacent in tailored suit and straining vest, raised his hand to interrupt her, a gold ring gleaming in a ray of sunlight from the window.

"Just a moment, Mrs. Lauria! Let's start with a few particulars. First of all we do not usually loan money without collateral..."

"But, you will hold my mortgage, Mr. Brewster. You will have my money and the house—until I pay it off!"

"...and your husband, Mrs. Lauria? Are you both employed?"

"Mr. Brewster! This has nothing to do with my husband! He won't be my husband for long. I'm the worker in this family!"

Aggie couldn't believe the manager had so many questions, wondering how she would handle the house on her own.

He had no idea the things she had to do that she couldn't mention, like bootlegging from that tarpaper shack thanks to the hole under the kitchen floor. Buying booze on payday, stashing it until the bars were closed, especially on Sunday, and waiting for the secret knock on the door, until Officer Raymond told her that the word was getting out.

She did not mention Hank. She could not bring herself to say he never paid support, even when the court ordered him to do so. Yes, they did catch up with him once—in the pool hall. Then he vanished and she couldn't even guess where he was.

The manager asked for details about her financial history and listened carefully about the house deal and the foreclosure her brother-in-law, the lawyer, told her about, the one with the back taxes owing that she was ready to pay. All she needed was $500. It was a lot to her, but it was probably peanuts to the bank. Altogether, $1,100 would get her in.

Of course, she would have to pay the lawyer, and pay for the divorce, too, but that wasn't any of the bank manager's business. Aggie was working night and day and knew down to the penny how much was coming in and where every cent was going out.

Frankly, she couldn't believe Mr. Brewster gave her so much time but they were getting along really well and he watched her carefully and seemed amazed at how much money she was making now and how much she made during the war. He asked Aggie all about it, and she explained it was a great opportunity, working at the war factory at the airport, riveting on the assembly line—darn hard work, too. The money was very good, almost a man's salary for a man's job, and because they needed workers so badly they even took her mother on the payroll.

He mentioned his board of directors twice, but he kept listening, so Aggie kept telling him her story, and she explained the technical job as well as he watched her in fascination. Then Aggie told him about her rewarding job at Square D, sitting on an assembly line, fiddling all day with tiny screwdrivers. "Little hands come in handy—since we get paid by the piece," she said.

"I take home more pay than anybody else does and the company provides health and life insurance and other benefits. My boss knows about the bank loan and says he would be happy to verify my income."

The manager let Aggie stew there, alone in his office, "While I check on a few things," he declared.

Once again, the seconds thumped along with the pounding rhythm of her heartbeat and the minutes stretched into agony. She ran every word she had said through her mind, again, and again, wondering if it had been enough or too much.

Finally the door burst open. She sprang to her feet.

"Let me congratulate you, Mrs. Lauria, you now have a loan," the manager proclaimed, puffing his chest like a movie hero.

A large triumphant smile spread across his beefy face that seemed even more reddened by his close proximity to Aggie as he shook her hand, his eyes darting back and forth from her cleavage to her face, down to the papers, over to her cleavage and back to her blue eyes.

Maybe his high color sprang from imagining his explanations to the board of directors. It looked like the loan did actually fall under the guidelines of their new initiative—just barely—maybe stretching it a tad and downplaying the "separated woman with children" part.

Aggie did not care about his assumptions. She had seen it all before and now she would handle him like any normal man and show up with a low neckline when she needed a favor. The man did not need to worry, she wished he understood that, she would be the best customer they had ever given a loan.

"Oh, you won't be sorry, Mr. Brewster. You'll see—there won't be one problem. I always pay on time..." She started to reply—then she found herself speechless, smiling, nodding, shaking his hand.

She gently closed his office door behind her and stood still for a moment, holding her head high, blinking in the sun's glow from the high front windows before she stepped briskly towards the revolving front door. It was a new dawn for her family.

The teller and Aggie exchanged nods with shining eyes, the former probably eager for lunch to share the gossip with her friends in the back room over their boiled egg sandwiches.

Aggie was thrilled Mrs. Madison might tell the other women working in the bank that a separated, single mother, with children, had just gotten a mortgage loan!

"Well, I guess it's Granny's doing," played in her mind. She told me I could do anything and today I believe her!

No Surrender

Chapter 10

His hands busy trying to keep his little brother from racing up the front stairs, or rolling around on the muddy lawn, the young boy hung back, and motioned to Mel—wait a minute.

Ronnie was proud that this house was now theirs, but he was not sure where his mother was heading.

As expected, the curious round-faced tyke escaped his brother and leaped forward with rampant almost-seven-year-old enthusiasm, ran up the front steps of the square box house and hollered "My room, my room!" as he had practiced all day, since their Mom said they were going to see it.

The boys had never had their own room.

Mel grabbed the doorknob, pushed against the front door and wailed to find it locked.

Ronnie stood still; he hung back to see which way Mom was going to go, up the stairs to the main floor, or down to the basement. His Italian grandparent's basement was damp and cold. "For the wine," his grandfather had always said, pointing to the barrels.

Ronnie had fond, now fading memories of the fruit trees and vegetable gardens at his grandparent's house, too, and the get-togethers under the overhead grape vines, with a lot of Italian mixed in with English.

Everything was different since they moved away

from their grandparent's house, and stayed here and there in apartments. They even had to live with strangers for a while, after Mom and Dad split up.

It was weird living with strangers, and no Mom or Dad. Just those people that had two kids of their own, and the parents thought their kids were better, and they took their side in everything.

Now Mom bought this house, their own house. That was the best part.

Mom had said there was no bathroom down there, but either way, he would follow along and hope for the best. Still, it was not easy to get a straight answer from Mom and plans could change, and as she always said, "Don't count your chickens before they hatch," and she was always so busy.

Ronnie had been hoping for something else.

"Too expensive," Mom had said, busy prying off the lid of a tin of blue paint that the father of her friend Jean had leftover in his garage. She had spread the daily paper on the floor and now stirred, and stirred, until the true color showed. "More rent from upstairs."

She held the back door wide open, waiting for Mel to scramble back down the front stairs and rush around the house to join her. Then he tried to push past her to head up the short flight of stairs to the main floor. Grabbed by the back of his jacket, halted in his tracks and lifted off his feet, he shouted "Hey!" as he found himself hauled up into his mother's arms.

"Whoa, boy! We go downstairs to measure up the basement today, remember I told you that?"

The tot looked down the darkened stairwell, quiet now, his mouth about to pout.

"We're going to fix it up just fine," his mother insisted, "down we go. Come on, Ronnie...this is our new house."

Now there was Jim, Mom's new boyfriend, downstairs with Ron's family. Jim did not like him or his brother very much, and there would be a new baby soon.

Maybe they would move upstairs then, Mom said, but for now, Mom, and Mel and Jim had no problem barging up the stairs, opening the door leading into the main floor, and casually walking down their hallway to use the toilet, so neither should he.

Eyes half shut, Ron lay on his top bunk bed and looked up at the ceiling that seemed to crowd his head. There had been three different sets of renters over the last two years, a change every few months it seemed, because Mom complained about this and that and when one family had taken a shower every night, instead of their own once-a-week schedule, they had to go, too.

The noise of this new family echoed around the basement.

That hard-heeled stomp was the dad upstairs, and run-fall-over, run-fall-over, was the brat, back and forth, back and forth, shrieking about some stupid thing. Then the kid would drop things or throw things, and the kid's mother shrieked about that, then even after the kid fell asleep, the parents still hollered, but now it was at each other.

No matter what he did, Ron could not stop the urge of nature that forced him to invade their territory late at night, and it gave Ron the creeps just thinking about announcing his needs and intentions. It was nobody's business what he did or when he did it. It was his age, Mom said; he would get over it. Besides, they would be upstairs soon.

Now he really had to go, and Ron amused himself by sneaking through the house at night with only moonlight from the windows and memory to guide him. Up the landing and hold his breath, softly breathing in and out, step and wait, step and wait, and slowly opened the door into their half of the house.

Night was not a problem: darkness was his friend when he sleuthed down the hallway to avoid bright patches from the streetlight that reached inside. With perfect balance, he never touched a wall or slipped on scatter rugs, and could hear the renter's rhythmic breath as the tubby man gasped in and snored out while the restless toddler gurgled on his squeaky crib.

It was not a perfect setup, but they would have a real bedroom to share, and soon their new tenants would be downstairs.

"Cut the lawn when you get home from school," Aggie called to Ron. Time was short, she had to leave for work soon, and her hands rhythmically wrapped sandwiches, washed stray dishes at the sink, and wiped crumbs from the kitchen table, leaving the older boy to get himself ready.

She passed a comb through her hair and fluffed it into a golden halo. Bending closer to the mirror for accuracy, she ran the tube of quite red lipstick over her mouth, ran a powder puff over her nose and opened a bottle of nail polish. Dabbing gently at the side of one nail, her head moved side to side to check the repair, then she capped the bottle with satisfaction and turned to inspect her own reflection.

Imagine this nice blouse for twenty-five cents at the Sally Ann, she thought.

She checked the time on her watch; she had to drop her youngest boy off at the baby-sitter. Mel had walked to school with a friend down the street, so there was only Ronnie to get out the door and she would leave, too, the house locked down tight, the way she liked it.

"Don't forget we're moving upstairs at the end of the month...there's a lot of painting to do when I get home. There will be new people down here." She was really talking to herself. She counted out change for the bus fare on the counter and scooped it up, ready to go.

"Take your lunch. I made you a peanut butter sandwich."

Behind her back, Ron grabbed his throat, tongue hanging out sideways, in a pretend gag at the mere thought of eating another one. He had similar gag reflexes on Mom's other food choices, too. He would hide cans of green beans, which he despised, at the back of the cupboard. If she found them, and served them for dinner, he put Kleenex in his socks and secretly transfer the beans, one-by-one, into his socks.

If he knew beforehand that he wouldn't like dinner, and would be sent to his room for not eating it, he would make a sandwich beforehand and hide it in his dresser drawer.

Aggie saw the whole gag act reflected in the toaster next to her, and pretended not to notice. That might give away one of her best secrets. Her kids thought she had eyes in the back of her head.

"Take care of your brother," she added, as always, just before the door closed.

The Wire Snapped

1958

Chapter 14

Just finishing her shift at General Electric, Aggie drove into the driveway of her bungalow on Langside Avenue. Something about the kids she had seen on the street caught her attention. Then it made her furious. Some brats had tossed Melville's two-wheeler onto the hydro wires. There it lay, stuck, half-hanging down and he was crying. She was so mad she thought she could kill them.

He had worked for that bike, at eight years old, delivering newspapers on his own route. They all had to work and he used some birthday money and a couple of dollars from his grandfather, Melville. He had looked around for the best second-hand bike he could afford, and there it was—dangling, green, on the hydro wires while Mel was jumping up and down in frustration with his fists balled trying to threaten them, and crying at the same time. All the while, the three bigger boys in their dirty pants and tee shirts, laughed and laughed.

"You little buggers!" Aggie flew out of car in a rage, ran over and grabbed the biggest boy by his collar, and swung him off his feet. She couldn't care less if he choked, and she whacked him good, smacking him like a windmill. She reached for the next brat to do the same—little punks, always picking on someone smaller. Girls will usually gossip and make trouble for each other—titter, titter—but this was brutal, criminal.

She yelled in his face, "Get up there and get that bike down or I will slap you silly until you do it!"

"I can't, I can't. Stop hitting me!" he cried out, with snot starting to pour out of his nose.

The other two boys had scrambled away, looking back over their shoulders when they mounted their bikes, feeling safe, holding their fingers up and making disgusting signals of what she could do to herself.

Aggie held the little creep up to the pole and made him hold on and shimmy up. He looked scared and she hollered at him, "You got up there once, you can do it again!"

The little brat clung to the pole. The wires were low, weighed down by the framework of Mel's small boy's bicycle and he looked terrified, his eyes big as saucers. He clung with one hand and reached out, tipping the bike, rocking it back and forth, but it only seemed to enmesh further and he looked at her, scared and helpless at the same time.

"Get down, stupid!" she called out, disgusted with him, but her energy faded. She had worked a full shift and still had to shop and make dinner. He was not like her boys; he was not thinking straight and she didn't trust him. She didn't want him to wreck Mel's bike.

"You little bugger!" she yelled in his face when he edged himself down slowly to where she could grab him. Then she took a couple of breaths to think and her voice got very quiet.

Holding his collar tighter than ever, she got real close, looking at him eye-to-eye, deadly serious. "You are now my son's protector. If anyone comes near him, I come to you first. Now get lost!"

Aggie let go of his shirt and he fell backwards, ass-first on the ground, scrambled away and shot looks back, but only to make sure she was not coming after him. The sounds of Mel crying and stopping, over, and over, and looking up to the wires, pulled her back to reason.

"Come on, Honey, let's go inside. I'll think of something." It calmed him down a little.

The city wanted to send her a bill if they took the bike down, and suggested it would cost a lot to fix if something went wrong—like a snapped wire.

Aggie was the one that snapped, but she was so tired of those bullies, and the fire department got the bike down, finally. They were not thrilled about doing it. She had to talk and talk, explaining the situation to everyone at City Hall it seemed, but for safety reasons they had to do it, in the end.

The best part of it all—was that they never saw the boys come near the house again, although it was just the beginning of problems for Melville.

Strange problems started for Mel then, and one day his grade four teacher phoned with a snotty attitude—as they sometimes do—and that surprised Aggie.

"Melville is becoming difficult to handle. He's also coming to school overtired and looks despondent all the time."

Aggie understood depressed was more than unhappy; everybody was talking about depression in those days, as if sadness and disappointment were just invented. She also knew Mel had told the teacher off for embarrassing a boy in his class by spanking him on his bare ass.

"There is an appointment arranged for him," the smart-ass teacher told her with a hint of triumph in her voice.

Why not? It might be a good idea to see how his mind worked, what he was thinking. He was quieter these days, keeping to himself, acting more like Ronnie, except Melville would have angry outbursts as if itching for a fight, and he broke the glass on the back screen door with a broom handle. Strangest of all, for no apparent reason, he cut up some dollar bills from his hard-earned pay into little bits on the kitchen table.

They approached the old two-story house for the appointment and it looked well kept, converted now into a doctor's office on the main floor.

A female nurse, or an assistant, wore a white smock and chatted gently with Melville, led him to stand on a weigh scale, all the while telling him that she had a dog named "Agnes" at home, and that "Agnes" always helped cleaning the dishes. Mel nodded, and nodded, told her about a dog they had at home back then. She listened carefully to all he said, and then took him inside to meet the doctor.

When Aggie asked him later, he said it was nice inside the room, with brown wood on the walls, and the doctor told him to sit down in a comfortable chair, like a barber's chair. Then he asked Mel a few questions, like what swear words he knew—encouraging him to open up and give him the real goods on the swearing. Trying to figure out his maturity level, she guessed. Then he started up a metronome, that time meter that musicians use, and the next thing he knew, Mel woke up a while later in the chair.

They finally told Aggie his problem was that he hated his stepfather—her husband, Jim—just like his brother, Ron did. Not a big surprise, but what could she do about it?

Try to keep things calm at home? Keep him away

from Jim.? Tell Jim that Mel was having psychological problems because of all of his step-father's drinking?

No, that would probably stir up more trouble for Mel.

Last hope, was it just a passing phase that Mel would grow out of? So much to think about, no clear answers.

Real Trouble

South Texas

Chapter 12

"It looks like there might be some trouble brewing in here, Hank," Norm said softly as he leaned towards him.

Everyone was getting plastered and more unsteady on their feet—everyone except Hank, a non-drinker, who sipped on his Coke.

Hank was having a good time. There was a small band playing lively music and the joint was jumping. He liked being able to sit around with friends, trading stories and jokes.

"Let's stay away from it; my fighting days are over."

"You took boxing, didn't you?" Norm asked.

"Yeah, until they started using me as a punching bag. So I took up Judo."

Their new-found friends around the table took time out from their banter about the women in the bar and started to listen.

One of them interjected. "So you learned that Jap Judo thing."

"Until the hernia popped. It felt like a knife jabbed into my gut. So I had to improve my communication skills, I was told."

Norm primed Hank, hoping he'd tell one of his favorite stories and for the others at the table who would hear it for the first time.

"You had fights after that, though."

"No more than I had to. There was one guy that came at me. I flipped the numbskull down hard on the sidewalk. There was a bottle of liquor in his back pocket and it broke when he landed. The glass stuck into him and he screamed and tried to roll off it but that just dug the pieces more into his rear end. He's probably still picking out the pieces." Hank was grinning now.

"After that, the bum crossed to the other side of the street when he saw me coming. He didn't know I couldn't really fight much with a hernia and couldn't run with it, but he left me alone after that."

The stale air in the bar grew humid, and the energy more rowdy as the night went on. The jokes and the stories became more, and more exaggerated and the people telling them got louder, and louder. Staggering replaced walking. Yelling and shouting replaced conversation.

Someone lurched into a table, getting up to go to the john, spilling drinks over the surface and into laps as broken glass flew in every direction. Naturally, a loud argument ensued, then the inevitable fistfight, which spread through the jammed bar like wildfire and it was only minutes before cops burst through the front door, grabbed a few people to break up the melee, then ushered them out the door to a waiting paddy wagon.

No one was spared. Everyone in that rowdy bar got a free trip to the drunk-tank to sleep it off. In the morning, after a fitful night with a bunch of snoring drunks, Hank got the news. They had checked him out and discovered he had an immigration problem. Aliens with a record of assault and weapons charges are not welcome in the United States of America. On top of that, they found the guns in the trunk of his car.

If that don't beat all. He had hopped the border back

and forth for a long time, and work remained available in Canada, or in the States, if he hung around the right places—hired with no questions asked. But now Immigration had him cold. All for being arrested with a bunch of drunks for disturbing the peace when he didn't even drink.

Now he had real trouble. He had his order to appear before a county judge in two days and Hank fully understood the consequences: he was probably going to jail. There was only this last gentle night of delicious freedom. It looked liked they wanted to keep an eye on him and make sure he didn't skip town, if the same man that he kept seeing in the dusty brown car was any indication.

It had been a game of cat and mouse,,and why not, he was annoyed with the whole farce. He had parked his car where it would be spotted, then went in the front door of a place and out the back. Hank liked the southwestern look of the town, and would rather spend his time exploring. It was interesting to walk down a few streets and see how people lived.

.

Tonight was the last night. Strolling the wide, open street, Hank enjoyed the red and blue neon lights on honky-tonks and restaurants, brightening now that the glaring sun dipped closer to the horizon. It made him nostalgic for the time ahead when he knew he would miss that view. Overwhelmingly delicious aromas wafted from the local eateries on the newborn evening breeze and the previously bare street quickly filled with couples and hungry-looking men seeking the grilled, roasted, or simmering food. A deep rumble in his belly answered the call. It was time to choose a place and settle in for the evening feast.

He relaxed into a comfortable seat by the window of the restaurant and ordered a large steak for his last meal as a free man. He idly wondered if the man in the brown car would spot him.

He ate contentedly while he enjoyed the pleasure of the sky changing into a purple fan with a radiant orange sun at its core. He smiled, as he had no idea when he would see a sunset again.

He never did have a chance to speak to the judge.

They let him rot in a small, stinking hot jail cell in El Paso for four days, with barely enough room to stretch his arms out to the side. His only food totaled two daily slices of bread with water, until his travel buddy showed up bearing coffee and hamburgers for him and his jailers—definitely a clever man, his friend.

Norm returned later, smuggling in thick juicy BBQ meat sandwiches on freshly baked bread, dripping sauce, the glorious aroma drawing the guards trailing behind him. Clever Norm had a large bag, enough for all and their families, and one for the cook, plus Export cigarettes that the southern boys loved.

Thinking ahead, Hank tucked an extra sandwich into a hole in the grey brick holding cell wall, carved out no doubt by many idle hands, that remained concealed by the thin mattress on the skinny bed.

The staff was so thankful that the county jail chef made him a big steak the next day, medium rare.

No one could tell Hank anything about his court case, despite his nagging. Why the hold-up? When is the court case? All he got was shoulder shrugs. Time dragged on with the only high point being the food that the cook sent him from the kitchen every day.

"Isn't there anything to do around here?" Hank nagged daily, tired of pacing the small cell and one hour a day in the yard.

"There's always something to do," a guard finally answered, tired of his pestering. "What can you do?"

"I can cook." It seemed a good way to get near food.

The cook was fat and black, with a shaved head, in love with his own wittiness, fond of slamming down the big saber shaped knife onto the wooden block and not averse to taking help from a prisoner, as long as the work was finished and the counter surfaces shone enough to see the man's reflection.

"Did you hear the one about...?" Hank started with a few dirty jokes and the chef stopped laughing long enough to make him a thick, juicy steak or other good things from the sheriff's reserve

The chef told Hank about his service on a Navy destroyer where he had honed his skills cooking for the seamen, and then the brass, and said he knew how to reward a storyteller.

"Hey, Hank. We have shrimp tonight."

"No, thanks."

"What?"

"I won't eat anything that swims, crawls, or slithers."

"You're Italian, right? Italians eat some strange things."

"Yeah, my dad use to walk all the way down to the city from the outskirts to buy eels, which took him most of the day. It was a real old country Italian treat."

He grimaced, remembering it all too clearly, and gave his audience fake shudders.

"Dad would bring them home in a burlap bag, and put them on the kitchen table, and the bag would squirm and bounce around. My mother would throw them alive into a big, hot frying pan and they curled up and sizzled until they were dead and cooked."

"The stink was worse than this place," he joked, but privately he knew he would have rather starved and his parents knew it, too, so they fed him something else.

"Your English is good for an Italian."

"Well, I was born in Canada. But even then my parents always spoke Italian at home, so I only knew Italian, and didn't learn English until I started going to school. The teachers would give me the strap if I spoke Italian, so I had to learn real fast."

When Hank promised to make the chef his secret Italian family recipe for tomato sauce, to create the best pasta in the world guaranteed to have his family drooling, he made a friend for life.

Time dragged on, one month, two months, and finally the Sheriff sauntered in.

"When do I get my hearing?" Hank asked him.

"You just had it. You have been 'Convicted with no court appearance and are to be deported back to your country of origin—escort provided.' Case closed."

The U.S. Government wanted him gone and assigned the same depressed detective that had followed him before his hearing, to take Hank for a three-day ride across Texas to Chicago, through a million jackrabbits crisscrossing the desert, morning to night, like a fun house shooting gallery, and him without a gun.

The clothes on the glum and rumpled man behind the wheel were a study in shades of dull brown from suit, and shoes, to necktie—he even had nondescript brownish hair. He said not a word throughout the drive of several hundred miles, and at night in a cheap motel the gloomy escort kept his gun in his hand, although he snored loud enough for a herd of the jackrabbits to thump around the floor and eat the sheets from under him, and Hank could have left at any time.

It did not matter to him what the man did, or did not do. Hank ate the hamburgers from cheap joints in little towns, paid for and handed to him by the guy with the deadpan face. To Hank, it was a free ride home courtesy of the American government, and he was ready.

All jail cells were full when they arrived in Chicago and, feeling right at home, Hank asked to be bunked in with a crowd of illegal Italian aliens, eager to hear their stories in his parent's native tongue.

"Pisano!" rang through cells, in great good humor.

The men surged forward, stretched out their arms and reached across the shoulders of others to grab his hand, and their stories spilled out. Smuggled over to work on the railroad, but only paid enough to eke out an existence, it was an old story Hank heard many times before.

The Italian prisoners had believed the old smuggler's myth that immigration is difficult, which was just part of a plot to extract their money, and when Hank told them to go back home and apply from there to come to the States, or Canada, someone tried to kiss his hand. Their old country abundance of gratefulness was embarrassing, but it still felt good.

He heard the news shortly after: the kangaroo court judgment barred him from the U.S. for five years, but he had no regrets. He would be free tomorrow.

A friend told him a while ago that divorce loomed in the offing but that felt like no surprise—his wife, Aggie, being pregnant with someone else's child.

It did not feel like he had been away that long, but when Hank looked back, he guessed it was three years at least, or more. He had not been keeping track, and time was funny like that: it just slipped away when you were not paying attention.

The next day he was on an early plane back to Malton airport, in Toronto, and that was that.

It Ain't Easy

1957

Chapter 23

"Well, if you want a divorce—you're going to pay for it. I don't have any money and I don't care."

Hank's blunt words rang in Aggie's ears, "I don't care," and it was probably the most truthful declaration he had ever made to her.

She had heard gossip that Hank was back in town from who knows where, but when she asked him for a bit of support for the boys, he responded that he would be no help at all, as usual. She did not bother to ask him where his money went. It was not any of her business now—all she wanted was help to raise their kids, but eventually he coughed up a bit for their food.

"You pay just enough for your kids to eat, to heck with their clothes or shelter," she shouted at imaginary Hank, remembering their bitter conversation while the blazing sunshine toasted her face and humidity teased out a trickle of sweat that formed at the bra line then dribbled down to her half slip.

It is a lucky thing to be working for an excellent employer, she marveled, but regardless, no matter how she looked at it, she simply must create extra income. Every cent she had went to the purchase and mortgage of her Langside house. It was all too much to figure out today.

She stepped up into the roasting oven of a Dufferin Street bus and settled in on the shaded side, close to the back door for a quick getaway, as time was racing and she needed to set up her station on the assembly line. She calmed a bit, smoothed her blue skirt, becoming too snug now, and then her crisp white uniform collar, suspecting it would need ironing before the bus had gone six blocks in this heat.

Aggie steadied herself in the rhythmic rocking of the bus that made her nauseous and turned to the window to focus on something outside, as that long-range perspective usually calmed her tummy. Then she quickly leaned closer to her reflection. Was that a wrinkle on her cheek? No. She smiled wanly, amused at her own relief, it was only a false alarm, her sprinkling of brown freckles catching shadow.

There was no air on this bus! After blowing across fields churned up to build new house foundations, dry-spell suburban scrub dust migrated through the measly-sized sections of the window that actually opened. There seemed no end to the demand for the next row on row of identical square box dwellings, only varying by two colors of brick, grey or sandy, and two styles of roof tile, grey or blue—take your pick.

Better bus service must follow, Aggie reasoned, but it would be many years too late for her and the boys. They would be ancient or in their graves before Toronto in general, Weston in particular, solved their suburban transit problems. None of it would do a thing for the people in Weston except suck up their tax money. What a mess!

The rapidly rising heat turned her chest beet red and a piercing headache crawled up behind her temples with fingers of lightening behind her squinting eyes. It seemed like all her problems were ganging up on her today, perhaps made worse by this wicked, muggy weather with no relief in sight. But maybe the most upsetting issue was the pending divorce that friends advised was terribly unbalanced—for men and against women.

Her friend at work, Jeannie, warned her when she first thought about marrying her new man. They had taken their time lingering in the air-conditioned lunchroom and craned their necks to stretch out the constant cramps from peering closely, and endlessly, at the circling line-up of tiny electrical parts prepared for soldering or assembly.

Jeannie had given Aggie the "I know what I'm talking about," glance while they picked out their lunch selections in the cafeteria yesterday. "You'll have to catch him in the act, there is no other way." Then she had insisted, "It isn't that hard, we can set him up."

Aggie supposed Jeannie was correct, yet wondered if she could do that to Hank, but, on the other hand, he would prefer to tell a lie in court than pay her anything.

Oh, the egg salad was good yesterday, finely chopped the way she liked it and that is another good thing about this job—Aggie reflected for the hundredth time—darn good cafeteria. Her waistband was snug, despite the old trick of adding elastic, and it would be obvious to everyone soon that she was pregnant.

It was the cafeteria lackey's job to take the trays off the table when they were finished, but he was nowhere in sight, so the girls did it for themselves, again. The slob was probably AWOL, flirting with the new girl employee in the alley behind the plant with his stinky cigarette hanging out of his mouth. That dumb broad was forever wiggling and giggling for a smoke, and Aggie and Jeannie wondered if she was selling a bit on the side. It was a stupid thing to do behind a busy factory, risking a hard-to-find union job for a quickie, but it happened.

"Some girls don't know when they have it good," her friend Jeannie had murmured, flicking back her long, brunette hair.

Aggie gratefully acknowledged that she personally had it good, now, intended to keep it that way, and hoped the baby she carried would have an easier childhood than her boys did when they were small. At least they lived in a real house now, and their mother was making good money.

They both had leaned their bums on the service counter, angled their bodies towards the chugging air conditioning unit on the wall, and Jeannie held up her hair to help the delicious coldness pass around her neck and down her back, between her shoulder blades.

"This thing is doing a bang-up job keeping the place cool," she mumbled appreciatively to Aggie.

"Considering the circumstances," Jeannie continued in their discussion of divorce, while opening the large staff refrigerator and pouring two enormous glasses of ice-cold water, "you'll have to initiate proceedings, you know, you're the one that wants a divorce. For a reasonable amount of money, lots of people will testify. It's done every day."

Jeannie shrugged her thin shoulders while she handed Aggie a full glass with one hand and held her glass to her own forehead and rolled it back and forth, obviously enjoying the ice-cold sensations.

"Some people do it for a living. It's called a paid correspondent. Probably the dumb broad outside would do it, but I would not trust her. Too stupid."

It made Aggie feel ill remembering that

conversation, or maybe the nausea generated from the midday sun amplified through the roof of the lurching tin can of a bus.

If Hank was in on the divorce plot, and pretended to be caught, then maybe she could stomach the lying. Oh, her "ex" flirted, flashing those dark bedroom eyes around at the girls when he was safely with his buddies, which was most of the time at the pool hall—but actually getting into another relationship? Humph! Really, he was entitled, but the issue had never crossed her crowded mind before.

Jeeze! She'd have to do some snooping. No, that was too much! She had to think of something else; there must be another way besides catching a husband or wife cheating.

Oh, and the crazy laws she had discovered! The rules stated that the person that left the property first got nothing. How could the law be set up so that everyone had to tell lies? At least that did not refer to her and Hank, as their divorce was mutual and they left the house at the same time, but they must play out the farce to get a divorce.

She felt her temperature spike, as if flames were fast-frying her brain. Who made divorce rules up? Men had first rights to children? What do men know about raising children? They can hardly be bothered saying hello to them. "Yeah?" they might say absent-mindedly if the kid told them something. There must be great dads out there, her father had been good to her, always productively working or building something in his garage, but not mean—not that Hank was mean either, just mostly absent.

Aggie felt more confused that ever. She and Hank had to make some kind of deal, she decided, the choke of nausea rippling up from her abdomen—she owed him that.

The problem was she was pregnant, now! She was roasting on this bus, now!

This young man, Jim, the father of this new life inside her, actually wanted to stay around and was willing to marry her. He crooned sweet passion into her ear, said it is now or never. That told her what her future would be, so something more must be done and it was going to cost her money—always the way it went in her screwball life it seemed.

It had changed her life when she met him, and Aggie remembered it clearly. It was the last of her day shifts and she needed groceries for the week to come, as there had been no lunchmeat, no porridge, no sugar, and no pork chops in the house that morning.

Everything seemed to run out at the same time and the paper bag she carried was very heavy, heavier by the minute. The boys would be already home from school, waiting for supper.

The radio weatherman was completely wrong, as usual. It snowed hard all afternoon, blowing sideways, and her boots were at home. Visibility disappeared off and on, in blinding gusts of snow.

She had stopped and stood still a few seconds to catch her breath and make sure nothing had slipped from the three bags that were melting as snow disintegrated the paper, and she wished for a car, but mortgage payments, bus fares, heating and groceries left nothing in the coffers.

Her mind had spiraled inward then, like now on the bus, searching for a solution in an endless loop of frustration.

A long truck had loomed beside her, and it moved very slowly as the sparse snow-bound traffic crawled.

The driver's head turned towards Aggie as he passed her, surprised to see a pedestrian, and that pissed her off a bit. What else would she be doing but walking when the busses had stopped running? Maybe he had not caught on to that.

Even though irritated, she noticed him. He looked like a handsome guy, but it could be the cold and the snow blowing as she had not seen him clearly, just a flash, and maybe it was the freezing-to-death illusion she had heard about.

The white truck stopped just ahead, motor running, the outline blurred in a swirl of snowflakes like a comic-book leviathan breathing smoke into the air.

She had to pass right by the passenger door but she was not sure where the culvert started. Then the door opened with the screech of cold steel, and he stretched across the seat and leaned out, waiting for her to catch up.

"You look kind of familiar—can I give you a lift?"

He said it while reaching his hands out for the disintegrating bags: his smiling James Garner looks, with the same black hair she loved, seeming very inviting under the dim truck light. She handed them up, gratefully.

His arm was steady as a rock when he helped her up into the front seat and the heater blasted heaven on her legs. "I'll drive you home if we can get up the streets in the snow. A lady like you should not be walking in this weather." He said it with genuine sincerity.

She thought, "A guy can't really fake that."

"I am so cold," she said.

"I'm Jim."

She was in love.

It would be great if Jim would get her a car but Aggie already knew the answer to that fantasy. He paid rent, that helped her with the mortgage, but the house would never be in his name. She refused to do that, called his contribution "room and board," so he gave her nothing else as punishment.

If he was working in town, or on the road, his car remained locked in the company yard and it was up to Aggie to get her own vehicle—one of the many things she had learned about him.

She had worn out her thumb hitchhiking and there was much time lost while she waited for buses, and rode buses, wasted time that she could have spent working. The suburbs may be the only place she could afford a house but the transportation stank.

Aggie dragged Melville in and out of cars hitchhiking, on and off buses, and stashed him in the back room of Melrose Cigar Store, on the weekend. She sold basic groceries and a variety of other necessities, but mostly the customers desired cigarettes.

Mel read the comic books where every second word was Blam! Now he loved that word. He mouthed the word over, and over, aiming his finger at passing cars, Blam! Blam!

"He's getting too big for that." Oh, God, now she was talking to herself.

Her skirt felt like mummy wrapping in this sticky heat, her nylon stockings strangled her legs, her garters dug into her thighs, and she could not be shaking like this at work.

She tried to concentrate, to collect her thoughts and it calmed her enough to make a plan. It was time to tap her meager savings, as owning a house cost so much more than renting, but at least she was the landlady and not making some landlord rich. She must remember to pick up a newspaper and comb the want ads for a deal on a car, and phone a friend who knew a wrecker.

This decision made her feel a bit better. With a car, she could drive to the plant on Saturday and Sunday, to make time and a half on the weekend shifts.

She had to be quick to put her name down because many people grabbed those shifts. The conveyor belt always hummed, ready for a hand to grab the next electrical part to solder, or polish, or screw down. It took steady hands with accurate fingers and those she had.

Ronnie would keep an eye on Mel, not happy about that, but at least her boys liked each other and everyone would like having a car.

For a few weak moments, Aggie let her head sink into her hand, her elbow balanced against the bus window. She was tired, utterly tired. Maybe buying her own house had been too much, or getting involved in a new romance too stupid.

Jim had a steady job and seemed to be mad about her, but he drank too much lately and got very jealous and pushy when he got drunk. But he swore to reform because of the baby.

Jim did other stupid things too: he drove drunk, and smashed his truck into a Ready-Mix concrete truck so hard he totaled it, and it ended up upside down on Yonge Street. In court, he said it was an accident that he was going the wrong way, and by some miracle they believed him.

He kept his job by going to AA meetings in church basements and the question always was: can you stay sober? Sober Jim would say, 'maybe, maybe'. But he missed sessions now and Aggie expected Jim would probably give up and give in to temptation, as he always did.

They still had the passion; that was the problem.

Like last summer when they rented that cabin at Wasaga Beach when it was so hot. It was just one small room, one thin bed and a mattress on the floor for the boys, a table and four chairs, but it was close to the water, and when they wanted privacy Ronnie and Melville could play outside.

Aggie and Jim went out to the car later, so the boys could sleep. A patrolling police officer saw the car rocking and shone his flashlight through the window. They jumped in shock, Jim hit his head on the ceiling and started to get mad, but she put her hand on his arm and shook her head, "No."

"We're married," she said in a flirty way to the curious cop. "The kids are sleeping inside and we don't want to wake them. You know what it's like to try to find a bit of privacy with kids around."

The cop shook his head and turned off the light.

Aggie sat up straight on the hard bus seat and squared her shoulders. There had been other pregnancies, ended too early, but for some reason she really wanted this baby. It reached out to her soul, and she would be the champion for her family.

She really did need a divorce, and that meant visiting her brother-in-law, the lawyer, again, letting him and everyone else in on her private life. It was going to be messy.

The lurching bus turned a corner to the last stop on the line, her stop, with the sun-glare radiating an inescapable halo of hot light around her body, mother and child.

Panic

Chapter 14

Panic pinned her freezing body to the cold driveway while her pulse pounded in her ears like a bass drum, drowning out all sound, which he could surely hear.

Gasping silently, underneath the car, Aggie watched his thick-soled work boots clump back and forth, crunching frozen ridges of yesterday's snow, close to her face. He stopped next to the right front tire, mere inches from her numbing hand and if he looked down, he might have seen the edge of her nightgown caught on jagged ice, shining now in the reflection of the porch light.

Jim turned away. His head jerked back and forth, probably looking for movement up the dark empty street or between the rows of identical suburban houses. He took a few steps further down the driveway, muttering, cursing, scanning the shadow-filled neighborhood, but never looked down where she lay shaking under the car on the oil-smeared ice and pavement.

Shivering with fear, snaking her bare arm along the frosted ground, she yanked the errant edge of flimsy pink nightgown back into the shadows and tried to think straight through the thunder of her own breath. If she made a wrong move, he was strong enough to make good on his threat to beat her to death. Many times he had sworn to do that and tonight he was so drunk the actual event would slip through his memory like the wisp of a dream, as violence always seemed to do when he sobered up. It would only affect her and her breakable boys, left behind to pay the price with a horrible memory.

Her slight body felt naked plastered to the deep ridges of frozen slush and her bare knees seemed to meld with the ice-roughened surface. She could not feel her toes at all.

He pounded further down the driveway to the street and stood there waving his arms. He snorted, called her name, cursed her and moved off the driveway to find her—kill her—or just beat her. He shouted into the deep black winter night.

"You won't look so good when I get through with you," he brayed, his hands on his hips like the Jolly Green Giant television commercial.

Aggie let her eyelids close a moment. He loved her beauty but hated the attention it garnered, but he did not seem to understand that. She had heard it all before. He'd fix her now! No more blond girl! No more girl to tease the boys at the bar! No more big tits to show around! Fuck the kids! Fuck her! There would be no more sober promises made, with such charming remorse, so quickly broken.

Thoughts and memories flooded her mind, her head throbbed from the stink of motor oil filling her nostrils and making her nauseous but, nevertheless, the cold ground pushed her into action. She must sneak back into the house to get the boys. Such sweet kids deserved so much better.

The front door was unlocked. He had chased her out that way, and it beckoned invitingly open, but now he would surely spot her if she made a run for it. She prayed the back door was unlocked, the only chance to enter the house unseen, but fright and shivers made it hard to think straight. She had to move out of the relative safety under the car, and she must reach the side offering shade from the bright and almost-full moonlight. She listened, hearing no crashing or thumping other than the sound of her own pounding heart echoing in her ears. It was time to get moving or be his regretful prisoner forever.

Aggie inched along in the scant amount of space between the slippery driveway that stung like freshly sharpened steak knives, and the undercarriage of the car. Slowly, she edged out from under her cold metallic cover and eased up into a low crouch for a quick look over the hood to follow his noisy progress.

"Aggie!!!" His head swung from side to side as he bellowed her name, hoarse now, and hurled insults that stung to the core as he moved unsteadily away down the road.

She could see him clearly, a handsome man when sober, his face now contorted from anger and consuming reckless quantities of liquor, and if he had turned around he would have seen her. He seemed impervious to the cold, and stumbled over clumps of unshoveled snow, lurching sideways down the road. He righted himself with awkward windmill arms and tilted away in the new direction that took him further from the house.

Aggie turned her eyes away, vaguely embarrassed by his actions, but this situation was nothing new in the horror of his addiction, not hers, and within that realization she found the courage to suck in a deep ice-crystal breath that stabbed at her lungs, but it was now or never.

Grabbed up trailing rags of her nightgown in one hand, her pale silhouette of moon-shadow preceded her through the dimly lit driveway heading for the deep shadow of the house. One hand found the cold brick wall to steady her and one bare foot slid quickly in front of the other, stepping with care in the black silence of midnight and avoiding toys and metal trashcans as best she could. Sharp pain zinged up the arch of an instep as she staggered up the back stairs—a gasp escaped, unbidden.

"Damn those toys!" The frantic words had zinged from Aggie's mouth in her desperate lunge for the door but as she touched the doorknob, her wet hand froze on contact. She yanked her hand back, then grabbed the knob again, and turned it holding her breath. Good, the door was unlocked and in a flash, she was inside her own familiar kitchen with the bolt lock slammed home, almost safe.

She raced through the kitchen and stumbled through the living room to reach the front door before he did the same. She slid the bolt firmly home, just in time!

She panted as her heart boomed a ragged staccato in her chest and she turned around to steady herself, to rest her back against the solid wooden door, but her escape had changed nothing. They were still trapped like terrified mice in a six-room cage.

Jim had sunk to ever-deeper levels of madness lately, and followed through on his threats when he was drunk, even viciously kicking in a basement window one night, to get inside.

Aggie said it was the last time she would forgive him. This must be the last time.

Aggie dreaded the dull thud of his hob-nailed boots pounding up the front cement stairs, but there it was, and immediately followed by banging on the heavy wooden door. The force of the blows, that awful clamor, had to be the result of a maniac long past feeling cold or pain, but it was hard to think of him as her handsome husband when he acted so insane.

Mad ravings of a long-time alcoholic rang in her ears—so many promises, so much forgiving—but the boys were frightened out of their wits, while the new baby boy was safely at her friend Sharon's house tonight.

A gasping sound made her turn around to find two sets of blue eyes as large as teacups staring at her frightened face, at her tattered mess of a nightgown, bleeding hands, and bare feet. Her two boys stood like statues, the younger in Christmas pajamas and trailing a clown blanket from his fist that hung down by his side. The sight seemed a world away from the fear that visibly surged through them all, while shivers shook her violently.

"He's drunk again," she said sadly, her voice cracking at the effort of speech. The boys nodded with solemnity.

Aggie held aside the window curtain to peek at her husband, the monster. The smaller boy was young enough to be frightened and confused again, but the older boy's face looked tight. He had seen it all before and she knew he had a butcher knife from the kitchen drawer hidden under his pillow.

"I know you're in there!" the man hollered, as the door shook. "Open the door!"

From the sounds, she figured he must have rammed his shoulder into the door with all his weight, again, and again, and she could not resist screaming, "That's going to hurt in the morning, you stupid bastard!"

The noise stopped.

She whirled around, her blue eyes wide open in panic, whispering hoarsely, "Grab your coats, we've got to sneak out the back. Quick, now!"

Pushing them ahead of her to the closet by the door, she reached in and threw out their coats and galoshes, crammed her arms into her own coat and jammed on the first shoes that came into her shaking hands. She yanked hats over their heads and pushed the awkward feet of the youngest into snow boots muttering, "Come on, come on, out the back door."

The small boy started whimpering when the back door started shaking harder than the front door had.

"Damn," Aggie grumbled. He had come around the house and that flimsy excuse for a back door would quickly lose the contest with his crazed brute strength.

"Ok, ok, now kids, we'll go out the front," Aggie whispered urgently. "Look, look, we're right beside it. Come on, come on..." She urged them forward, her voice becoming a shrill breath as time trickled away. She rose to her feet, steadying herself on the door jam and trying to look brave.

"We'll have to run fast, fast, like the wind" she cried as she turned the front door lock, threw the door open and stepped outside with the smaller boy by the hand.

She heard the man kicking ferociously at the children's playthings and the snow shovels in the driveway, reminders of home life that blocked his path to his target.

She gasped. He almost had her.

Aggie hauled up the younger child into one arm, staggering with the heavy weight, his bulky coat as big as he was, and reached to grab the older boy's hand, and she ran, yanking him along beside her. Slipping, the smaller boy kicked his feet in alarm while the bitter wind bit into his mother's neck, and her exposed legs and feet, as she skidded on the icy surface in yellow summer shoes, the first shoes in the jammed closet to come into her hands. Yet, the scent of freedom tantalized her in the frigid air, and a fresh courageous energy filled her exhausted body, and renewed her spirit. If she could run fast enough, carry the bulk of the boy far enough, they would escape and never have to endure this torment again.

Her husband was gaining; it was not hard to do. He'd beat her to a pulp when he caught her, he shouted.

"Hey, there!" rang out a new baritone voice. "What's going on here?"

Aggie's breath caught in her throat. It was the police—saved!

The cruiser slid to a stop across the street while the red beacon light pulsed a rotating vigil.

Aggie staggered towards the opening car door as one officer stepped outside to hold it for her, and held his arms out to take the wiggling boy, that he gently deposited beside her when she settled in the back seat.

The same police officer ushered the downcast older boy to the passenger side of the vehicle and motioned for him to sit in the back seat, also. Ronnie then sat stock-still like a rock, his skin drained to ghostly white, his eyes straight ahead and a twitch around his mouth that indicated his jaw setting as firmly as a mask. His mother knew he detested feeling trapped—that scowl betrayed a dangerous anger brewing deeply in his heart.

Still shivering, with an emergency blanket around her shoulders and in the full blast of the heat in the vehicle, she leaned across Mel, and put her hand on his shoulder.

"Ronnie," she inquired earnestly, but he looked straight ahead and did not answer. Not wanting him to feel anger towards her, in this night already filled with a thousand hurtful emotions, she acknowledged, regretfully that he was growing up too fast and pulled her hand away.

Tears of relief and sorrow swept Aggie's cheeks as she leaned towards her smaller boy, his eyes blinking, looking bewildered as he sat quietly beside her in his deep red winter coat, but he was not responding. When the patient police officer slid in to the front passenger seat and reached to answer a call, that action caught the smaller boy's attention and Melville pulled away from his mother as if she was not there, his eyes locked onto the receiver in the man's hand.

Reprieve flooded Aggie's heart—Mel would be fine now. The new gadget intrigued him and he was in the care of the man in the front seat with the same welcoming expression in his eyes that Aggie's father gave to her. That affectionate look on the police officer's face was impossible to fake.

The officer smiled benignly and leaned closer to the boy to let the lad push the button on the side of the unit while he called into his division. He gave their address to the person listening and reported on the situation as another police car pulled up.

The senior officer stood solidly planted, still in the gleaming snow like a steely-eyed television cowboy ready for a shoot-out, his arms loosely by his side and his thumbs hitched lightly to his belt, slightly behind his holster.

The sturdy man's voice sounded relaxed, and yet commanding, when he called out to her husband.

"Where do you think you're going? Come over here and talk to us."

The drunken man waved his arms, complaining loudly, and then the rant trailed off to blubbering about how he suffered because of his wife, while the revolving police cruiser light flashed the color red off and on in his face.

Back in the cruiser, the officer turned to Aggie, and gently told her, "Go back in the house now. We'll deal with your husband."

Never, never would she tolerate another drinker, Aggie moaned, still shivering and her head throbbing from the stress. She hated alcohol, she told them, and she worried aloud because it was the second time this month that this had happened.

Shopping USA

1958

Chapter 15

The thin-framed boy reluctantly sat up straight when his mother's husband, Jim, slapped his leg off the armrest of the chair and growled, "Move your carcass and help your mother make sandwiches!"

Ronnie's face stiffened into a sulk, his eyes straight ahead looking at his brother. He muttered under his breath, "I don't like peanut butter." Especially after the sandwiches sat for a few hours in the car, when they became dried out gummy globs, he thought.

"You're as useless as tits on a board," Jim grumbled.

There they were sitting around again, waiting for Aggie to get herself ready after everyone else, her fair hair still in round wire curlers while they had to sit and listen while she yakked forever about beds that did not make themselves.

The minute hand on the clock clunked boldly like ominous warnings, from slash mark to slash mark as Jim spoke out to no one in particular, "It's one o'clock already."

He turned towards his wife with his hand raised and a finger pointed at her accusingly, "If you were not on the phone for an hour gabbing to your friends about what you're going to buy, we'd be gone by now."

"Well, Joan is doing us a favor, minding the baby at her place for us, I had to tell her when to give him his bottles and all that," Aggie responded, "I had to be sociable."

He grunted for an answer.

She turned away to continue packing the sandwiches, but her eyes slid towards her husband. It wasn't an hour, she mouthed to his back as he stomped the other way.

Jim stopped pacing back and forth issuing orders about what had to go in the car, although he did not trust the boys to pack it properly, his way, and ended up doing it himself. He thrust his hand through his thick black hair, turned on his heel in the middle of the kitchen, and announced, "I'm hungry."

"But, I just finished making sandwiches for the road," Aggie protested, spinning on her heel to face him.

He ignored her. "Well, I'm hungry now. How about you boys—you hungry?"

His dark-eyed glare locked to their eyes for the first time that day, slowly swinging back and forth between them.

"Sure, sure," they echoed each other. He was not yelling yet, but they figured it would be safer to agree with him anyway.

Jim grabbed the paper bag of freshly made sandwiches off the counter beside Aggie, who stood with her eyes raised to merciful heaven, and he threw it their way, "Then pay attention."

"No, not those!" she protested as she rescued the bag and stuffed it into her big purse on the floor beside her. "Eat the ones on the plate; these are for the trip back!"

Aggie heaved a sigh and plunked the plate of quickly thrown together lunch sandwiches also made of peanut butter, in front of Ronnie and young Melville, then turned back to the counter and leaned her hip on it now for support. She shook her head in exasperation, the big wire curlers seeming to move independently as she reached her hand back into the brown paper bag, almost empty now, and decided to make more just in case—boys get hungry anytime. Ronnie snuck over to the fridge to get some jam to add to his sandwich.

"And," she spoke to the air, "I still have to fix my hair."

When the boys were busily munching, Jim shot a look at Aggie's back, turned towards him now, and quietly opened the door to the basement, while shooting a "shut your mouth" look at the boys. Then he stepped inside and stealthily closed it behind him.

Jim returned quickly and was silently beside them again. The boys leisurely chewing continued. When Mel's eyes grew big and round, and blinked fast twice, Ronnie almost smiled back, thinking his brother was clowning, but then realized it was a serious signal. He snuck a quick glance around the room and his eyes became gloomy. Now both of the boys knew and sat wondering what would happen when Mom saw the bottle of beer in Jim's hand.

She heard it—the fizz of the cap snapped off with the bottle opener and she whirled around, the sharp knife poised and her blue eyes narrowed as she stared at the grown man's taunting gesture, breaching the "no booze allowed in the house" rule like a truant child looking for trouble.

Jim's head arose, anticipating her disapproval, his arrogant eyes shooting a dare he knew she would not meet, not today, not when they were heading out to cross the border and shop. He had paid his portion of "food and board" money that went towards the mortgage—not that she would ever put his name on the house. Maybe he'd have another beer, too, if they did not get out of the house soon.

Aggie turned away, looked steadily at the counter to focus and finish the job and tossed a couple more sandwiches into their take-away bag.

Safely out of the line of fire, they could sit on the front stairs of the house and eat their sandwiches in relative peace, and she was satisfied just knowing where they were and that they were safe. The freshly sharpened knife still in her hand, she waved it like a bandleader's baton and called out the boys as the door swung closed behind them, "We have to go through Customs on the way back...don't wear your jackets...we're buying jackets when we get there...for school."

"They grow so fast," Aggie muttered to herself. "And now the fool is drinking already and we haven't even left the house." She shook her head again as she finished her chore and wiped her busy hands on a kitchen towel, then started yanking the curlers from her hair, asking the woman in the mirror why she was under the spell of Jim's rugged, matinee-idol looks and his loving. It was still a mystery to her, but she was.

It was true that she endured the daytime hours of arguments and accusations for the passion of midnight when the house darkened, the children slept, and no matter how she squabbled with her husband through daylight hours, his hands sought her body, and his throbbing mindless manhood, as always, aimed in her direction.

She shrugged. There was the baby to consider, the son he always wanted, not the two hand-me-downs from Aggie's first marriage that he could not pretend to like. That added up to three children needing to be clothed and fed and a mortgage to pay.

Today she did not want to set off his powder keg

temper, and he knew it.

"So where is that place for cheap stuff?" Jim grumbled as soon as they crossed the border and hit the bustling Saturday traffic in Buffalo, New York. "Hurry up—pick a place...they all look the same!"

Aggie bounced with excitement and craned her neck to look right and quickly left. "No, we need the big store I found last time. We already talked about it, remember? I'm sure this is the street. Look, on the right, there it is—that big red sign—look at all the cars! Quick! Park! Look out for that idiot on your right! TURN IN NOW!"

"These are cheap," Jim said agreeably, holding up a pair of pants obviously too small for either of the boys.

"Oh, they're cheap, but they can't be that small. It doesn't matter if they're a bit big, they're growing so fast. I can't believe Ronnie is eleven and next year he'll be even taller..."

Aggie picked and speculatively pecked her way through special sale piles like a magpie hunting mice. The boy's arms were jammed into sleeves that invariably seemed irregular somehow, and the legs on pants were too short for the eleven year old or ridiculously long for the seven year old. They were leftovers from who knows where, but on the good side, the price may be slashed to next to nothing. There were also some ends-of-line stuff from better stores but they were in limited sizes.

"It's just a matter of choosing carefully. Look, these are nice," Aggie enthused, shoving more pairs of pants in Ronnie's direction. He looked surprised, as the boys' opinions were mostly ignored, but in the end whatever Mom showed them was the final decision.

Ronnie got a man-sized grey suit, with a jacket too

big, the pants a foot too long, and the waist huge, but by golly it only cost $5.00, and he would fit into it someday, Mom said. They got Mel's pants two-for-the-price-of-one and cheap to begin with, and a big grin lit up her face. God she loved shopping in the States.

"I need a drink, Mom, I'm really thirsty!" Mel looked wilted now, straining for breath in the dusty old clothing emporium and that broke the spell of the piles of sale items. "Well, just wait a bit," Aggie said, bending down towards him, "you stand here a few minutes. I'm just going to take a quick look at the shoes."

Leaving the wreckage behind, they carried their choices to the front counter, discarding items as the bill approached the allotted amount and in the end, it was the gigantic gray suit, pants for school, some shirts, two seriously discounted warm jackets, socks, and underwear. Naturally included were a few pairs of extremely cute and shockingly cheap high-heeled shoes, nightgown, blouse, sweater, and skirt. Jim got himself a couple of plaid flannel shirts for work and some socks.

The boys totally lost interest in the new clothes once they left the store and lagged behind their mother as if their feet were stuck in wet concrete.

"I'm thirsty," Mel repeated to his older brother, looking up into his brother's blue eyes, so like his own.

"Can we get something to drink, Mom?" Ronnie ventured.

Jim shouted, "Haven't you had enough for one day? What do you want next? The moon? I want a beer, but I don't have one!"

Aggie's eyes rolled—it sounded like three little boys in the car. "OK, OK! Boys! Let's find a movie. Jim and I are going to do some things and we will come back and pick you up when the show's over."

"WOW!!" chorused the boys.

"The movie is only one more block down this street, I saw it when we drove in," their mother assured them.

Jim looked suspicious, his dark eyes clouded, brows furrowed as if driving a few more blocks would be an inconvenience.

Aggie's blond curls whirled around as she faced Jim, and her steely blue eyes fixed him with a stare. "Then we'll do our stuff. OK?"

Without waiting for response, she turned back to her boys and smiled. "Everybody happy now?"

The boys nodded "yes" while their eyes danced with glee, but both of them were too smart to say anything aloud.

The theatre was not impressive when they saw it, but they were quickly out of the car and their mom bent over and counted out some money in their outstretched hands.

"We'll be back to get you when the movie's over. Here's ten cents each for the movie, and 10 cents each to buy some pop and a chocolate bar."

Mom jumped back into the car with Jim and they were gone, swallowed up by downtown Buffalo traffic.

Hands jammed into their new jacket pockets, holding their movie money tightly, the boys looked towards the dirty old movie house. Rusty colored paint peeled off the marquee, and what had looked like enticing current posters were carelessly slapped on top of a thick layer of former offerings curling up at the corners, or half ripped off the wall by passers-by. However, it was an adventure to be in Buffalo, a place that they had heard about on the Buffalo TV stations that they got in Toronto.

Mel's eyes rounded and stared at a six-foot tall scene where submarines were exploding and men thrashed in the sea and shouted at each other with their mouths wide open, possibly drowning. "Yeah, Ronnie, this looks good!" he said, motivating his older brother.

Ronnie's head bobbed, too. "Yeah, yeah, it looks good."

Eyes glued to pictures in a magazine in his glassed-off wicket, the scruffy teenage ticket seller mumbled "double bill" without looking up, "ten cents each."

He took the twenty cents in one hand and lifted the other to his mouth for a long drag on his cigarette, then tilted his head back to exhale a perfect smoke ring with a superior look in his eyes. Leisurely, he pushed the red tickets through the semi-circular hole in the glass wicket for the boys to grab. He gave a crooked smirk at their eagerness as if he was almost bored to death, before re-opening his magazine.

Ronnie wrestled the heavy theatre door open to let his eager little brother rush in ahead of him, and then hurried to catch up before the boy wandered too far.

Melville stood still with his small nose wrinkling, sniffing the air in the middle of the dim lobby and stretching his mouth experimentally, this way and that. "It smells funny in here."

Ronnie prodded. "We've got 10 cents left. What do you want to drink? The movie is going to start soon."

He impatiently watched his brother's wide eyes and his slow progress towards the shelves of glistening packages. Once Mel was there, he stood staring at the array of drinks and candy as if drawn by magical powers.

"Do they have Orange Crush?"

"No, just orange something...or Coke...choose one."

Mel was not finished talking. "Look they've got Milk Duds, like we saw on TV...and Circle M pop!"

Hands clutching their treasure, they turned and faced the ratty velvet curtain separating the candy counter from the theatre seating, and held it aside, barely noticing the cloud of stale smoke and grit that puffed around their heads. Inside, they stood still a few moments while their eyes adjusted to the gloom.

There were no other kids, only three or four scruffy slouching men scattered around the theatre as if they tried to be as far as possible from each other, while a cigarette smoke trail, caught in the bright light of the movie projection stream, snaked upwards toward the gaudy, painted ceiling far above.

Blasted by sound, snacks and drinks balanced in their arms, Ron took the lead, looking only at the right side and, with a head bob, indicated the row he wanted, as Mel followed.

He kicked aside a nearly empty popcorn box and a couple of crushed candy packets, and they sidestepped across the sticky floor to the last seats by the wall, their favorite spot.

Ronnie tried to explain what was happening on the screen to Mel, but that lasted only for about a minute, until bombs started exploding and they both contentedly crunched and munched their popcorn.

The boys sat mesmerized as men hollered over the boom of depth charges rocking a submarine to one side, and then the other, on the brightly looming screen, then the men lost their balance and skidded across the skinny walkways and grabbed for handholds, or looked worried checking the instruments, and some died.

One sailor argued with the Captain, and wanted another man with special badges to take over.

For a while, it seemed like the Japanese sailors in a big ship were smarter than the American sailors in the submarine. Some depth charges hit the American sub with blasting noises and killed some men, and it seemed that all the American sailors would die, so the Americans argued about who was a better captain and the best plan to trick the Japanese. They shoved dead American bodies and garbage into a torpedo tube and blasted them up to the surface, and the trick worked.

The Japanese captain saw the floating garbage and dead men, and thought the American sub had sunk.

Then the Japanese started to go home, so the Americans snuck up behind and torpedoed them, and nobody was mad at the Captain any more.

The boy's eyes never left the flashing images; they forgot about the gum and garbage under their feet. The pop and candy disappeared, robotically lifted, hand to mouth as a newsreel told them things they didn't know, or particularly care about. The lights went on dimly for intermission and they blinked their eyes, looking around and then at each other, as they were bored with no money left for candy. Time stretched out endlessly before them, so they tipped their heads onto the seat backs and looked at the ceiling, far above, covered with weird and faded paintings of fat baby angels with rounded wings. Mel ducked his head during the upcoming features when a spaceship seemed to zoom right at them and the boys nodded with enthusiasm at each other—yeah that would be good. After that came some cartoons, which was better than looking at the ceiling, and they laughed when Popeye got whacked with a plank and Olive Oil said, "Oh-h-h-h-h! Popeye!"

The second movie had stern looking men in uniforms around a big table with little flags on sticking pins that they put all over a map of the world. They talked too much about complicated army things and that made it hard to follow.

Then other men with blackened faces crawled through endless tunnels and blew them up, so more men came. They worked hard to dig the first bunch out and some buildings blew up, too, and some of the rescue team blew up because they did not get out in time, and but mostly the men talked about it later, over, and over again.

Finally, the theatre lights came on brightly and they looked a bit startled and then dazed. Their eyes had grown used to staring straight ahead at the screen in the darkened theatre, and they blinked several times, re-adjusting to the real world.

They moved up the side aisle quietly, steadily, with hands in their pockets and heads scrunched down into their collars.

The tow-headed boys stood on the sidewalk after the movie, shoulders sagging, waiting for Mom and Jim. Strangely worn out from the battles on the screen, and hungry, lunch far behind them, they found some comfort leaning back against the nicked and aged bricks of the theatre.

It was beyond the time Mom said she would return and the passing yellow buses, with green sides, had lost their charm of being different from the red ones at home. Buffalo looked the same as Toronto except for now when the neon lights on all the bars, budget stores, and loan company storefronts grew brighter than the setting sun and even the grocery store had a neon sign blinking "LIQUOR" in red, off and on. Mom said that buying booze in a regular store was illegal in Canada, so that explained all the bootleggers at home, and the boys knew what bootlegger meant.

The passing crowd changed, and Ronnie edged closer to Mel so his little brother could lean on him if he wanted to. Groups of two or three men laughing, or complaining loudly—maybe drinking already—replaced the families with shopping bags that had scurried past in their haste to be home.

He couldn't do much about it if somebody picked on them, Ronnie figured, but he would try to protect his little brother as much as he was able.

"I'm hungry," Mel decided, looking up into his brothers blue eyes as if Ronnie could solve the problem.

"Well, so am I," he agreed. "Maybe Mom has more sandwiches left."

"There! That's Mom!"

Aggie jumped out of the car wearing a new dress and chattering, her blond perm bouncing, cheeks two drinks rosy and her smile wide, happy to see them safe and sound and waving a hand for them to hustle.

"Sorry we're late. It was further away from here than I remembered, and this rush hour traffic! Come on now, climb into the back, it's a long drive home and we've got to cross the border."

Jim's face seemed red, contorted, frozen into a flushed scowl with his eyes staring out the front window, and his head swung left and right, checking for a break in traffic.

"Let's GO!" he growled, although it sounded like "Letsh go-o, sh-shtoopd kidz."

Jim slurred something about..."if you knew where you were going!—if you remembered anything!"

Aggie countered, "...if you left earlier, hadn't needed that last beer...now we had to park illegally..."

Jim shouted, "Shut up! Shut up!" while he slammed the steering wheel with one hand, again, and again, and then he was rigidly quiet in the car while they drove through the city. Ronnie and Mel were frozen like two stones in the back seat.

The crowded city thinned into suburbs, and then all farmland as they approached the border crossing in the quickly falling night. Aggie ventured, "We need to change clothes."

She saw no sign of houses, only a silver glow shining in the fields, moonlight on fallowing harvest cuttings between the tall trees of the perimeter, planted long ago as sentinels to block the icy winds and protect precious crops.

"Turn right there, into the side road."

Parked next to the gutter of the road, Aggie and the boys clamored from the car, and had to raise their voices to rise above the loud bubbling rush of yesterday's rainfall swiftly moving past them.

Scurrying now, as night quickly fell, she hauled their purchases from the car within the small range of visibility cast by the car's interior lights. She and the boys began the drill of donning garments tightest to loosest, one on top of the other, so the border guard would only see two bulky boys.

She tucked in the boys shirts, and Ronnie's long pants rolled up slim, and put the too-big grey suit on him over top. In the gloom of early evening, he looked like a chubby boy with a small head.

Mel looked like a little straw man with collars sticking up willy-nilly.

Aggie slipped on her new pair of pumps and the blouse, sweater, and skirt on top of what she already had on. The new strap sandals, plus a pair of slippers, were shoved into her purse with the nightgown, and a miscellany of papers, wallet, and beauty essentials were spread over everything. Accomplished in a flurry of motion, they were ready to go. She would do almost anything to avoid paying duty.

Mel whispered to Ronnie, "I'm still hungry." Ronnie nodded in agreement, snuck a glance at Jim, and gave his brother the "not now" look.

Jim stayed slumped in the front seat, behind the wheel, yakking out his drunk-talk. "You're always on my back, always complaining. My money goes towards the mortgage, too, you know...I help pay for the house...and the furniture...", although he said "alwaysh" and "housh."

Aggie and the boys hurried, squishing the empty paper bags into baseballs and pitching them across the culvert, grinning when most of them fell into the racing water and disappeared into the churning eddies almost instantly.

In case she did not hear him the first time, Jim yelled out at her, "I bought that furniture, I said!"

She called back without thinking, as if she was talking to a friend, "Just a lot of cheap junk!"

Jim erupted from the vehicle in fury, bellowing, "Shut your mouth! I'll kill all of you!"

He headed towards the back of the car, slammed his open palm hard on the car window of the back seat where the boys had scurried inside and growled when they jumped at the shock. "I've got an axe in the trunk!"

Ronnie's eyes blazed open wide, his mouth gaping.

Mel cried out in terror, his face screwed up as his eyes desperately swiveled between Ronnie and his Mom but found no hope, so he dropped his head into his hands and sobbed.

Aggie's mind spun. She failed to account for how drunk Jim really was and regretted her words. She and the boys trapped on this empty road in the blackness of night with a mindless alcoholic who lived for the craziness of guilt-free unconsciousness.

There must be something she could do—she altered her tone.

She stepped away from her sons and spread her hands out to her sides in beseeching supplication. "It's

OK, honey," she cajoled. "It's nice furniture. I was only kidding around. Let's get back on the road and go home."

He stopped, one hand on the opened lid, his other arm reaching inside the trunk.

"You know I'm grateful for all you do. I couldn't do it without you. We'll be at the border in a minute, need to look good for that. Really, honey. Let's go home and get something to eat. I'll cook something for you—I know what you like."

He pulled his head out of the trunk and his eyes squinted with suspicion, ready to make a dive for the inside, in case she proved to be not sorry enough. "OK, but keep your fucking mouth shut. I helped buy that fucking furniture."

His free hand now jabbed his own chest. "I pay the god-damned mortgage and don't even own any of the god-damned house!"

He slammed the trunk shut and crashed his fist onto it, hard, making the boys in the back seat jolt again, terrified, as if a shock wave ran through them.

Mel was quietly sobbing and Ronnie was rigid. To move in any direction was to be noticed, so he stayed perfectly still, stiff, his face showing no emotion whatsoever.

"It's getting late now, Jim. Let's get back on the road, and get home."

Griping, Jim edged along the side of the car to stay upright, and half fell into the driver's seat.

Aggie got in quickly, closed her door ready to go, and smiled to the drunk in the driver's seat. "It will good to get home, Honey. Everything is back to normal."

Ronnie looked over at his younger brother.

This was normal?

Mr. Hyde

1964 era

Chapter 15

"Barbados, that's right," Jim, answered Aggie, his voice dripping sarcasm.

Hands firmly planted on his hips, his menace searing into her mind, he stepped closer to her to emphasize his words, until only the yellow plastic laundry basket stood between them on the weed-ridden backyard.

It was temptingly close, making her want to heave the basket up and dump the still damp sheets all over him, especially when he leaned closer, daring her to object to his latest bright idea.

"Haven't you ever heard of it?"

"Of course I have." She flicked her head and rolled her wary eyes, thinking fast, but did not pause folding the bed sheets. They were fresh off the line and the weak October sunshine was dissolving, eaten up by a bank of rolling black clouds that meant one thing to Aggie: the rest of the laundry would have to hang on lines strung across half of their basement, adding to the prevailing autumn dampness.

A strip of lightning split the darkened sky, a roll of thunder would surely follow. Autumn chill cut through to the bone but she hated turning the furnace on too early in the season. She told the boys to wear more sweaters because oil cost money.

Hoisting the laden basket to her hip, she maneuvered it up the steps from the yard and into the kitchen, trying to ignore Jim stomping behind her as a petulant boy summoned to the principal's office. The still damp sheets might as well be up here for now. She would sort it all out later, when he left her in peace.

Aggie filled the kettle, set it to boil and stared at it in her exhausted stupor that, nevertheless, did not interfere with Jim's campaign for her attention.

"We have to decide, you know. These tickets are a bargain because Frank can't go, and he's trying to get rid of them."

"So, what does that have to do with us?" Aggie turned her head to look straight at him, in his stubborn stance, he was not going to go away quietly, she might as well face it. She turned towards him, her arms crossed and shoulders dropping in resignation.

"I've been working really hard! I need a change from this..." Jim swung his arms and swept a pile of folded laundry onto the floor to demonstrate his disgust with all things domestic.

He advanced on her with the scent of alcohol around him—stinking like a beer hall after closing. "You can leave Vincey and Lilly with a friend that baby-sits. Bring her back a bottle of rum or something. It's only a week."

"I'll have to do more than that," Aggie started, "a boy and a baby..."

Jim was yelling now. "You have a job. You make money—work it out! It's all paid for, food and booze...I am going...and you better go, too! I'm trying to do something good for us."

With that, he smartly turned on his heel and stomped down the steps to the driveway, the metal storm door banged shut and rattled in its frame, his truck door creaked loudly as it opened, and echoed into the kitchen when it slammed shut. The beaten-up motor, badly needing service, turned over with the rumble of excess force on the accelerator, and in a roaring rush, the noise was gone.

Aggie stood still, her face immobile. She had witnessed his tumultuous exits a hundred times but it was not a good thing that this felt normal.

Shrouded by her sloppy old housecoat that hung like a bag around her, bigger all the time, Aggie pondered how to change her life. Ten pounds more had dropped off her body since her daughter, sweet Lilly, was born. With the baby fat melted, her skin on her face was taut, and her ribs stuck out like the skinny old horse that pulled the rickety milk wagon when she was young. The horse staggered sometimes, snorted out his nose in protest, and she wished she knew how to do that.

Every time she looked in the mirror and noticed the dryness of her browning hair, the dullness in her eyes looked back at her with no emotion. It was discouraging. It was afternoon, and she was still in her housecoat and her hair was still in curlers.

With a sigh, Aggie lifted the well-used old kettle and poured the boiling water into the waiting pot to join the tea bag. Relieved with the familiar sameness of the trusted motion, she felt better, and in a few minutes, the tea would work its magic and soothe the pounding that was starting up in her head.

Inside her head, revolving thoughts spun out.

She would miss her little girl, too. She was at work so much it seemed as if she had missed the early baby stages and heard about it from the babysitter. She had taken Lilly there fast asleep sometimes, and brought her child home ready for bed, and Aggie did not want to miss a day of her upcoming school years.

Now this Barbados nonsense would eat up all that

she had saved and she knew that somehow that would be the outcome. Jim would be short on his contribution to the household because he bought the tickets, or something.

Her eyes drifted around the cluttered room as she sat down to eat her breakfast, only lukewarm tea and oatmeal and here it was 1 p.m., but at least the last of the laundry was on the clothesline and some of it dry, lying in the wicker basket beside her rickety ironing board. It seemed that board was up permanently nowadays. Someone needed something ironed all the time. Ron had learned to do his own. Oh well, she sighed, it is a good thing for a boy to know how to take care of himself because he was fussy and she did not have a lot of time.

Must think about Barbados. She would take her new popsicle-orange short skirt, for sure. That was a fun end-of-summer sale with piles of really cheap stuff, as cheap as the States. Imagine that, a skirt with matching sandals and now she would wear those on a real ocean with a barbecue on the beach and that could be wonderful fun. She paused to take a bit of lunch and smiled. Someone said the food at resorts was often good, and all included, like the booze Jim had told her, and maybe she would get fat and jolly.

She paused, and her shoulders re-tightened to their accustomed wary position and her happy expression faded, replaced with familiar grooves of worry. With Jim and free alcohol, something was bound to go wrong.

The long and bumpy bus ride from the airport to the resort enchanted Aggie, despite the thought that the springs in the bus seats had worn out long ago from the hefty passengers that rode it every day.

She leaned forward eagerly, as the scenery was so

different from home, and her newly cut and blond hair flicked from side to side while she took in formal gated-estates. White with red brick roof tiles, they stood within private walled gardens of fruit trees and vines that spilled over the walls and hung to the ground.

Against the starkly blue sky, tall green-topped palm trees swayed in the breeze wherever she turned and she tried to see it all at once.

The locals in Barbados wore loose clothing in the intense heat: the women's blouses in brighter colors that complemented their dark skin—red the most popular, with elaborate stitching, and their skirts skimmed their ankles. Some young girls chose the fashions of the States, tight and short skirts and sleeveless blouses, and the older women looked them up and down with scornful expressions and turned away.

Fair-skinned businessmen, descendants of colonial arrivals, were dressed in custom-made suits with shirts and ties and removed their jacket if they sat at an outdoor café, folded it with care, and placed it carefully on the back of a chair. Their women, much fewer of them on the streets, dressed with casual and unquestionably expensive elegance.

The tourists stood out like sore thumbs. The women with permanently curled hair favored brightly colored dresses, short skirts or Capri pants, and wore or carried the large woven straw hats sold at the roadside stands. Their portly men loved Bermuda shorts and outrageous floral patterns on their shirts that flapped in the breeze, to prove to themselves they were on holiday in the tropics.

Great smelling food seemed to be cooking everywhere in small restaurants and food stands, making Aggie hungry, but the fully loaded bus passed quickly by.

Farther out of town, groups of boys kicked soccer balls around in grassy fields beside small schools, while little girls in uniform stood in groups, heads together, sharing comments and giggling. Large orange flowers bracketed the roads standing tall on top of long green stems and resembled orange birds' heads with beaks and a purple headdress that included golden antennas. It was a great deal taller than the extremely expensive version in the florist shops at home and the bus driver mentioned the name—Bird of Paradise, and Aggie agreed; this looked like paradise to her.

It was all a delightful change from the gloomy grayness of the Toronto suburbs, growing colder by the day with nightly frost coating the remnants of summer and yes, any day now they would get a dump of snow.

More in the countryside now, the bus narrowly missed small herds of goats. They passed food stands with thatched roofs that had a couple of rustic tables set up beside by the road. Native artisans sat beside a small table of their weaving or carving, watching regretfully as the potential business zoomed by, while their plainly dressed little children ignored the bus altogether, and played kid games batting rocks with sticks in the dust.

Everyone on the creaking old bus had sour faces now, tired and irritable. Aggie figured they were as tired of the dust blowing in from the road as she was. A weak cheer arose then quickly fell when the last curve of the road curled into the resort driveway in the late afternoon. Many of the passengers, like her and Jim, had missed lunch altogether.

As they drew near, the resort stretched out on one floor, fronted with blooming red flowers on thickly twined bushes. Aggie could see through glass doors to the lobby, then through to the eating area and all the way through to the darkening sea, and she longed to leave the rattletrap bus. Jim's glance caught her eye, his head nodded towards the exit and she nodded agreement. The practiced team gathered their hand baggage, as did the other passengers, and everyone scrambled for the door at once as if it really mattered who got off the bus first, as if the food supply would vanish. This had been an extraordinarily long day and it was time to fill their stomachs.

Enticing aromas wafted from a fully loaded grill as soon as their feet were on the ground. The door opened and they would learn to their everlasting pleasure that the grill stayed hot morning to night luring them to eat, eat.

The bus driver grinned and loudly called after them, while they rushed away, that he would unload the luggage and formal dinner was later—this was only late lunch or tea, as the English would say.

"Don't forget to check in! You need your identity card to eat in the restaurant."

His voice faded behind them as Jim grabbed their room key, and they sprinted down the hall like little children, to wash their faces and hands before they ate.

The room was nothing special, a double bed with the bedspread of a tropical motif of palm trees, a couple of relaxing chairs, a decent closet, and a small bathroom holding a sink and shower stall that had a yellow pineapple stencil in the center of each tile.

The best part of the functional room was the wide, glass patio door, and once they flung back the drapes and heaved it open they faced a large manicured lawn studded here and there with a flambeau, a workman starting to light them for the evening, and a wide sandy beach. Rhythmically, darkened waves with frothy white caps crashed on the shore in front of them, leaving a skirting of bubbling white foam, while diamond bright stars sparkled against the blackening sky of an early tropical sunset, with no city lights to dull their show.

It would be wonderful in the daytime, too, quite impressive, just what they hoped for, as portrayed in the photo on the brochure and the best part, for Aggie, was the heat, just like summer. Sitting outside under the stars was magical—a summer evening in early November, that she dreamed Florida would be.

"I'm so pleased," she ventured. "If the food is good, it's just what I wanted." She cast sympathetic eyes to her husband, as he looked exhausted but still enthused, and proud of himself. He nodded several times in response, reached out and put his arm around her shoulders so they could enjoy the view side by side. Everything would be all right tonight.

As the glorious tropical sunset died away to an ethereal glow, a small band of musicians set up their instruments and played intricate melodies during dinner. They wore ruffles on the sleeves of their loose white shirts that shimmied as the musician's hands flew over their steel drum pans, or whacked rhythm on tall drums, or on smaller drums held close to the body under one arm. Their tight black pants, banded with a red sash hanging from their waist, swayed with their hips, also in rhythm to the engaging and exotic calypso beat.

Aggie and Jim danced that first night, afire with the exotic experience of the soft and warm ocean air that seemed a magical elixir on their skin. They kissed tenderly while they swayed together under a star-studded black sky that looked so close a person could reach out to those brilliant lights, pick them out, and admire them like glistening jewels.

Snug together, at their table for two, Aggie spotted

something funny and burst out laughing, then shared the joke with Jim. Local single women, that their waiter said were nicknamed "Barracudas", wafting clouds of throat-catching floral perfume on their copious breasts bursting out of low necklines, were asking men to dance—even some married men with their wives. Forward women, they unabashedly slipped pieces of paper in the men's pockets and the men, and the management did not seem to care, so the visitors assumed it was business as usual.

They did not come near Jim and her. "Maybe," she whispered to him, "we seem too deeply in love." He whispered something naughty back to her, his lips close to her ear, for her alone to hear and she played coquette, seemingly delighted but a little shocked and turned her head away.

He drank too much and Aggie did her fair share. Back in their room, the patio door slightly ajar, smelling the fresh ocean evening air, they enjoyed the intimate pleasure that kept them together, each finding the other beautiful in the glow of the balmy tropics and rum, wondering why they fought with such ferocity.

They woke in the morning with blistering headaches, wore sunglasses by necessity and vowed to take it easy on the rum punch this bright new day by the sea. That promise held one day for Jim, as his hangover melted away.

His hand to mouth with rum punch, a freebee for guests, started at lunch the day following and continued on a crowded boat cruise. Through the toasting ceremony with the captain, he drank them back as fast as he could lift the tasty liquor, then started lurching sideways when he walked on the deck as if it was rough seas.

Aggie edged away, and turned to lean her forearms on the railing, lost in the view of the rich blue of this deeper sea, the white froth on the waves washing against the gunnels, and salt air on her face, sweet to her senses, while sea creatures raced the ship in the open expanse of the sea. If she looked the other way, he would simply be another drunken tourist on a cruise and she would be free to plan how to make this kind of beauty part of her life, someday. She believed with all her heart she could make it happen.

The crew was mildly sympathetic until Jim kept it up, one free drink after another, and he fell down the steps almost knocking the captain overboard. The crew cringed away from the couple, and Aggie was tremendously upset.

They fought ferociously as he sobered up. His embarrassing ways galled her, ruined her holiday, she said, but finally they made up and pledged to spend the entire next day together.

It was nice in the resort but there was nothing else for miles. She could hire a taxi to prowl through the cheap shopping in town but the prices, when converted to American dollars, were no bargain. "Walking out alone is discouraged for safety reasons," the notice on the door had informed them, "and please use caution if visiting the town." Therefore, any money they spent would be in the kitschy gift shop.

With only two days to go at the resort, Jim decided he wanted to swim after a leisurely breakfast, because he wanted to see Aggie in her bathing suit again, he said, and they could not go home without a suntan because he wanted to make them jealous at work. He was on his fourth or fifth strong drink and sucking it back like Orange Crush at a kid's picnic, when he headed for the water.

She had lagged behind to test the sand and it

seemed to dissolve under her toes, soft, but riddled with sharp shell bits, beautiful to look at but hard on softened feet grown used to high-heeled shoes. The waves were stronger than they had looked from the table where their drinks waited, and they drew back with a lot of suction on her ankles. She almost lost her balance when she stepped back, not sure about it at all.

Stretched out on a lounge chair with her sunglasses on her eyes, ready for her tan, Aggie was not enthused about the rum punch handed to her—it was too strong, too much rum, so she set it aside. The lounge chairs looked like a safer way to get a tan and she was satisfied with her decision, happy for the peaceful moments, and she laid her head back down.

Then the hullabaloo started. She raised her head to look around, noticing that one man had stopped turning fish on the barbecue, dropped the spatula to the ground, spun around, and wildly waved to several other men while he ran towards the water. They dropped rakes, threw down bundles of laundry, stopped working clippers on the greenery and raced to the shore. This had happened before and they knew what to do. Aggie idly wondered what was wrong and craned her neck to see. Jim's head rose above the waves and then disappeared from view.

"Help! Help!" The sound of arms smashing the water and a man calling out and spluttering, and the people shouting, was barely audible over the waves slapping the shore.

"Yes, that's my husband." Aggie put her head back down and resumed her suntan. Serves him right—he could drown for all she cared.

The well-trained employees fished him out, flipped him over on his stomach, and pounded his back until water gushed from his lungs.

Jim was quieter that night, sober for a change.

Apparently, salty seawater did not agree with rum punch.

The next day, the last full day, he disappeared after breakfast. Their trip was over in the morning, there was an early plane to catch, and he was gone. Probably found a crap game, she figured, and who knew what else. She felt deserted.

Whatever worries built up inside her in the afternoon, slowly simmered down to cold anger. She sat on the lawn in front of their room staring at the sea, wondering what to do, and how to do it. She did not have her plane ticket—Jim had the tickets—so she could not leave. Then she heard a commotion in the hall: shouts, punches, grunts, the sound of two or three men scuffling, and the thud of a heavy body thrown against the door that rattled the hinges.

"Fucking bastard!" She knew that drunken slur, "Aggie, open the door!"

If she didn't, there would be more yelling and screaming. When she unlocked it, the door burst open wide and he stumbled inside.

Pretending to fix her hair in the mirror on the dresser, she could see his sorry face, so as calmly as possible, she asked, "What's going on?"

"I want my wife." He grabbed her arm and twisted.

"Here I am." She was not going to give him the satisfaction of whimpering or pleading.

"Come on, let's have some action!"

"Not now, you're drunk!"

"So what? You're my wife, that's your job!" He yanked off his jacket and flung it over a chair.

"Not when you're stinking drunk, it isn't!"

He shoved her onto the bed, ready to mount, but she wrenched herself free and toppled him over onto the floor.

"What's the matter with you?" He grabbed for her arms. "I paid for this vacation, I want to get fucked!"

"Come back when you're sober!"

"Fuck you! I'm going out to get FUCKED! I'm going to fuck a black girl!"

"Why don't you sleep it off a bit? We can eat something, and do that later." She tried to sound calm.

"Get out of my way! I'm going out!!"

Knowing nothing good could come of it, but trying to engage him in conversation anyway, Aggie asked, "Where? We've got a great place here."

"Bullshit!" he shouted as he staggered into the bathroom.

This was her chance. She grabbed his jacket, found the plane tickets in the inside pocket, and snatched hers.

Aggie grabbed her purse, and threw her stuff from the dresser top into it. Picking up the closest shoes, she heaved open the patio door, and ran for her life. There was no time to get anything else. He would have to bring all her clothes back with him—if he was able. At this point, she did not care.

Aggie stood in the shadows around the side of the building for a few minutes, listening, then edged around to the front. She had seen taxis waiting there several times when she had passed through the lobby, but there were no taxis waiting there tonight, and no one at the deserted front desk to call one, so she had to keep moving.

Keeping her anxious eyes questing back and forth, first through the glass to the brightly lit lobby—but there was still no sign of guests or staff—and then through the lobby to the back lawn where flambeaux shone and dancers gyrated. The doorman shook his head, when she asked about taxis, and pointed down the road, dimly lit now that daylight was fading fast.

Aggie kept to the shadows, yanked off her shoes that wobbled and slid on the rough stone and grimaced when uneven bricks cut her tender feet.

Close behind her she heard the bellow. "AGGIE!!"

Not daring to stop to see if she was spotted, she ran hard until she saw some buildings, then wove between them as the overloaded purse slammed against her, regularly slipping down off her shoulder, and needing a continual pull on the straps to keep it in place.

She stood on another road, now, her chest heaving and the heavy purse at her feet. A taxi passed her by, then another as she tried to flag one down. The driver's eyes widened at the sight of her staggering in bare feet on the stone road; they did not want any tourist trouble.

She tried to walk again, sweat pouring down her face, her moistened palms losing grasp of the burden that felt as if it was filled with cement blocks.

Trying to look calm, she burst into unbidden tears of despair. How could she have trusted him? Why was she so stupid? If he was near alcohol, he drank. This happened over, and over again and would destroy their marriage and he could not get that through his thick skull.

He was two people: Dr. Jekyll and Mr. Hyde, was what her doctor told her. He explained the story about a scientist, Dr. Jekyll, who tried to make a potion to make him more powerful but it backfired so that when he drank it, he turned into a monster that killed women horribly.

Aggie had left Weston with the normal Dr. Jekyll, and here was the monster, Mr. Hyde, transformed into a horror and the potion was simple—alcohol...and Jim loved it...and did not believe he was as bad as everyone told him he was when he was drunk, .

A vehicle slowed beside her, startling Aggie. It was a

taxi and a kind face peered out over the steering wheel at her sitting exhausted, holding her purse cradled in her arms.

The driver leaned out of his window. "Taxi?"

She thought it was the fair thing to do, to tell him the truth, so she looked him in the eye and told the tale.

"Yes, I want a taxi but I warn you, my husband is drunk and he's looking for me."

His round, brown face showed concern, with a hint of kindness. "De rum is bad. What you want, lady?"

"My plane leaves at six o'clock in the morning. I need a hotel where he can't find me. He will look for me until he passes out." Aggie knew she looked a wreck, her shoes ruined from the cobblestones, her feet cut and bleeding, her short orange skirt dirty now, and her short blond hair that must be standing on end.

The driver thought seriously for a long moment, hands gripping the steering wheel hard as if it would get away on him. He looked at her again, shaking his head back and forth and he heaved a sigh. "I help you. You stay in de hotel. I take you t' safe hotel, no problem. You stay inside. No, no, open de door." He shook his head seriously back and forth. "Only 'fo me, open de door," he emphasized, pointing to his chest. "Very bad men in de town."

This made Aggie pause, wondering what kind of set up it could be. She may be jumping from one problem into a bigger one.

That was before the sound of a drunken holler echoed down the street. "Slut! Whore! I'm goin' to kill you when I catch you."

Oh, god. He was still on his feet and really drunk tonight. It was a wonder he found her at all, but he had a tireless instinct for doing that.

She looked at the shocked expression on the taxi driver's face peering into his rear view mirror and he looked scared himself.

"Yes, yes!" She scrambled for the passenger door before he changed his mind, while the driver leaped out, grabbed the purse and flung it into the back seat with her.

He hustled into the front seat, pushed the accelerator to the floor with his door hanging wide open and they sped away, tires squealing, a comet of stones spewing out behind.

The dimly lit passageway to the clerk's booth was disgusting, littered with torn band concert and movie posters and a layer of filth, a warning to Aggie not to hold great expectations.

The counter clerk's suspicious eyes stared at her from his scarred mahogany face, and with a strange smelling cigarette in his mouth, followed her every move. She felt that it would be better if the floor opened up and swallowed her, but the driver flicked his eyes to her face and boldly stepped in front of her, his hands waving in the air, conversing in rapid patois she could not follow.

He turned to her and relayed how much it would cost and Aggie handed over the bit of money demanded for the room, realizing how massive a man he really was, bigger than her by far, his arms like thick tree branches filling the narrow space in the meager hallway.

"Come, come!" He grabbed the purse and shooed her like a chicken up a flight of uneven stairs to the second floor and down a hallway. Once at the door of a room at the back, the driver smiled, trying to reassure her.

"It safe. No one evah dream you come to dis hotel. Worst place in town, but you must stay here, in de room." His voice was low, his words so jumbled, it sounded like a buzz in her ear, but thankfully he saw her confusion and enunciated more slowly, "Juz stay in de room."

The compassionate look in his eyes showed his concerned for her—Aggie could see that.

He promised to return at daybreak, at least that's what she figured he was saying in his patois English, but she had no way of knowing if he would, or would not come back, or what else could happen to her in this urine soaked sanctuary.

"I come fo' you at five," he repeated several times, holding his broad hand up with palm open and fingers spread to demonstrate the time on the clock he would return. Then he tapped the numeral on her watch to make sure she understood, as if repeating it in his elongated vowels would ease her panic.

He still looked uncertain, so Aggie nodded, over, and over again to prove she would stay put, all the while thinking that at least there would be a closed door with a bolt lock, although history had proven it was possible to kick a door down.

She sat rigid on the rickety old wooden chair in the dingy, airless hotel room, her hand clutching the handle of her battered purse for security and preparedness. She steeled her mind against overheard and frequent raging arguments, and women's screams from the rooms, and the loud throbs of island music and the laughter in the streets outside, where it was black and stank from open sewers.

She vowed not to sleep but awoke occasionally with a jolt, and told herself the sound was the scurry of rats she heard and not an intruder. Her eyes drifted longingly to the bug-ridden bed, willing it to be something it would never be, clean, but habit had her wanting it anyway.

She waited, and waited, and she imagined the black sky growing lighter and lighter, and the stars becoming ghosts that haunted the brilliance of dawn.

Finally, her chin on her chest as she curled in the chair, Aggie awoke with a jolt to a short toot on a distinctive car horn. Jumping up to the window, she recognized the driver she remembered from last night and with a breathless gasp, she waved to him, concerned about the worried look on his face, and then he spotted her. She held up her finger as if to say, "one minute," and the driver nodded and folded himself back into the driver's seat, engine running—ready to go.

Like a maniac, he maneuvered the cab through light dawn traffic while he flung his gaze from the road to the rear view mirror checking who was, or was not, following them. Then he looked back to the road again, while Aggie sat in the back and clutched the back of the passenger seat for balance, hoping, hoping, they would be on time.

The tires squealed protest pulling into the tiny tropical island airport. There was barely time to board the plane, and ticket in her hand, Aggie dug out all the money she had left in her purse, and held it out to him.

He shook his head, "No," and patted his heart.

Aggie figured that was to show her that he had deep feeling for her situation.

"You a fine lady; you be safe now."

She put the purse down and held out her hand, that he grasped in his giant hands, and they both nodded and nodded—strangers bonded forever over an act of kindness—and he smiled, his lips curling in a satisfied grin. Mutual understanding had beamed from their eyes that portrayed they would, each one, never forget the other.

The people at the check-in counter were a little surprised that she didn't have any luggage, but managed to get her through in time. Her husband was nowhere in sight, which suited her just fine.

It was better if he missed the flight altogether.

Some Fun Tonight

1965

Chapter 17

Ron stayed where he was, lounging on the well-worn couch, enjoying the quiet of the house with his mother and stepfather miles away on the highway, heading for Wasaga Beach, again.

He had enough of that so-called holiday with long, hot bumper-to-bumper drives on the highway and a maniac behind the wheel. It would have been alright if they stopped to buy a hot dog or a hamburger, but all they ever got was a peanut butter, bologna, or chopped boiled-egg sandwich. And when you got there, you ended up being a blood bank for the mosquitoes.

Besides that, he liked to keep a distance between himself and his stepfather as the antagonism worked both ways.

Ever since he was a kid, he hated those sandwiches in his lunch everyday, and in high school, when he had money from a bicycle delivery job at the drug store, he ditched those whenever he could, to sit on a stool at Kresge's lunch counter and devour a hot meat pie with gravy. It was his money; he earned it, so it was his alone to spend.

It was extra quiet with his younger brother and little

sister gone with them. It was just Mel and him at home now, and they both looked a little dazed from the unusual silence without Jim hollering, "Don't forget to put this in," and, "Get over here and help." His mom had rushed around, too, flustered, trying to remember everything, and the girl pouted for attention because she wanted lunch, and young Vincey was unhappy there was no room for his bicycle.

Finally, finally, the last sounds from the loaded to the gills 1959 Chevy, with its gigantic butterfly fins on the back, faded down the street as the phone rang.

It was Larry, from the Department of Highways, where they both worked in the mailroom, and a co-conspirator in their plan tonight.

"Are your parents gone?"

"Yup, time for the party. Mel is here but he's no trouble."

One car pulled up in front of the house and screeched to a stop, and a surprising number of kids scrambled out the flung-open open doors, leaped up the few steps and barged inside, with the driver squealing his tires as he peeled away on the quiet suburban street.

"Where's the booze? We brought beer!" No one bothered with glasses. Beer caps popped, heads thrown back, the instant crowd plopped to the floor looking around, poking each other in jest and the joy of being out, and free, no parents anywhere around, and flipped through a stack of records. One guy, in a hurry, lurched to the stereo record player and had Little Richard booming "Long Tall Sally," as if he had lived there all of his life.

Ron, Larry and Mel had a lot of catching up to do, so they did, upending their bottles of beer and guzzling them down, and then Mel wandered off to visit at a friend's house with a bottle hidden under his coat. At fifteen he was thrilled to be able to drink some beer.

"I'm hungry. Is there any food around?" someone asked.

"We could go down to the doughnut shop and get some doughnuts," Ron offered.

"There's a car in the driveway." Someone was observant. Mom's dark blue 1957 Buick, her pride and joy, and the only car out there, was a lot of temptation.

Ron's enthusiasm dropped again. "Yeah, but I don't have her keys. My mother always takes those with her."

Some guy threw out what sounded like a good idea. "I could hot-wire it, to get it going. You can drive, can't you?"

That was all of a dare someone else needed. He said he knew how to do it—hot-wiring—he'd seen it in a movie. He tried, but success eluded him.

"We could walk down," Ron said. "It's only about a 15 minute walk."

Cackling, giggling and weaving, the loud and motley crew made their way down the darkened street to the doughnut shop in Weston.

Someone was wearing a housecoat, and the bozo decided to flash a passing car. That passing car happened to be a cop car that screeched to a sudden stop and turned his flashing red light on.

The kids split in all directions.

Ron ran down the street, looking for somewhere to hide with his heart pounding and his stomach feeling queasy, as more cop cars converged on the rowdy collection of inept drunkards. He dived at a high dense hedge and smacked into wire mesh embedded in the center, then stumbled as he bounced off it. His head swiveled right and left, looking for a direction to get out of here and find a place to hide out of sight.

He jumped over a fence and headed for a doghouse,

the only shelter, half-hidden by a bush. It must be a big dog, he figured, but it still scraped his shoulders as he pressed himself inside and tried to pull his feet back, holding his arms tight around him. He could hear the sirens waa-waa-ing and cops yelling as he lay frozen with fear. Eventually the noise died down, and he crawled over to peek over the fence. The cops had gone away, and the suburban night was quiet once again.

He slunk home, not feeling so good now, and opened the door to the stink of stale beer and alcohol, and found empty bottles everywhere, some smashed to bits and stains growing larger on the rug, beside the cigarette burn holes. His brother could help him get rid of the evidence and then Mom would never know, except Mel was sleeping over with his friend. When he came back home, Ron would make him swear silence.

He could have used the help to clean up though, Ron muttered, and gingerly picked up empties and drained half-empty bottles into the sink. He gagged from the stench as he felt around for sharp bottle fragments, cigarette stubs, but they littered everywhere. He opened all the windows to air the place out and cut little pieces off inconspicuous places of the carpet to glue into the cigarette burns.

His mother flung the front door open in mid-morning, her arms loaded with all she could manage from the loaded car, packed just the day before. Aggie's hair, barely combed, stuck out in unexpected places and her eyes were black underneath, as if she had no sleep, at all. Grimly, she surveyed him, and then the room, with a dangerous look on her face. Her breath sucked in, and her voice rumbled like thunder as she demanded in full force, "What happened in here?"

Ron replied, trying to be casual, "Oh, I had a party."

Aggie steamed, and her voice rose like an opera

singer. "How many people were here?"

"A couple of guys."

"A couple of guys couldn't have done this! Are you kidding me?"

Ron rushed to re-assure his mother, "I'll do some cleaning today!"

"Yes, you will! You will do it all! And you'll pay for any damage!"

Jim did not butt in as he used to do, and said nothing for a change. He had been backing down since Ron stopped him from beating on his mother a year ago when he was punching her and tearing out her hair. He was finally big enough and confident enough from his Karate lessons to knock him down and kick him down two flights of stairs. That rude awakening ended the physical abuse of his mother. Jim was not the tyrannical boss of the house anymore and Ron made sure he understood that.

Aggie looked around more carefully, studied the rug, the bags of garbage he started to collect, looked at her son again, and strangely, with a minimum of lecturing, she let it go, expecting him to fulfill what he promised.

It was all strangely quiet that night.

Hooked

Chapter 18

"SCAB! SCAB!" the strikers screamed at the interlopers, who dared push through the arm-to-arm protest circle around the workers' entrance, to grab the temporarily available jobs.

"NO—NO—TO AUTOMATION!" they chanted alternately, pointed fingers jabbing the air, over and over, like attacking rattlesnakes.

Legally barred from overt action, like fistfights that could get you fired, strikers resorted to occasional "accidents," reported but never proven. Smacks on the head, or jabs to the gut with a STRIKE placard on a wooden spike were a common story, but strangely, the witnesses to those injuries vanished.

The cheaper non-union workers, sliding into the factory door in the ensuing commotion, punched the time cards and clicked more pay per hour than they ever dreamed possible.

"It's payback time," Aggie whispered loudly into the phone, stretching the cord as far away as possible from the kitchen where the kids wolfed down dinner and then looked around for pie. She had no time for baking now, had run into the A & P and found three for a dollar. It did not look like much apple in that skinny pie, but as long as it was sweet, they would eat it.

"Meet me at Dufferin and Wilson, Maggie, at the coffee shop, and call all the people you know, the more the merrier, I know Tomas is coming. Wear something black because tonight we are going to teach those night shift scabs a good lesson about stealing jobs and they'll get the message: one way or another we're getting our jobs back."

"Are you sure, Aggie? What if we're caught?" Maggie's voice got higher and thinner. "I don't want to go to jail!"

"We won't go to jail," she countered quietly, her blue eyes looking darker now and flicking around the room, mentally gathering up the clothes, boots, and hat that would partially disguise her. "Just meet up in the coffee shop. We'll drive over to the yard, but park a block away from the gate. My friend Sheila will be on the inside, see. You remember Sheila, the dark-haired girl from the Union dance last Christmas, the one doing the loud singing? Anyway, she'll open the gate a little bit. We'll be quick and quiet, in and out in the dark. Can you keep your mouth shut?"

Like coffee house Beatniks, the eight black-clad bodies jammed into a back booth, drinking coffee and mumbling subversive politics.

"I still don't like it," Maggie insisted, shrinking down, trying to compact her 5'8" frame, and looking even bonier than she actually was. "If one person tells, we're all out of a job!"

"And worse..." Bob Baker lamented, slowly shaking his head to, and fro, the baseball cap on his huge skull hardly hiding the blond buzz-cut peeping out the back, and he yanking his non-descript black jacket closer to his body.

"Oh, Bob," Aggie said tiredly, "get that silly cap off. Everyone knows who you are. You stand guard by the car and whistle if anyone is coming. O.K.?"

Relief flooded Bob's cherubic face.

"Have you got the knife, Tomas?" Aggie flicked her eyes to Tom, who sat silent and sullen, deep in the darkest corner of the booth.

"You bet I do! And I am ready to use it." His swarthy face wore a determined look, and his deep brown eyes squinted in anticipation. "There are wrongs to right."

Aggie decided to stay close to him, in case he overdid his part to play and tried to get even with someone in particular, but nonetheless he had a right to be here; a mortgage, a sick wife, and three small kids to feed were impossible on strike pay.

"Damn scabs." Tomas mumbled to himself but everyone heard him and felt his pain.

"Well, I have my knife, too," Aggie assured them in a low tone. "You all know what a good baseball arm I have—well, I can slash a tire!"

They paid their tab, quietly, and split their group into two cars. Now that the chore was imminent, they drove the highway fast and silent, ten minutes to the industrial plaza, with its lights ablaze for the night shift and filled with their temporary replacements: the enemy.

Each car had a driver, a watcher, and two slashers primed to puncture, rip, tear, or slash as many tires as possible in seven minutes, and then they had to leave— no matter what, as Sheila's break would be over then and she had to get back on the job. If she was caught, well, they had to make sure she was not caught. Sheila had little kids, too.

Black figures moved through the night with only a few grunts, soft curses and thuds.

Whispers of running shoes on tarmac, followed.

Seven minutes later, faster than a lightning bolt, the squeal of quickly closing gate metal shivered through their veins.

Shaking, satisfied, the two sets of car doors clicked shut as quietly as possible and the drivers pulled out, slasher crews intact, racing each other on the highway, hooting and laughing, drunk on power and waiting for tomorrow.

Damn her mother, anyway! Aggie could feel her teeth start to grind with stress. Things were going along at a steady clip since the strike ended and now her mother was dying!

She sat down hard on her kitchen chair, gave the table a push for good measure. The metal salt and pepper set tipped over, the saltshaker starting to roll off, and Aggie caught it in her right hand in one smooth swoop. "Safe," she said automatically. It was not a baseball, but it was the only bright moment of her morning and, as she set the shaker back in place, as the impossible thought drilled painfully into her brain— my mother is dying now to spite me, now that things are going well.

She had fought so hard to get her job back after the lay-off, Aggie mused. First came the strike action, and then the union wrangling a new contract, and if she left now all that she had fought for would be lost: a decent pension, paid holidays, a secure job, and it gave her a headache that turned her temper to dreadful.

She got up quickly and headed for the living room, then leaned back on the burgundy couch, grateful for the little matching cushion that fit perfectly under her neck. Miraculously, there was no one home but herself, and her thoughts seemed to echo around the room, an endless cycle that began and ended with the reality that there was a line-up for her job. No one left the highly paid technical work, it was hard to qualify for it in the first place, and her riveting experience during the war did that for her.

That's right, she moaned, no one left a high-paying

job guaranteed by contract to increase wages year after year, so why was she expected to do this? Her mother had three daughters and Aggie was the one with the highest paying job, but no one else would take her.

"She's so nuts!" her secretarial sister, Bea, judged explicitly, the sound of her pen tapping on her desk in irritation spelling out her mood.

Aggie could just see Bea ensconced at her desk with the latest office equipment, her blond hair fashioned in a simple and sophisticated style, her clothes business smart, and her face squinting up in distaste at the thought of being in such company as the sick and spiteful old woman.

Nancy, her other sister, the one married to the lawyer, said, "She's so mean, she upsets the family. I couldn't possibly have her here, and Jordon won't even drive me to see her." She turned to yell at one of her sons, her voice reaching an exasperated pitch then falling to a low moan, accompanied by the wooden chair that creaked as she sat down hard. "They don't listen to me. I can't cope with any more, I just can't cope!"

She knew Nancy had probably not combed her own hair for a week, and it would be murder to put her mother there, and she entertained that thought for a moment, but had to face it in the end, there was no choice—she had to quit her job and take her mother in until she died.

"It's always about mother," Aggie said to her teacup. "She has hooked me again.

It seemed she was always paying for the sin of being born, but at least this was the last time. Their duel would be finished, and her excellent job would be, too.

Her boss was sad to see her go. "You're a natural, Aggie: good dexterity, small hands, and a reliable employee. You have been an asset to our company. Nevertheless, the contract says, no leave of absence unless it is for your own health."

His face became stern "Don't give up the life insurance policy, though, it's a good one. Make sure you pay it every month."

"Oh, I will, Mr. Hunter, I will."

"I'll call you, Aggie, if a position opens up, in case...you know...you're available, but you realize how it works—there will be others in line—full-time employees, first dibs and all that. We just don't do part-time."

"I know, Mr. Hunter, I know."

"We will recommend you highly."

"Thank you, Mr. Hunter."

She closed the office door quietly, for the last time.

Legs on Rye

Chapter 19

Aggie tilted the cradle of her new slim-line, little red phone, admiring her lucky purchase, and she told her friend Mary all about it. There it had sat, brilliantly red, with a sticker that said fifty-cents, among a pile of second-hand household appliances at the Salvation Army Thrift Store. The cashier had agreed: if the sticker said fifty-cents, then fifty-cents it was.

Aggie untwisted and re-twisted the red cord on the red phone, while her foot bounced up and down in time with her conversation.

"Does it work?" she had asked the cashier. The woman shrugged, she told Mary.

Aggie had pressed her for an answer. "Can I bring it back if it doesn't work? You're really sure it isn't just decoration."

"Well," the woman had sighed, with a shrug. "We don't usually get fifty-cent items back."

"And didn't she just plug it in to make sure it worked!"

Her search for a comforter, warm and fluffy, but light, to put over her mother, did not work out.

Aggie had taken her back to the hospital twice but the woman was still shivering, or in spasm, Aggie wasn't sure what. Her arms and legs, especially hands and feet, felt ice-cold to the touch and this was strange because her head was hot, moist, as if life itself was seeping out of her in sticky sweat. That old bird was still alive, down the hall in Aggie's bed..

"So, anyway, when I came out of the Sally Ann, I picked up a newspaper—got to check on the jobs, I thought—now that my mother has screwed up my life again. There was an ad for the Triumph Hotel looking for a waitress in the lounge.

"You know the place," Aggie went on, "where I worked when Vincey was on the way? That the two brothers own? The baseball players? It's their retirement business, I guess. That's a good job you know, lots of tips, good for lunches."

She added with a tone of satisfaction, "I'm just going to have to work lunches there until my mother decides to die. I can get a woman down the street to look in on her, see. Mother mostly sleeps then. She's awake half the night. I will have to put her in another hospital for the very end."

"Oh, come on, Aggie," Mary protested, "you can't be working night and day!"

"I have to," Aggie protested. "I still have the house bills and her pills to pay for!"

"Yeah, bills and pills," Mary knew all about that.

Aggie thought for a moment, trying to think of something to cheer up Mary. She had her own problems.

"Oh yes!" Aggie enthused, "I'm having fun at the Triumph—the lunch specials are pretty good. There's a big board up for the daily choices and the local businessmen come in. A couple of days ago they had red snapper, and huge corned beef sandwiches on rye bread. The men love those."

"Remember those black satin hot pants I bought?"

"Yes, I do" Her friend laughed in anticipation.

"I wore them yesterday and one man looked me up

and down, head to toe, and said, "I'll have legs on rye!"

Mary laughed, "Oh Aggie, you're a riot!"

Aggie laughed all the way to the kitchen, as far as the cord could stretch, pleased that she could reach the kettle. She took a minute to fill it and set it on the stove's largest burner on high. The talking continued while she fished the tin of tea out of the cupboard. The idyllic decoration of Chinese women with paper parasols always seemed to sooth her—a prelude to the tea.

"I need to get out, see," she went on. "I seem to be here all the time. Except we did go to a family function and I got to dance with Lilly and we did everything, the polka, and that new dance, the Twist! It was so much fun to see that little girl catching on. She is naturally graceful.

Other than that, I am only gone about three hours a day and Vincey is in school, not that the boys could really help with this. Mel's gone to live with his dad and Ronnie has moved out. Jim used to yell at the older boys all the time for some reason. I think he was jealous."

"Why would he be jealous, Aggie?"

"Because he has no education; he'll always be a truck driver. I picked Ronnie up from the bus stop one day when it was raining really hard, and Jim blew up because he didn't care about him getting soaking wet."

Aggie thought a moment. "I kicked Jim under the table."

Mary burst out laughing. "That must have felt good."

"Yes, it did."

"'Let him walk,' he bellowed, so I kicked him in the shin. He was so surprised he didn't do a thing!"

Aggie stopped for a moment to catch her breath, and then dropped her voice to a serious, tone. "It's been hard around here with my mother so sick. I haven't seen you or anybody else for ages."

"I was flying around the city before, night and day, going to work and to the hospital, but it was better than this. Now it's like prison having her here. I feel like I'm going mental. I've got to make money. Good jobs don't grow on trees. There is just no sign of her dying."

Her friend made appropriately sympathetic noises, while Aggie got up again to fill the teapot with the boiled water and plop in the tea bag.

"A woman will come in during Mom's major nap. Really, all day is one big nap. She's asleep more than she's awake. When she's awake, she's miserable. I don't get it at all.

"There, did you hear that? She's in my room, in my bed, and banging on the floor with her shoe; can't you hear it? I sleep on the couch—no wonder I'm so tired. Jim is angry all the time, but mind you, it doesn't stop him from getting friendly, if you know what I mean."

Aggie just wished she, herself, could sleep. She tossed and turned on the sofa bed in the living room, and jumped at every sound. In the first place, her mother had a smell on her that was not human anymore. It was as if she had one foot in the bed and one foot in the grave. Just changing the sheets made Aggie feel nauseous.

Her mother's hair looked like straw. She screamed at Aggie if she tried to comb it and complained if she didn't. Dying sure didn't look like an easy thing to do.

She had always been miserable—now she was miserable and sick. Moaning loudly, she blamed Aggie's Dad for everything, as she always did, or blamed Aggie.

Dad would not take her mother. He had buggered off to Florida, with three pals in a trailer park and he would not budge. In love with palm trees, he said. You have to come here. Done his time already, he said.

Me, too, Aggie grumbled to herself.

It seemed her mother had totally forgotten about her other two daughters or her son.

That was fair; they certainly wanted to forget about her.

"Damn my sisters," Aggie told Mary, "leaving all the caretaking to me, just like the old days. Because I'm the eldest, they said. Sure, sure."

She stirred her tea as she spoke, so hard it almost tipped over the rose patterned cup, and set the spoon down firmly on the saucer, making it ring.

Habit. That must be the reason she took her, Aggie thought. Just a darned habit to say, "I'll do it."

Like a dare, really. If someone said "I'll bet you can't do it," it rankled her gut.

"Just the other day I was talking to somebody, trying to get some help, and finally got a call back," Aggie complained. "Then a woman from Lilly's school was at the door and of course I had to take the phone call and mother was banging the floor, and everyone was mad at me, as usual. I get nasty looks from everybody around here all the time, but somebody please tell me how to split myself in two! All for a woman who hates my guts!"

"Well..." Mary interjected, "have you ever thought about helping to open the Pearly Gates for her? I've got an extra heavy pillow, you know."

"What do you mean?" Aggie responded in a conspiratorial tone.

Then she caught on and burst out laughing. "Ah, go on! Thanks for the laugh. You're always kidding me!"

"Well, then, you could sneak away tonight, when she's asleep," Mary urged in her best mystery voice. "Give her one of your tranquilizer pills. We'll drive down to the Masonic Hall, an hour down, an hour to play, an hour back. They always have a good band.

We'll dance ourselves silly and sneak back in the house like the old days."

Aggie threw back her head and laughed again. "Oh, don't tease me. You know I'd love to do that! Remember the night we tricked our parents into thinking we were baby-sitting, at the same place? ...and neither of us even went there?"

"Sure do," her friend agreed. "Our fathers pounded on the door when we didn't answer and woke up the whole house! Don't know what made them suspicious that time."

Aggie sighed again. "I'll get back to my life soon. We've got a lot of dancing to catch up on."

"Someday it's going to be my turn," she told Mary, but now she had to get busy because the moaning was getting too loud and might wake up her daughter. She often fell asleep playing in her room.

She really hoped there was more medicine to quiet her mother down.

"Gotta go," she said, regretfully hanging up her cute red phone.

Little Blue Pills

Chapter 20

The doctor in charge had checked her mother's nametag: "Agnes O'Hara." He did not know why she was quaking, either, and did not care. They signed her over to Aggie, put her mother in a wheelchair, ignoring her loud moaning, and helped to push it to the doors of the hospital, where they left them.

"Bring her back in a month if she is still alive," he told her.

It was Aggie's problem now.

Trapped until her mother died.

It played over, and over in her mind.

Trapped, trapped.

This waitressing is too much...it's exhausting, she mumbled to herself. A few hours a week to shove a little change into her pocket, when she could talk a neighbor into sitting with the grouchy, sick, and half-mad old woman that had the shakes, and stank to high heaven, too. It did matter how much Aggie scrubbed her mother, avoiding the protesting hands slapping at her, cursing her; the woman still smelled as if all her poison leaked from her skin, and it did not make her any more agreeable.

Day and night—night and day, the horrible situation robbed her time with Lilly, now growing older and putting her dolls carefully on small chairs, with their hair perfect, dresses and little outfits straightened out smoothly, tiny socks pulled up and shoelaces tied. She could see her only girl, and her last child, taking time in the morning before school to comb her own silky blond hair. Lilly didn't ask her mother anymore.

The days flew by, torn between lunchtime waitressing and home, and there wasn't much time for a catch-up phone call to a friend, so she leaned on the wall trying to gossip with Mary, like the old days, but she didn't feel a shred of youth left inside herself; all she felt was tired.

"Oh yes, Lilly is fine. She's going to school now. Jim's all sunshine and roses when it comes to Lilly.

Vincey's in grade ten, but he's not getting very good marks and I don't know where he is half the time. He has booze on his breath, too, and hangs around with his pal, Fast Eddy, and wants a motorcycle because his crazy friend has one."

Mary was blunt. "Teenagers are hell—especially boys. I haven't had one night's sleep since my Georgie turned 14! Now he wants to be called George."

Aggie listened to her friend's tales and woes for a bit, to be fair, and did some more complaining herself, but she had to go.

She wheeled around when she hung up and heard her own voice played back on the recorder, loudly, and it sounded staccato, yak, yak, yak, then a screechy laugh, and more yak, yak.

Her daughter was laughing at her, and her husband's eyes beamed triumph.

Aggie snapped. She screamed at him, "You had to ruin it, didn't you!"

She yanked off her shoe and went crazy smashing the little red tape recorder to bits as Jim leaped up yelling. Faces contorted, and both blazing mad, they spewed threats and words of hatred that fed the fire back and forth.

He could not leave well enough alone, and that was the end of that.

"My husband is on the road all week and drunk at home on the weekends—fights, violence. I'm loosing my mind, Dr. McMillin.

"I'm so tense my neck is stiff, like I'm always waiting for something awful to happen and my mind is spinning.

"I'm working part-time, looking out for Vincey, and I worry about Lilly with all this yelling going on. I have no time or energy. And now I have my crazy mother. I need Valium to tide me over."

"Look, Aggie, Valium is very addicting and it doesn't really solve anything. I'll give you some samples but I recommend you go to Florida for a holiday."

She almost cried with the thought of medicinal relief, at last.

"Take your father's advice, Aggie. Relax—it will change your life. Find someone to look after your mother for a week; just one week will show you what I mean. Fly down to Florida and rent a car. Stay at your dad's place, he's always offering."

At least she had her little blue pills to help her out now.

Aggie phoned her dad, pacing back and forth as far as the telephone cord allowed. "It's time, I'm going nuts and I have to get away. I'll find someone to look after her for a week—someone I don't care about too much—they probably won't speak to me after that."

Melville, senior, went to Florida every winter and enjoyed the visits of younger people. Thankfully, her dad was always glad to see her. "You're always welcome here, Aggie. We'll make room somehow." She embraced that calm note, to help her carry on.

Aggie was reading the map, vaguely aware of her little girl in the backseat.

"I need to pee, Mommy."

They were in the middle of nowhere so she tried to ignore her for a minute, because Jim had missed the highway, again! "Take this right. No, turn now—you missed the turn!"

She mumbled to herself. "It looks too small for a highway, but it is. Where are we now?"

Lilly said she had to pee, again.

Aggie ignored her.

Something caught Lilly's eye. "What are those small bushes, Mommy? Does it snow here?"

"No, it's too hot for that," said her dad.

"Stop—I want to see what it is."

"We have to keep going to get to Florida tonight."

"Yes, stop," her mother intervened. "Show the kid something. It's her trip, too."

As far as they could see, fields spread in every direction with only the skinny black ribbon of road separating one spiny patch from another.

"Oh, wait a minute, that's cotton. You know, like cotton balls at the drugstore. Colored people pick it. Wonder where they are?"

"Maybe they're in the restaurant, Mommy."

"Oh, Christ!" Let's get out of here," her daddy grumbled. "What the hell are we doing out here anyway? Its four o'clock—we're not going in any goddamn restaurant."

Mommy chirped in, "—that's why we have peanut butter sandwiches."

"It's kind of scary, Mommy," said the little girl,

quietly.

"Don't be silly. It's really quiet, that's all…"

Aggie thought to herself, "We better get out of here, though. Too quiet. Like a graveyard. Not even a bird chirping."

They all looked around, no cars, just the crossroads. Which way to go...hearts thumping now.

"Where's the Sun?" ventured Aggie.

"Who cares!"

"The sun is in the west now, it's 4 o'clock. Turn left. We want south, remember? Got to get there tonight. Find the highway, gas up and keep going."

"I'm tired, Mommy. Need to lie down."

"Alright, you can bundle up your sweater for a pillow and put your jacket over you. Make a pee first, then take a nap. We'll keep going."

"But, I'll get my bum scratched!"

"Shut up," her Dad growled. "Do it and get back in the car. We're driving straight through."

At the beach, stunned into silence as bolts of moonbeam shimmered on the water and soft evening breeze caressed their relaxed faces, there was no cause to fight.

Aggie asked a local man to take a picture of them in the failing light—a picture of her, Jim, and Lilly leaned back against her father's legs, his hands on her shoulders.

The ocean drive wound around the sea as she searched for her father's place, contented now, passing beach after endless beach with palm trees that reached to the moon and room to exhale.

Aggie and Me

1973

Chapter 21
Author's View

When invited to the home of my lover's mother for dinner, with my two children, it seemed a landmark occasion even though we had been before, in 1969, when we were a real couple.

Back then, Aggie stuck her blond head into the club door on an autumn afternoon in mid-town Toronto, and smiled as she glanced swiftly around the large room, curiosity satisfied, and invited her son and me, and my two children, to Christmas dinner.

Christmas 1969 -Vincey, Joey, Ron, Janice, Arlene, Aggie, Lilly

I had heard stories about Aggie, her thrift and her style of travel, with numerous peanut butter sandwiches on the road to here or there, but it was clear she garnered respect from the two sons that I knew. We did not have a chance to talk in depth; she was in her usual hurry.

It was hard to explain "the club" to Aggie. The dignified building on Avenue Road, in mid-town Toronto, had been many things over eighty years of its history. In bygone days, horse-drawn carriages had delivered clients to lawyer's offices, then it transitioned into an art gallery, and the last incarnation before us was an antique shop.

For Ron, and me, it was a cool establishment with a cavernous main floor set up with tables, chairs, and the walls painted black, with deep red velvet drapes on the long narrow windows. Turn-of-the-century tea tins and bric-a-brac sat in gilded picture frames and rock'n'roll bands such as "Leather" played on weekends. A former military police woman gave Tarot card readings in the afternoon, while my children played outside or in the small kitchen or upstairs in our living quarters.

The august edifice oozed with history and passion, and it was a fine place to entertain local DJ's and pass the weekend of Woodstock in 1969. While the children played outside in the shade of a spreading tree, Ron's brother Mel dropped by on his motorcycle, with his long reddish-brown hair down to his shoulders.

Longhaired passersby waved a cheery hello, and we stayed tuned to the radio for the exciting news that wrote an exclamation mark on our culture: the half a million people that showed up in a little town in New York State, for a music festival.

Aggie's million duties, on the following Christmas day, were exhausting to even watch, and far too hectic for us to share a conversation. She plopped down on the arm of the sofa for quick photos, her blond hair cutely coifed and her skirt a mite short, but her knees pressed tightly together for modesty, as required for a woman in that groovy, show-your-legs era. In a flash, she rushed away to other hosting demands, and I would learn was her normal speed of accomplishing anything.

It never occurred to us that our situation was

unusual, a younger man with a woman and her two children, or it did occur to us but the arrogance of youth brushed it aside. We lived in an era where beads, headbands, trekking through foreign countries, pretending you were not part of the establishment, did not have a job and just hung out, day in, day out, was "cool." Throughout written history, there has always been some type of hippy, hipster, wanderer or rebel on the shy side of radical. Most of them, like us, were weekend hippies that worked or studied during the week and always knew where their money was coming from, or when to panic.

Eventually, we left the club with the angst of failed-endeavor blues that ate up our time and emotions for a couple of years. Sometimes, money and relationships simply slip away, and we parted company.

He called, sporadically, and once landed at my door with a fabulous carved wooded jewelry box from a journey to India, no explanation. Then the door closed and that was it for another year or so. Life went on.

In 1973, after a phone call and months of planning, Ron and I, and my two children, had returned from an extended trip to Europe and Asia, in a Volkswagen van we purchased on the streets of Amsterdam. The irony for me, after joining his quest, was that he did not intend to reside in Toronto—now he talked of heading out west with his brother to pan for gold, which was code for "be free of responsibilities." I suspected the hepatitis he had contracted on the road trip to, or from Afghanistan, still lingered. No matter the cause, he was not ready for a family.

He had been dreadfully ill when we made it back to London and holed up anxiously in a dowdy and dimly lit hotel room where the bedsprings died fifty years before.

Despite his protests, the longer we sat in the

straight, stiff-backed old chairs and listened to Ron's every ragged breath, as the endless hours ticked slowly by, the less likely it seemed that we would board the early morning flight.

I thought Ron was perishing and called the harried hotel doctor who, lucky for us, was a practical but kind man once he finished his examination. He looked carefully at me in a long, embroidered Afghan shirt with baggy cotton pants, at the big-eyed eight year old girl huddling close by my side, and disheartened ten year old boy sitting on a cot across the room, holding his head in his hands. With a thoughtful frown, the man put his stethoscope down on his lap, and looked again at the feverish and shaking man turning a brighter yellow before his eyes.

"I am supposed to report this," he said, with an officious look hardening on his face.

"We're on an early plane," I responded in an even tone, looked at my children and then back at the doctor, fighting to keep the quiver of desperation from my voice. "All we have left are the airplane tickets."

After a long silence, while he looked at us again, he told me, "Well, his color might be from the light of that orange lampshade, but I'll give him a shot anyway."

Ron was too out of it to realize there had been a long, thick needle shoved into his upper arm.

"You get him on that plane in the morning."

"Yes, doctor, I will."

He looked into my eyes searching for understanding. "When he's home, take him to his own doctor."

"As soon as we arrive," I replied, nodding. "We have a physician in the family."

There was no charge for his visit.

We all agreed: he was not there.

Time changes things, and now, at the end of 1973, here we were after his recuperation, facing the future, my lover almost well and talking of moving on—although I found that incomprehensible—when his mother invited us for dinner at her house, again. Awash with mixed feelings, I still looked forward to seeing Aggie. I wanted to know her better, and maybe, this time she would find time to talk.

There we stood, my brown-eyed children still wearing their embroidered shirts from Afghanistan, and a deep tan from our exotic journey. My girl's long brunette hair gleamed with a hint of russet, and my son's hair was blond, almost white from the desert sun.

We faced Aggie's yellow brick suburban house, a square box, similar to several others on the street, reminding me of the house I had lived in through my school years, when my parents were still together. The door opened into the small foyer and jammed-full closet, and this time, a tantalizing aroma of roasting meat meandered through the hall.

Warmed and rosy from kitchen heat, Aggie's friendly face soon beamed before us, topped with a perfect cut and style of blond hair, her customary crowning glory, and I though to myself how handy that must be, to be a practiced stylist, instead of tenuously clipping my own bangs.

A small, slim woman with a twinkle in lively blue eyes, she talked her steady stream of welcoming consciousness, and took our jackets. Passing through the living room, all heads turned right to stare at a huge wallpaper mural of a tropical scene that was new to me, spread over an entire wall, and she waved a hand towards it, as if to say, that too, is mine. An imitation palm tree stood in front of it, five feet high, with a wooden monkey hanging on for dear life and an alarmed look on its face. A merry laugh burst out of me.

"Oh, that's precious!" I exclaimed.

We greeted his younger sister and brother, the children from this second husband now sitting heavily at the head of the arborite kitchen table with an undisguised look of mild disgust on his face; that had not changed.

Aggie's fair, slender, and pretty girl, Lilly, about ten or eleven, my son's age, with a sprinkling of freckles splashed across her subtle nose, looked carefully through her curtain of white blond hair at me, and my boy and girl barely younger than herself. Her brother, Vincey, older by a few years at 16, tall now and robust, like his father, was a typical teenager and looked anywhere but at us.

I had no idea what they had heard, or not heard, about our little temporary family. Their brother and I had been together and apart before, and shared Christmas when these children were a few years younger. I only knew that my lover habitually kept his lips sealed and did so now.

Like a spinning doll, Aggie performed each task as a professional host to make us feel welcome.

"I made a roast tonight. It always goes well with mashed potatoes, and then you get the brown gravy, see? There will be dessert. I had a bit of time and made a pie to go with the ice-cream."

She looked at Ron for a response but he was absorbed looking around the room. He had not been there for a while and, one way or another, he would never live in the same house as his stepfather again.

Aggie never did stop the quick rhythm of talking and moving whether she cooked, or served, ate, or bobbed up and down to cut up homemade pie and make coffee, as if the years in-between our gathering had not touched her. The corners of my mouth turned up into a spontaneous smile as I watched and wondered where she got the energy.

Regardless of the negative attitude from her husband, Jim, Aggie made us feel entirely welcome. I knew she had worked a variety of jobs from the assembly line of machine parts for airplanes to waitress, hostess, and it occurred to me what a talent she had, this ability to act quickly with precision. Yet, the situation felt absurd; I was a separated woman with two children and my lover's mother was a mere seventeen years older than I was, but performed as if she had twice the stamina. Well, that is four planets in Leo for you, I figured, in living, bouncing color.

Ron said "We were in Afghanistan," which left his mother's face blank. She must have known that, but kept busy, her head tilted as her hands moved with the art of practice, alert for more explanation.

I chipped in, trying to keep it simple, "We went to Europe first, flew to London and took a ferry across the channel. In Amsterdam we bought a Volkswagen van. People stand on the sidewalk and hold a sign with their van model and the price, and take you to see it—that's why Ron studied the Volkswagen manual before we went."

"Oh." Aggie said, her surprised blue eyes wide as if it was all news to her. "My mother is from Scotland. Maybe I'll get there sometime."

Aggie had her own problems and pleasures, I knew that much. Trapped in a marriage with a chronic drinker given to fits of alcoholic rage, with two more children that she loved added to the two young men she had already raised, she had to carve out her own pleasure whenever she got the chance. As long as her children stood on their own two feet, were educated, stayed out of trouble, and no one asked her for money, she did not feel obliged to tell them what to do.

Yet, there was a deeper layer to her; a calculator in her eyes that comprehended every action in the room and weighed the consequences of taking action, versus pretending nothing was happening, a useful talent we all use, but she could have taught graduate lessons.

I decided to phone her later. A silent acknowledgement, and great inquisitiveness, had passed between us and I wanted to know her better; I found her admirable.

Moving through the living room on our way to the door, gazing again at her calling card, the tropical scene in the living room, it told me of her dreams, her love of Florida, and although I would not understand its true importance for many years. I was simply grateful that she accepted me, this tall, skinny woman with long brown hair that wore the short skirt and thong sandals of our tribe, and obviously still in love with her son.

Like Father

1974

Chapter 22

Vincey told his story, after some hesitation, while he looked around the counselor's small office. He hadn't known what to expect. On one short wall was a filing cabinet and a jammed bookcase. On the longest wall, a large window overlooked the flat plateau in the middle of nowhere.

He knew his mother had paid good money to get him here, to the special school, to give him a chance, she said, so he knew it was important to do his best and be honest.

"How did you start drinking?" the counselor asked.

"I think I got the taste for alcohol from both sides of the family—both sides. My dad was a punch-drunk alcoholic. It was strange because his Dad's parents were quiet, religious, and his sisters were sober as nuns, living lives of recluses, rarely leaving the top floor of their house.

"If anyone wanted to visit them, they had to tip-toe up the stairs and knock on their door like mice tapping. I didn't really want to do it, because it gave me the creeps, but our mother said we should."

The counselor looked at him solemnly. "What did your father, Jim, do when he got drunk?"

"He was always loud and nasty, oh yeah, rampaging

over this and that, any excuse to rant and rave, like when he got busted for drunk driving again, in his truck when he was away on the road. I don't know how he kept his license. He ransacked a hotel room with rowdy friends he picked up on the way last year."

"Sometimes my mother was home," Vincey told him, "but often she was out working."

"That was our weekend if Dad wasn't on the road, booze and fights. He would threaten to kill us all when he was home, especially Mom. He beat up on her regularly. Then he acted apologetic, crying, vowing not to drink again. We never knew what we were walking into when we came home.

"I remember the time Dad was trying to push Mom down the stairs and my brother Ron pushed him down there instead. I was really proud of Ron for that. I'll never forget Dad's face. He was shocked. I don't think he touched Ron or Mom again."

It was hard to tell whether the counselor was surprised or disgusted. A lot of the kids here had the same kind of story to tell, so either he was used to it or he hid his reactions well.

"My mom liked to have fun but didn't need alcohol to do it. It was lucky Mom was like her father, Melville O'Hara, who knew how to stay sober and how to save a buck."

Now that Vincey felt comfortable with the man, because he did not push him or demand anything, it felt good to get the memories off his chest; to tell someone that had heard this kind of thing before.

"Dad always had a trucking job. He got an inheritance from his parents and bought his own truck, then hired it out to a kid without checking his age, and the kid wrecked it. His insurance didn't cover the driver because he was under twenty-one. Dad hardly ever missed a working day, but blew a lot of money on booze.

"Dad could be nice now and then, when he was sober, take an interest in my inventions, especially when Lilly was a little girl. He acted as if he could make it up to all of us by being nice to her. He tried to pretend he was like that all the time.

"Dad often talked about changing his ways; for years he talked about that. My mother took him to a lot of clinics and programs. Nothing worked. Maybe it worked for a week or two, but payday meant buy-booze-day to him, a habit he could not break—bank to liquor store like clockwork.

"Laughter and brawling, and shouting, made him feel important, I guess," Vincey said, "or powerful, or something.

"Dad was always pushing and shoving with somebody, his friends or my mom's brother, Uncle Chuck. Dad didn't dare to really fight with Chuck or he would have ended up dead. Chuck won every time.

"After a horrendous battle, when Dad and Uncle Chuck tore up the living room and wrecked everything in it, and the cops took them away. Mom had to pay the bills and buy new furniture, but she finally got him out of the house. It had taken her almost twenty years.

"My sister, Lilly, ran to the neighbor's house to call the cops. They only took them away because Mom dug out papers to prove that the house belonged to her. She showed it to the cops while the two drunks threw things around, wrecking everything.

"Finally, Dad got arrested while my little sister, Lilly sat in the back of the cruiser. I just got home and saw her there. Our little black cat, Noche (that means 'night' in Spanish,) was in her lap and she held onto him with a steel grip. I thought she was going to squash him.

Just after that Mom thought it was best if I come here to finish my education."

On the next visit to the counselor, he asked if there were issues in the other side of the family, that could have led to the need for alcohol."

"Well, my Uncle Chuck, Mom's brother, was even worse with alcohol. He loved anything that gave him an excuse to rage like a maniac. He was pure evil. He had no conscience. 'Born without it,' Mom said, 'a problem in the head.'

"Mom said her father was a normal caring man but her Scottish mother, Agnes hated the responsibilities of the world.

" 'Maybe it was all too hard for her,' Mom told me. She came to see what this country was all about at 17 years old, and quickly had four babies, no money...but times were hard for everyone then. A heel of bread was a good breakfast, sometimes food for the day."

Vincey continued. "It meant that Mom, Aggie, shouldered her mother's work and grew up fast caring for her two younger sisters, Aunt Bea and Aunt Nancy, and her baby brother, Chucky, and we knew what trouble he was, always fighting, and not listening to rules."

"Do you have any thoughts about why he was like that?" the man asked.

"Mom said that Chuck inherited his mother's desire to escape and put it into alcoholic rages, hatred of anything or anyone that stopped him. He sure didn't get it from his father. My grandfather is straight up.

"Uncle Chucky can't see past himself. He's a really selfish man," Vincey said.

"A couple of years ago I worked for Uncle Chuck for a while. He was so unpredictable that one day he'd drive me around in his convertible and the next day his lip would curl in hatred.

"Chuck got irritated one afternoon when we were roofing and I was handing stuff up to the workers. It was a stinking hot day and the foul smell from the black shingle tar had us coughing and choking. One man complained and Chuck threw him off the third-floor roof we were working on. The man died, silent and twisted on the dirt. Chuck turned to me and he growled—'if you talk, I kill you, too.' I lowered my eyes and turned away, and kept working."

"The scariest summer of my life," Vincey confided, "Chuck is one tough customer.

"Like a wild man, Chuck fought everyone—the cops, the Mafia, he did not care.

"Crazy Uncle Chuck did kill a man on the street one day. When it went to trial, it was called the 'One Punch' murder charge, and made a career for the lawyer. It was around 1963.

"The lawyer just got engaged to Aunt Nancy. She was pretty in those days. She always had her hair nice and smelled good. He took the case even though it was his first criminal trial. It was all over the Toronto Star for months on end. Mom hoped Chuck would get a long, long time in jail, at least get him out of our hair, but despite witnesses, Chuck pleaded self-defense, got a suspended sentence, court adjourned.

"He was a complete prick to me," Vincey said. "He booted me around like a dog. I guess, when you get away with murder a couple of times, the law doesn't mean much to you."

At that, the counselor took off his glasses and massaged the bridge of his nose with his thumb and forefinger, in a gentle pinching motion.

Vincey wondered if all this violence, from all the alcoholism in Vincey's family, was finally getting to him, so he backed off from the brutality in his life.

"I'm a good rider, you know." Vincey continued his reminiscences, "I was never pulled over on my motorcycle for that by the cops, but I had my first impaired driving last year. The lawyer is married to our aunt, now, and he took care of the legal mess, including the head butt and two black eyes I gave the cop while I was in tight handcuffs.

"When the court date came, I paid nothing. I had a good job, too, making $100 a week at a rubber factory, but had to give some to that goofball lawyer."

He paused, "Lawyers do come in handy."

" 'You paid nothing because that lawyer is your uncle,' a cop said one night when I was leaving the Beverly Hills Hotel in Weston. My 500 Triumph MC fell over and he called it resisting arrest—I had to punch him out.

"Another night I was so drunk downtown that a cop in the family, somehow related to my father, took me home; Vince was his name, too. I'll never forget him. It wasn't his jurisdiction, but he took me home anyway. After that, Mom decided I should come here."

"Did you leave good friends behind?" The man seemed to ask strange questions but Vincey thought, why not? He was here anyway, he might as well tell him.

"There was a good friend of mine—we called him Fast Eddie because he was so slow. We went to St. John's in Weston, together, and were in the same class at Pelmo Park School. We got to be friends, drinking behind the school on the weekend. You know, he's probably still living with his mom."

He paused to laugh.

"One afternoon we're hanging around outside the school and a woman cop pulls up beside us and says,

'Get in the car.' I thought her badge number on her hat was funny. I'll never forget it, 1-2-3-4, so I grabbed her hat."

"She says, 'I'm going to arrest you.'

"Fast Eddie says, 'we're not going anywhere, and he opened another beer for me. She came towards us but we split up and ran home between the houses.

"We jumped on my motorcycle, laughing. and took off through the underpasses in Weston, a beer in my hand in broad daylight, her hat on Eddie's head. Fast Eddie liked it so much he wore it on Hallowe'en.

"Fast Eddie had a garage full of doo-dads that our cousin, Gordon, the lawyer's son, also a lawyer, found fascinating. He spent hours in Eddie's museum of useless motors and parts that almost took over his yard, too.

"'Your cousin, the fucking crook!'" Fast Eddie called my cousin that, but he used Gordon anyway when he got hauled in for driving without a license. He and Eddie were both natural-born collectors of junk.

"Gordon shows up like Colombo, car smoking, falling apart. You could hear that old rattle-trap coming a block away, the old Pinto his mother had given him smoking so bad we had to pull over—no oil. He drives Eddie to court for the never-ending lawsuit and his car is smoking.

"The judge looked over to Gordon and the dumb jerk was nodding off in court! He was just lazy in the mind.

"I beat the shit out of him up on Keele Street for that. "Yeah, some people, like Uncle Chuck, are born violent and some are just born crooked, like Gordon."

"Fast Eddie started growing little pot plants, only sativa, before the bud. Someone stole his plants and he got so upset—yeah, (laugh) it was me. Then Mom sent me away to this special camp, 'to become a well-rounded, better person,' she said."

The counselor told Vincey he sounded like he knew how to take care of himself, and they would work together to make sure he finished his education with a useful trade.

Vincey was satisfied.

Elvis and the Clock

1978

Chapter 23

The clock was a lying demon. If Aggie was working, time flew, and if she was dancing, the dial hands spun so fast they attained orbit, leaving a stardust trail of hot musical licks and unfulfilled romantic dreams.

Time was a trickster and always had been; it liked to play games without warning. It sprang forward and let bright lights suddenly shine in her half-closed eyes when dancehalls closed, and revealed the totality of her last dance partner. More wicked tricks shocked her when she looked in the bathroom mirror in the morning, in the strident bright light that evidenced a suddenly much older woman than the last time she noticed.

Aggie decided to betray "Time the Imp," right back, and take revenge for his plans by retaining the bloom of youth. She would stay healthy and never, ever stop dancing, and disallow time to let her down and ruin her life. She knew, instinctively, like breathing in and out, that there were too many exhilarating things yet to happen.

She reached her hand to the right and punched up the volume on her car radio. An Elvis tune was playing on her favorite station: Elvis—her timeless, ageless, innocent joy—her reprieve from the memories and demands that yanked her attention back and forth in a dizzying whirlwind. At least Elvis was, until he weakened and made a sorry string of silly movies and then sank into drugs and booze, like a backwoods sot with a still, out behind the barn. But that would not, could not, spoil his soul-melting voice that presented the hope, the dream of romance alive and well, just a heartbeat, a turn of a dial away, a distraction she did not have to share and no one else could ruin for her.

Her affair with Elvis started long ago, Aggie remembered, as she drove home from work, as tired as tonight, on a summer evening in a borrowed car with the windows open and the soulful music cranked to distract her from thinking about the meager meal she had to feed her boys. There were three boys then, one just a baby, and a new man, Jim, quickly losing his appeal as fast as he lost his temper and found a bottle.

Thanks to the bank loan there was the house, but not a lot left over. Usually she took the bus, or stuck out her thumb and swore to get her own car every time some creepy man with a scary grin on his face presumed too much.

She had taken a deep breath, trying to unwind in a borrowed car, soften her tense grip on the wheel and let the empty road disappear in a black ribbon of asphalt spilling out in a continuous fountain in her rear view mirror.

A sound from the radio had caressed her eardrums like a breeze across a river on a hot summer day. Soothing, smooth, the seductive voice spoke to her personally. "Love me tender," the man sang, "Love me true, all my dreams fulfill."

The words were laughable; no person could do that

for another person. Yet, Aggie knew it was everyone's secret dream, the quest that drove a woman from man to man, or a man from woman to woman. "For my darling, I love you, and I always will."

The voice itself filled space, needed only soft accompaniment, and let silence separate the words, one from the other, and the liquid richness of this man's voice was tone perfect. She had waited in anticipation to hear his name, Elvis.

Jim's long-haul driving job had suited Aggie just fine, at first, with only her two boys, she remembered. Funny, that was the first job Elvis had, too, driving a truck somewhere in the boonies of the southern states for Crown Electric Company. She smiled thinking about all the bits of information and the tokens of Elvis she had collected over the years.

Every song Elvis recorded seemed to speak to her personally and that gave her hope, even through the toughest times, that there would be one special man that she could trust. It seemed hard to spin the wheel and have all the good things at the same time, but it was worth a try.

Aggie drifted to years long gone, when Jim was away on long-haul drives and she started her first preparations in early winter, right after Christmas, to go to the Collingwood Elvis Festival.

"Come on, Aggie," Sharon had urged, "we can run away next summer, pack sandwiches, drive all night, and sleep in the car."

She found a large penny jar, that used contain pickles but did not have that funny smell any more, and built an Elvis fund. A nickel here, a dime there, stowed away in a concealed crevice in the closet.

What a crew that was, she and her friends; Sharon

and Mary; skinny troublemaker Carol; and the redhead, busty Judy. Once at the festival, they hit the afternoon rehearsal for the Elvis imitator's show, their women's Capri pants traded for girly crinolines. They made wisecracks and chewed bubble-gum in their own troupe that could rock and roll, and cheer with the best of them, out for laughs, crammed into wooden stands normally used for outdoor baseball games, and they created a tradition.

It was as crowded at rehearsal as it was at the sold-out and expensive evening shows and raw energy had pumped through the sweaty crowd jammed together in humid mid-summer heat and it rocked the stands. The girls screamed and laughed, whooped and hollered when twirling spotlights lit up a white, black, or oriental, turned-up collar, shaky-leg, sexy Elvis. They held up their hands protectively, to avoid blinded retinas from millions of reflecting sequins on costumes of strutting, groaning, sometimes overweight, scarf-waving Elvis Pelvises.

Aggie chuckled to herself, on the darkened highway, alone in her car with her memories. She felt she understood Elvis's denial of time, and maybe she and her friends could do that road trip...but no, not this year...chances were slim in all this confusion.

Now it was twenty-odd years since it all began with Jim, and still she drove the same blacktop road and oncoming car lights zoomed by—wanted nothing from her. There were no personalities to deal with, only the flash, flash of headlights lighting the trees and they flicked by, looking rigid, lifeless, like cheap dime store Hallowe'en cardboard, crafted into artistic skeletons with their leaves mostly vanished into the crisp, cold air.

Now this cracked shell of a marriage was dead, too,

and soon it would be officially behind her.

As that realization settled into her mind she relaxed, and a tease of a smile wedged in the corners of her lips as her head slowly moved from side to side with a look of wonder spreading across her face. That evil man had known how to goad her, how to make her look like she was the problem, but the last punch was hers. He would not be home tonight or tomorrow night, or ever.

Soon it would be winter, but she would be free.

The older boys had eagerly headed out west before the final curtain fell, and now her youngest son was finished with all the education she could talk him into, plus training for a trade, and he would head off somewhere, too, following his wandering brothers, she figured.

It was hard to keep her mind on the future when she was still haunted by the past. Aggie remembered the nerve-wracking stress of making serious plans when Jim's addiction counselors confirmed that the likelihood of him giving up the drink was slim to none. Jim had not made the acknowledgment of alcoholism, they said, and it was time for her to think about an entirely new life. The last thing they said, before the door closed, was "Find a man with a job that loves you." Aggie knew, deep inside, that they were right.

She shook her head thinking about that final terrible day with nosy neighbors gawking, while her drunken husband shouted and cursed with her insane brother— her treasures smashed to bits as the walls spewed plaster, which did not stop until the law took him away, because it was her house.

She would sell that house. Too many ghosts of bad memories lived there and it was time to move on—she had something better in mind for Lilly, and for herself.

Now that he was gone in an alcohol-soaked, love-nest with another woman, Aggie finally had the legal proof she needed for divorce—the papers beside her on the car seat. She and her daughter were free to set out on their own and Aggie nodded.

She breathed a profound sigh of satisfaction; she was on her own clock now and could spend her time exactly as she wanted.

Perhaps the best idea was to sell it and get out of town, entirely, make a fresh start. One thing she knew for sure, Lilly, her youngest, would be in a peaceful home with her, regardless of what happened between her parents.

Aggie checked the time again, to see if it was too late to drop in to her brother-in-law the lawyer's darkened house to have the papers signed—a nice house on a good street with distressed people inside. Sure, her sister would complain about the late hour, but there was one dim light on, and it was only midnight. Her sister did not have to keep one eye on the clock and work night and day.

All her husband had to do was sign his name; how hard was that?

Aggie flipped the lid of the seat divider open, picked out an audio tape by rote, slipped it into the dashboard deck, and leaned back in readiness as her lips curved into a smile.

The familiar strains of, "Warden threw a party in the county jail," blasted from her dual speakers. "Jailhouse Rock" could always do it for her.

Elvis may be bloated and almost collapsing on stage, but time disappeared when he sang to her—he was still, "The King."

Girl Talk

1979 era

Chapter 24

Aggie poured boiling water into the teapot, to join her favorite tea bag, and sat down to wait for it to steep. It was a good time to take a break now, with the sun slanting into the picture window in their snug, little house. She had been waiting tables all weekend and she really needed a break from the monotony of Monday chores.

It was delightfully different now, living with her growing-up-fast girl. She did not mind folding her daughter's pretty, yellow sweater or pairing her socks fresh from the clothesline. Without hesitation her girl would do the same for her mom.

It was incredibly different from when they lived with Lilly's father. No, it was not smooth sailing then, when that irritating man loved to get Aggie's goat. That really was a silly expression but it did describe somebody butting against you, over and over, determined to get on your nerves.

He enjoyed getting the kids revved up high and then laughing, leaving Aggie to look stupid. Like when he drove like a maniac with the kids in the car, with all the windows rolled down, because their faces were hot from all the running around at her Dad's farm. It blew her hair up into a cyclone on top of her head and she complained that she had bugs in her teeth, and they all laughed at that. It did not worry the driver that the slightest accident could kill them all.

His mean energy fed their private war, waiting for the next bomb to drop. No wonder she had a hair-trigger temper in the bad old days. In the end, all of her three boys could hardly wait to flee out west. Finally, the police took her husband away.

Peace at last.

It was not worry free, though, when they lived by Lake Simcoe. In their first winter, a sudden high-wind blizzard left Lilly and four other youngsters huddled in their lakeside school with the hydro shut off, and no school buses or parents able to reach them. Aggie knew she had to do that, or die trying.

Her little 4-cylinder Mazda, bought cheaply as a repossession from a desperate man, was a hearty little red car, unpredictable in this lakeside weather, but in Aggie's unshakable mind, nothing could stop her.

The frigid blast from the Arctic roared unimpeded over the ice field of the lake and it raged around her tiny car, trying as hard as it could to blow the flimsy vehicle clear off the road, yet the little Mazda motored through that worst of storms.

She left her car at the entrance to the school parking lot, a field really, barely visible under drifts of snow compacting into ice and she wondered if she would find it again when she returned.

Her useless gloves discarded, heart racing and her rapid breathing heaving her chest, she dug frantically into the icy mound lodged against the school doors, like a demented dog that just knows there is a bone in the ground.

Inside, the shivering students called out to her in great excitement so she yanked the door with all her might and opened it a crack, giving them hope, so she dug harder, with the white wind blasting against her as she anxiously labored.

Finally, she scraped her slim form inside, and stamped snow off her boots while the children milled around and eager voices shouted in her ear as she distributed her pockets full of mittens and the extra scarves from around her neck, that she brought from home.

The only voice she really heard was Lilly. "Mom, Mom. I knew you would come!"

The kids shivered in their light coats, cold to the bone with the heating off for hours, Lilly told her. Aggie pulled hats over their heads, protecting them as best she could and they worked together now, pushing their combined weight against the door.

Now there was just enough space to let the bundled brood edge out one at a time, bowed against the force of the wind, and they held on tightly, mittens to mittens, single file, as she led them. They kept their mouths closed to keep out the biting sleet that bore down on them from every direction, and she shouted, "Keep holding hands! Don't let go!"

The wind snapped her words into the cold sky as she pushed forward through the night that stabbed and stung, and she looked back, time and time again, and counted the chain of doubled-over children to make sure none had fallen behind.

In the car at last, kids sat on each other's knees with their heads bent over, squished against the roof, one lay down across their laps, another squatted between the front and back seats, whatever they had to do to close the doors, and leave Aggie room to shift gears.

With great satisfaction, she slammed the driver's door shut without an arm, boot, scarf, or glove in the way. Everyone cheered when the motor turned over twice and coughed, and then the little red hero jolted to life. Hurray! The hearty little Mazda ran smooth, mounted snowdrifts like an army tank and chugged them home.

Once inside the warm, familiar coziness, huddled in front of her fireplace, she patiently called the thankful parents, one by one. It was a pleasure to assure them their children were safe, warm, fed, and bedded down for the night.

Older now, her girl looked in her mother's eyes and Aggie felt incredibly lucky for all the times when Lilly would linger, share a cup of tea or ask to borrow the new coral blouse that looked "amazing" with their blond hair. They talked about doing hair for others as a job, and current hairstyles, cuts, curlers and perms. Doing hair was a fine way to make a living, Aggie knew.

This was all quite opposite from her experience with little sons who yanked at her hand in their early years to keep her close to soothe their little fears. Later, and quite suddenly, itching to be free, they refused to touch anybody's hand, especially their mother's, and born with one foot out the door..

One day, while she was in high school, Lilly asked, "What are you doing, Mom?"

"It's the Twist, remember? Want to dance with me?"

"No, I can't. There is a man coming to the school to talk about free driving lessons."

Her mother kept gyrating to a song on the radio, one foot out and pointed like a ballerina, her backside swinging back and forth in a happy, irresistible dance.

"Come on, girl. Two minutes."

Laughter filled the kitchen—they still had fun. .

"Are we moving again?" Lilly sighed when Aggie thought it was best to be closer to the city, and chose a condo in Richmond Hill, just north of Toronto.

The rhythm of life continued, and now Aggie replaced sandals with boots for Canadian winter. Thank goodness, for end of season sales and the Sally Ann. It was amazing what people gave away! Some items were brand new, in original shoeboxes, and bought for next to nothing.

She pulled out her tall snow boots, lined in fleece, and shook her head There had been no early warning. She was unprepared in her short-skirted uniform and snowdrifts on the icy streets immobilized her car.

There she was, cold and alone, three blocks from home, and yes, that storm defeated even her mighty Mazda.

Lovely warmth had kissed her face as she finally made it inside, and slammed the door shut, stamping that damn snow off her shoes and shivering violently, rubbing her hands together briskly to bring them back to life, and then she shivered again.

As the heat of the room bathed her skin, Aggie breathed in deeply and allowed the cozy blanket of home to settle around her body in an unmistakable sweet cocoon of love, and slowly, she smiled.

A delicious aroma curled into her defrosting nose that night and gradually Aggie realized the sweet smell was freshly baked and still-warm cookies. Lilly had baked and cleaned it all up, knowing how soothing it would be to find neatly arranged cookies on a pretty plate trimmed with pink flowers.

Beside the plate was the recipe propped up against a mug, written out on a piece of lined paper, and Lilly's schoolbooks sat arranged with care in a pile on the counter, ready for morning.

Leaning over the plate, Aggie inhaled the sugary

sweetness for a moment, quickly snatched up two cookies and devoured them. She would never be able to look at that cookie recipe again without tears in her eyes, recalling her daughter's empathy, and that forever touched her heart.

What If...

1980

Chapter 25

Her dad had been talking about Florida again, teasing her on the phone, as soon as she got in the door from work. "What if you could avoid winter altogether?" he prompted.

"I would wear sandals year-round," Aggie answered and laughed, "I could have as many pairs as I wanted and I know there are huge discount stores in Florida. I remember those."

Aggie thought about Florida a lot, especially after the last cold winter. Now, she turned her head to look out her condo window and sadly, the flowers in a couple of planters on the balcony were sagging from last night's nippy air. She decided that yes, she and Lilly would take a very long drive one of these days, all the way from Richmond Hill to the sunny south.

Lilly did have her driver's license now, but it still made Aggie grin when she thought about Lilly at the driver's test.

Lilly had practiced by changing the gears in Aggie's standard car while Aggie drove, but on the day of the test, she froze. She would not budge from the car. Aggie opened her car door and walked around to the passenger side, where Lilly sat like a stone.

"What's the matter?"

"I'm so nervous."

"Put out your hand," Aggie commanded, dug around in her purse, shook a little bottle, and tipped a blue pill onto Lilly's outstretched palm. "Just take this pill, Lilly; it will help you stay calm."

"I don't know, Mom, what if it puts me to sleep?"

"I don't think it will, your teeth are chattering." It was risky, but it was 1978, and everyone was taking them.

Happily, Lilly had passed the driving test at 16, but Aggie still did not trust her about everything. At a teen dance, when it got late, it meant nothing to Aggie if she showed up wearing her nightgown and sexy pink slippers. She still asked around, "Do you know Lilly? Have you seen Lilly? I'm worried about her, see?"

Her daughter was humiliated, but fortunately, Lilly's new friends thought it was funny.

They also thought it was unusual that Lilly was allowed to sit in on real estate deals—none of the other parents would tell them anything—but Aggie thought it was crucial for Lilly to learn.

Aggie's phone rang again, and she picked it up, then sat and gabbed for a few minutes, just to pass along the latest newsy tidbits. Even here in Toronto's outskirts gossip was always amusing, like what the municipality was doing, or not doing with the roads, or what color of low-neck sweater the dumb puffy widow with the sharp beak was wearing at a local coffee shop, thinking she would catch a man.

"Maybe we should go to the bingo tonight," Aggie offered. Lilly was recovering well from having her tonsils out and maybe this would perk her up. She was legitimately old enough now, at eighteen, and they shared the mother-daughter miracle of enjoying each other's company.

"Bingo!" Lilly screamed before someone else could, and jumped up from the long table, blue eyes blazing open, her bingo numbers winning the fifteen hundred dollar pot!

"Mom! Mom!" She turned to Aggie as if to confirm the truth of the miracle.

"Yes, yes!" Aggie cried, and opened her arms for a tight hug.

Lilly accepted the receipt the dealer handed her, whispered "thank-you" and waved it in the air like an Olympian winning a gold medal.

Without another word, they grabbed their handbags and walked quickly through the smoky room, heading for the cashier to collect Lilly's winnings. Cheers and applause equaled the number of glares from career "bingo Grandmas" they left behind, but that did not stop Aggie from giving the caller and helpers some of the money, twenty dollars all together.

"If we want to keep our luck, we have to give it away," she said but they kept moving, both scared someone was going to jump them for it. The place was packed.

Their standing deal for wins was a fifty/fifty split, and once outside in the fresh air, teetering on their high-heeled wedged shoes, they tossed the stacks of twenties skyward and laughed their heads off in the parking lot, while they scrambled and tumbled against each other with joy. Then they had to count and recount madly, and stuffed crumpled bills into the necklines of their peasant blouses and the waistbands of their miniskirts, just for the fun of it. They were careful not to leave one blessed twenty-dollar bill behind on the black tarmac, still hot from the summer sun's blast.

Between fits of giggles, as they sat in the local coffee shop with their two blond heads bowed over a paper napkin like conspirators, Lilly listed her budget numbers with Aggie's old ballpoint pen, quickly running out of red ink.

"Oh! We shouldn't be doing this in red," Aggie joked. "We need a black pen for this. In the black—that's where we are now."

The gangly bus boy put up his finger to signal, "Wait a minute," smiled from ear to ear, found a black pen quick enough, and then put a hand to his mouth to stifle a giggle. This win was infectious it seemed and his grin made the girls smile wider.

Aggie sat back to give her space.

As she bent to her task, Lilly's blond hair fell in a curtain obscuring most of her face. The Genie of Aladdin's Lamp offered a great gift, her mother knew, and it required a good deal of thought.

She watched Lilly focus, straighten her shoulders as she felt the future settle on them, and the sprinkling of Lilly's freckles, splashed across her nose, looked darker somehow against her excited blush. This was a one shot deal; Lilly had better get it right.

The bus boy, whose name was Darrell, he told them, busied himself clearing dishes and wiping surfaces in the almost empty coffee shop, except for the winner and her mother, and he looked happy, heartened.

Aggie thought the boy was genuinely thrilled that this could happen to someone he knew, and saw his glance dart to Lilly. Perhaps he knew her from school. Well, she mused, I wonder if he will find the courage to approach her, or will Lilly seem to be a goddess now?

Aggie focused on the money; she was clear where her half of the win would go—her seven hundred dollars. That was not the point right now and she had sat back and crossed her knees, her hands flat down, one on each side of her on the blood red imitation-leather bench seats of the restaurant booth. "

Might as well get comfortable", flashed across her mind. It was rightfully Lilly's decision where her money went, but Aggie was ready to jump in at any moment.

Lilly started with her goal, half talking to herself and half to her mother. "The technical high school hairdressing course, the full course with the license, costs $1,700."

She enumerated her income, starting with the seven hundred dollar win, paused to glance at her mother, giggle, and then carried on.

"Tips from the part-time job reasonably steady, plus my money..." Lilly mumbled. She tallied carefully, multiplying the average amount of wages, and tips, by twelve months of future work, and added the sum to her seven hundred dollar bingo win.

Lilly sat back in her seat, looked at her mother, and declared, "I think I can do it...it will take a year of payments, but I can do it." Her crystal-blue eyes blinked, and shone.

Her words ran faster. "I can work all day, Sunday, too, I can...."

Lilly's voice trailed off; a small smile on her lips and her eyes filled with a faraway look, giving the impression of being in her future, perhaps saying "Thank you, God," knowing she was a disaster as a waitress.

As she told her Mom on many occasions, she had dropped meals, forgotten to put in orders, burned bread, and hated the drunken men, constantly repeating themselves, with a cocky attitude while they looked her over.

Her eyes opened wider; she blinked rapidly and looked triumphant, and that spoke as loudly as words—that which had seemed too extreme to envision was now a reality.

Lilly inhaled deeply and looked towards her mother

with a question in her eyes, seeking the older woman's insight and approval, Aggie figured. She could almost feel her daughter holding her breath in her anticipation.

Aggie nodded in pride and full support. She would prefer the girl invest her money in real estate. She understood that market, it had served her well, giving her both a nest egg, and an income, carefully banked, but her daughter deserved her own dream. Whatever she did, Lilly held the cards of honesty, and dependability, with grace and a smile.

Aggie cherished the opportunity to give advice while she still had power to help Lilly with a decision. She had seen the longing in the eyes of the bus boy—all male eyes in the restaurant, actually, and Aggie was a looker herself, but Lilly still possessed a naivety of beauty, not yet awakened to the ways of the world.

Soon, Lilly would move freely in new social circles with her gentle nature, and would find a male so attractive that, in the underhanded way biology has of making fools of us all, she would fall for him, for good or ill.

Aggie marveled as she considered their symphony of co-operation. As the Sun and the Moon wove their dance in the sky, so did the two women, with few complaints or problems, their dual system gently rotated, sharing space. When one saw a new hairstyle, they both tried it. One would be the cook while the other cut hair, a game for two, played for fun, experience and profit.

Aggie then followed Lilly, taking the hairdressing course one year behind her. What fun that was! The students ribbed her for being so much older and she did not mind, even when they called her Granny.

A chilly preview of winter wind nipped the heels of

autumn, curling the last of the leaves into crispy bronze, spinning them into a spiral of stragglers in a miniature cyclone that scudded across the lawn. The local apples had been plentiful and delicious this year; maybe baking a quick apple pie would fill the place with "welcome home" smells when Lilly returned from her long day. Aggie would be at work by then but Lilly would know she thought of her.

Someday, too soon, Lilly's focus would be a full-time job and she even talked about trying her luck in Toronto and would live who knew where, without her mom.

"The question is," Aggie said aloud, "whether I can live without her."

Turning away from her reverie, she had Florida on her mind. She was close, very close, to accepting her old friend Jake's offer to buy her a place of her own, down in the warm and sunny Sunshine State, no strings attached. He was in love with her sister, Bea, but could not convince the reluctant woman to marry him and consequently took Aggie under his wing instead. He remained such a good friend, a protector since grade school, really, who expected nothing in return but a bit of friendship.

He told Aggie that she richly deserved something just for being herself, that she had done her best for everyone else. She was so close to her dream of Florida, that if she got a three-season waitressing job she would take Jake up on his offer, and have a permanent trailer where it is warm in the winter.

Imagine missing winter—imagine that!

Take a Chance

1984

Chapter 26

Aggie checked her watch. Time was flying. Soon this sunny Monday morning would be a memory and she did not want to waste any more of this fresh spring day. She checked her lipstick and her hair in the small mirror hanging at the perfect height beside the front door and slipped on her favorite shoes. It seemed the right time to make her move.

As she stepped out her door, a flock of excited seagulls frolicked overhead, calling their welcome to the transformation of wintry weather into sunshine, and they dived and rose again into a brilliantly blue sky that hosted high puffy clouds, scattered like a few cotton balls spilled from a bag by the Moon.

Today, Aggie intended to pick up her good friend Sharon, and they would go to Lake Simcoe and accomplish something she set firmly in her mind last night. She had noticed a "Waitress Wanted" sign in a window at Big Bay Point in Innisfil, a couple of days before—an interesting lead worth following up.

A chef was restoring the former landmark, The Breeze Bar, famous for its burgers, and he was keeping as much of the 1950's décor as possible and updating the kitchen. Aggie thought that was clever. Why mess up a good thing?

She asked around, and someone else called it a gold

mine. That was music to her ears.

She pulled into an empty spot a couple of blocks away from the restaurant, and the women sauntered past a few shop windows with nothing new inside. It was a mystery how the small stores stayed in business at all with so few sales.

Aggie spotted the promising structure they sought, set back on broad property with signs of construction in motion: a hydro truck, a carpenter's van, and a tall hearty man hustling along with long rolls of white paper tucked securely under his arm. Maybe floor plans, she speculated, and Sharon stopped with her to watch him enter and stamp mud off his boots. Before him was an impromptu carpet of unraveled brown paper floor protector, and an inviting door chime sang a pleasant melody as the door closed behind.

She looked at the card in the window. The notice, trimmed in red, still advertised for a waitress. Good.

"This must be the place." She looked inquiringly to Sharon and her friend raised her eyebrows and nodded, smiling in unspoken agreement.

The recently opened establishment seemed inviting, unpretentious, and would not cost a whole paycheck for lunch, hopefully. The upper part of the door, freshly painted white, had small squares of glass giving it an elegant old-world charm, and on the door a hanging sign stated, "Open."

Aggie reached for the door handle, curiosity aroused, and soon the two women sat comfortably waiting for service. She appreciated the ambience of the large and well-lit room, and looked towards the makeshift partition, from where the obvious signs and noises of reconstruction were coming. It was easy to see the new layout roughly formed and the layout showed great potential.

A quiet, but untrained and uninterested young girl,

likely from the local school and hoping for a summer job, plunked down two menus of the usual lunch fare, always with an creative twist.

She took their order for tea for Aggie and a coffee for Sharon.

Aggie was quite pleased when her tea arrived with its own delicately patterned blue china pot, but the girl wandered away again.

After returning, and hemming and hawing, the girl took their food order. She had never done this before, obviously, but having no reason to rush the women took their time. They chatted while they waited and sat back to take in the peaceful blues and grays of the refreshed décor.

Rewarded for their patience, they enjoyed the well-presented and tasty food when it finally arrived.

"That was really good." Finally full and satisfied, Aggie was impressed. "I like it here."

Sharon agreed and then asked, "So, how's Lilly?"

Aggie relaxed back into her chair before she responded.

"You know she finished her hairdressing course and went to Toronto for a job. Well, I went with her to look around for an apartment but everything was really scruffy—and so expensive!"

"We thought one of them was all right and she moved in, but when she tuned out the light at night, there were scuttling sounds that scared her. When she turned on the light, she saw hundreds of cockroaches on the floor and the walls, and that frightened her horribly. She had never seen one before and didn't know what they were, so she called me."

Sharon made appropriate noises of disgust and sympathy.

"Lilly was in a panic and I told her to call the landlord and demand a refund, or we go to the police right now. She threatened and wrangled, handled it well, and got all her money back, and then we had to go apartment hunting all over again. I think she's happy with her new place, finally."

"I guess winning that money was a wonderful help," Sharon offered.

"Oh yes," Aggie agreed. "But it was awful when both of the places we worked burned down while Lilly was in hairdressing school—it left us up the creek—and we had to start from scratch."

Searching for jobs simultaneously, Aggie had told her daughter it would all work out as usual, and lucky for them both, it did. They found new employment and Aggie sold the place she owned at the time and invested in Barrie. The house had a lot of room and rental potential for a suite, as soon as she fixed it up.

Sharon was properly sympathetic and reminded Aggie she could do anything she set her mind to, and of course the right person would get the suite making money for her.

They both drank more tea or coffee as Aggie rambled on, trying to be practical about what she should do next in life and mentioned waitressing.

"Maybe I should stick to cutting hair; maybe I'm already pushing the age limit, especially in a place like this. It would be really busy in the summer."

Sharon leaned over her ample arms crossed on the table and stared earnestly into Aggie's blue eyes.

"Why not, Aggie, no one knows how old you are! You don't need to tell anyone...lie! Simply lie. Besides, you sure do not look or act fifty-eight years old, darn you anyway. I show every year on my face—and more!"

"No, you don't," Aggie lied. "It's just that he will find out later."

"And, you will have proved how wonderful a waitress you really are by that time, right?"

"Right!" Aggie echoed. She did not worry about her skills; she had enjoyed herself and done a great job bartending at the local golf club the week before, and that hectic gig was a slam-bang operation—full speed ahead for several hours, if she counted the clean up. That was when the slippery helpers disappeared immediately after the contents of the tip jar was totaled up and doled out.

"I'm sure Swiss Chalet will take me, if this young guy doesn't."

"Of course they will."

"Of course they will," Aggie affirmed, psyching up for the task ahead, "and there are always my haircuts."

She picked up a remnant of fresh and tasty sandwich, too good to waste, and washed it down with the last drops of her cup of tea, then pulled out her compact from her handbag and chose a lipstick to refresh the coral color she was wearing.

"See you later," she chirped with a musical note in her voice.

She shimmied out of the restaurant booth, walked self-assuredly across the newly laid carpeting while admiring the renderings of exuberant wild life in original paintings hanging on the pine wood walls. The effect struck her as elegant and rustic at the same time.

Perhaps, she considered, the waitresses should wear blue uniforms to match, and a hostess could wear her own stylish clothing.

She liked this lakeside town and this restaurant. It would be a pleasure to work here, if the food was consistently good and if the owner had a like-minded nature. It was no fun otherwise—not worth her while to start the job.

As she approached the cherub-faced younger man, Aggie's blue eyes lit up with courtesy and her cheeks creased with the charming smile of a professional greeter.

His attention was obviously elsewhere, his head bent over a long list of figures as he leaned against the bar, his forehead wrinkled in concentration.

"Hello, I'm Aggie. I notice from the sign in the window that you are looking for a waitress, and I am looking for a permanent position, for evenings, as a waitress and hostess. Do you have a few minutes to talk?"

Startled slightly, his eyes readjusting to the real world after cruising column after column of numbers, the man looked straight at her.

She knew he saw a blond and neatly dressed woman standing before him, hopefully of indeterminate age.

She was not a girl, no one needed to tell her that, but she hoped her confidence spoke of her years of experience, and that her energy of willingness said so much more—said it all. She looked like she could handle the job, and what she did not know she would learn.

He was so young. Aggie thought he might not know what he was doing, and somebody in the restaurant should.

His eyebrows creased and then his eyes lit up. Aggie grinned as it hit him—where they met.

"You were tending bar at the country club last week. I was there, too, do you remember?"

"Yes, I was!" she exclaimed, pleased that he remembered her; she had recognized him as soon as she entered the restaurant.

He had walked into the club dining room and looked around calmly, taking it all in, and watched everyone going through their paces while the dining-room servers hustled, setting up with practiced rhythm to handle the crush of people soon to enter the banquet room.

The band, busily absorbed, had adjusted final screws on the drum set and tested speakers for volume, or tuned strings for clarity. Finally, they sat back and wolfed down a cold drink while a couple shared a smoke. They looked prepared to entertain for a long night of club members drinking and dancing to their groove on the too-small dance floor.

Aggie, and the young man before her, had exchanged fly-by pleasantries but she had been in motion, racing the clock to get the set-up perfect before the final speech was finished and the big rush for the bar began. There was no time for idle conversation.

This man had been taking it all in, too, and now she knew why he looked so intense that night. He had been assessing the layout of the bar and the drinking habits of his new town. What a perfect audition! She grinned at him and he did not hesitate a moment.

"You could start this weekend, if that's all right with you, though I must say it really is just waiting tables—I usually handle the bar." Then he did hesitate. "It could be unpredictable for a while, if you want to take a chance. I'm very new here, just feeling my way around town."

"Yes," Aggie agreed, "but it's a small town, and I've already heard your place mentioned once or twice, but haven't seen an ad for it. Wasn't sure where it was..."

They nodded, together, each of them obviously engrossed and thinking of ways to spread the word that Davidson's was the new place to be.

"So, it will be pretty easy to get the word out, you know, talk it up a bit," Aggie hinted. "I'm good at that."

They both wore a grin at that comment. It seemed she was already working, and he outlined his goals for an organic garden to grow as many of the herbs and vegetables as possible, and spoke of the search for a source of healthy meats. The more he voiced his dreams, the more excited she became.

She smiled spontaneously, pleased as punch, "I've been reading all about that! I can't find anywhere to buy organic food in town; a few people think I'm nuts to even bother. That's such a good idea...a garden of our own."

The burly man bustled back through the door with another armload of tubes of paper. A layer of sweat shone on his brow and Aggie glanced at his worn coveralls and blue cap with a lightning bolt insignia above the brim, which probably meant electrician.

"Here are the plans for the front walkway, no problem with the Town...and your new lighting ideas have been passed."

"Thanks, Fred."

The young owner of Davidson's restaurant turned towards Aggie again.

"I've got to get back to work now. Could you be here by 3 p.m. on Friday? We can run through our system of doing things, and by the way, I am Dan, and the restaurant's name is "Davidson's." Uh—can I have your phone number in case something comes up?"

"Of course" she replied, thinking quickly. "Please let me know by Thursday if there is any change in your plans." She thought she could always get that job at Swiss Chalet if he changed his mind.

"Funny!" she told Sharon a couple of weeks afterwards. "I showed up on time for work on Friday and I have worked every day since, and Dan, the owner, never did ask my age!"

The friends had a good laugh about it on the way to the wooden beach walkway, not wanting to miss the misty orange and purple halos of the lakeside sunset gleaming off the darkening blue, tranquil water.

The Real Thing

Chapter 27

It was like a dream come true for Aggie, that a young chef with the vision of fine dining took a leap of faith in a small town by a lake, in cottage country, and it seemed they were in sync from the start.

Aggie had questions. "Who is your butcher?"

"Well, I am."

That surprised her. "What do you mean?"

Dan leaned a hip against the kitchen counter, his eyes took in the room, and he slowly smiled in an ironic fashion, perhaps amusing himself with memories.

"I knew, somehow, that this is what I was meant to be—a chef. It surprised my parents, even though I was completely at ease in a kitchen."

"In the course I chose, they taught me everything: that the process begins with the purchase of a cow, and the importance of knowing where it was born, what it fed on, and then butchered for a specific purpose. Until you are hands-on with the meat there is no clear understanding—the cut is the destiny of the steak, and once you see and taste the results, it is not something you easily forget."

Aggie nodded and then shrugged. She had seen many a cook ruin good meat. She had done it herself in the old days, in a hurry, and it seemed like she was always in a hurry back then.

Dan responded, "Oh yes, a stupid chef can destroy it,

usually not allowing for the time it takes to get the meat from the grill or the oven to the table, onto the fork and into the mouth, and meanwhile, it is still cooking."

Aggie bobbed her head in agreement.

"In short, Aggie, now I can use the best meat supplier and tell him what I want."

"So, now we cook!" Dan joked, picking up Aggie's eager spirit. "We will convince with cuisine, plant the garden, stock the bar and open the door. It isn't Toronto, New York or Paris, but I can afford it for a while."

He also made sure she understood the sobering reality: that the property, the renovating, and purchasing of the supplies, had stripped his finances bare.

"We just have to cut corners," she pronounced. "Do it ourselves."

By the next day, Aggie's granddaughter, Cindy, stood on a stool at the sink, a huge adult-sized apron brushing her feet as she moved the dishrag back and forth over the plates. She had so much soap in the sink that when she swished the dishes around in the water, the high piles of suds spilled over on the floor.

That solved two problems; the dishes were washed and the girl was happy. To everyone's amusement, Cindy liked to wash dishes, and soapsuds were cheap.

Aggie cut Dan's hair as he sat on the stool in the centre of the kitchen, a confused look on his face, as if he did not know whether to laugh or cry. He flinched involuntarily at the first few snips. He liked to pretend he was scared while he sat with a huge towel around his shoulders to catch the shreds of hair.

"I feel like a guinea pig!" Dan teased, trying to make Aggie nervous.

"I've done it all my life," she protested. "And I've got

the certificates on my wall to prove that I'm a pro!"

She gabbed to distract his attention, while they batted around new menu ideas, a pot of something yummy stewing on the stove, beef maybe, and herbs, and scrumptious sauce that made them hungry with the delicious smells.

"We know it's all going to work," she added, "we just had to have patience."

"Patience!?!" Dan spluttered and then started to laugh, and had a hard time stopping.

Aggie joined in. "We don't know whether to laugh or cry, but we always have something to eat!"

It did not hurt their business a bit when Aggie's birthday rolled around in August. The first year, her friends had come for dinner and a band showed up as the restaurant was closing.

Davidson's rocked for hours and the next week the story went around and they were fully booked. Aggie knew how to get things done, how to make folks come back for more. Her boss, Dan, knew how to handle public relations, and how to court the press, and in short order, their smiling faces were in the local paper.

Every year after that, her birthday was a party with a band booked in advance, and local musicians joined in as their gigs ended along the lakefront, and over to Barrie. Beer flowed and the word spread— Davidson's was the place to have good food and a good time.

Sometimes, it got wild. One year, when every local johnny bought drinks for the house, Aggie danced on a table in her pink cowboy boots, blond curls swinging, until she fell off, into the arms of several men willing to catch her.

She was 70 years old at the time, and Aggie famously joked, "Too bad no one took a picture of that!"

She moved among the tables, placing set-ups here, flicking errant crumbs there, as troubling thoughts played, over, and over in her mind. "Tonight is booked solid and two servers off sick, just because a concert is on. All the part-time girls are "sick" at the same time, too. We need another pair of hands."

As she lay down the last carefully folded blue cloth napkin, one at each setting, and plunked the cutlery neatly beside it, Aggie noticed movement outside the door. A young woman, with hunched up shoulders, stood staring at the sign posted in the restaurant window. She looked a bit of a mess, as if she had not slept in a week. She shook her head and squinted, to read the "Waitress Wanted" sign, and hugged her oversized yellow sweater closer.

Aggie mumbled to herself, "How hard can that be? Come in, or don't come in."

Yes, it looked like she was going for the door.

Aggie leaned through the pass to the kitchen. "We have a young one coming in—rather straggly looking—have we heard from Eleanor?"

"No!" Dan's deep male voice rang from the walk-in freezer. "If she's alive, hire her!"

Aggie looked the twenty-something girl over, noted her restless eyes glance towards the cash register, flick away and back again, and in jerky sequence the girl's survey slipped around the paintings on the walls, anywhere but Aggie's eyes.

She is here for cash, not a long-term job—Aggie figured, and probably does not live in the area, having not seen her around. Her clothes looked slept-in and there were circles under her eyes. Too bad, she would have been a pretty girl if she cleaned up her act and stayed off drugs.

People with nothing to lose get careless.

"The sign outside says that you need a waitress."

The girl raised her head slightly and tried to smile, "I'm Susanna." Altogether, the result was comical, as if her shoulders had heavy dumbbells resting across them and it was a problem to move leaden lips.

"Yes, we do. Let's sit down and talk about it, over a coffee. Have you eaten lunch?" Aggie knew the answer; the girl had no breakfast either.

She led them to a deuce, pointed to where the girl should sit. Jeeze! The kid was so dopey she might have to drink the coffee for her, too.

Aggie left her there and stuck her head in the kitchen. "Can you make a quick chicken sandwich? This one looks like she might faint."

Loud Dan muttering followed Aggie backing out the door. Swinging to her left, she reached for the hot coffee and filled a cup in one practiced arc.

Probably a summer rat, Aggie figured, left behind when the drug market pulled out a couple of weeks ago, as well as the crowds along the lakefront when parents got their children back to the city, and back to school.

Fortunately, less people milling around did not affect their evening restaurant or bar business too much, until almost winter. Aggie would be gone soon, as well, to Florida, a place where real winter never came. Anyone who could get away did so, including Dan now and then.

She placed the life-saving brew in front of the girl with the squeezed up, morning red eye of a pot smoker, and the downturned depressed mouth of the speed freak that ran out of pills. She looked a mess, actually; she could have brushed her hair better and she could have bathed, but at least the caffeine would get her talking.

"Oh, coffee...hot coffee." It looked like it was hard

for her to formulate any words but those and Aggie got busy with something else, keeping an eye on the scraggly girl.

It was all no surprise to Aggie—the girl looked desperate, as if she wanted to shrivel up and die, and she seemed to shrink where she sat, squeezing up her shoulders and her eyes.

Aggie walked over to the table and sat down again, but the girl looked away from her, and then she turned back, a resigned look in her eyes; maybe she had decided to be honest.

"I haven't worked for a while. I saw your sign in the window and I think I can do whatever you need—I did it before, at a lunch counter. I really need a job." It was all she could manage and her gaze slid back down to the table.

A bell rang. Aggie pushed through the doors to the back and there was a quick exchange of loud conversation in the kitchen that ended with, "Oh for God's sake!" from Dan.

The only thing the girl seemed to care about was the hefty sandwich on the blue patterned plate, the thick cucumber slices beside it, and the clump of parsley, and her hands found it before it reached the table. She picked up half and tore off a hunk with her teeth.

Aggie left her to it and methodically set up tables while she ruminated, "Please, please, let someone else come in within the hour. If we hire her, we won't be able let her go for seeming to be sneaky."

She did not bother making up a check for the sandwich. They could be stuck with this girl for a week, or a month, however long it took her addiction to need something badly, and maybe rob them blind, and Aggie only hoped it would not cost them too much.

Dan would have to watch her like a hawk when Aggie left town because she did not trust the girl as far as she could throw her. She had seen addicts before and it was just a matter of time, but it was better than nothing tonight.

In The Stars, Wild Love

November 1989

Chapter 28
Author's View

I was disgruntled and out of sorts.

According to the rules of astrology, the three-month span I elected as the best time in the last five years for romance, leading to marriage, was drifting by like the last lifeboat from the drowning Titanic.

My astrological reputation hung in the balance and all because of this waiting game.

Oh, there were offers, four proposals that summer actually, but when the one proposing is not the man that makes your heart sing, if the front of your brain is conjuring picket-fence scenarios while the back of your brain is flashing red, "NO, NOT HIM", logic says to wait. Several good men had been turned away without rational explanation—only a simple thank you, no.

I had not cared about love that lasts forever for a long while, and romantic adventures had come and gone quickly by, but this year was special for me, and I did care. My heart and my astrology chart said it was due, so where was this anticipated event? Wild love ruined me before, yet to settle for less than the real thing would be a swindle for both parties.

Tension gripped the back of my neck and squeezed, continually tightening, restricting my breath like a boa constrictor around my shoulders. My doctor confirmed it was as hard as a rock and consequently she suggested I talk to a shrink, a psychiatrist, to try to work it out. I was clenching my neck, my shoulders—they were not clenching me.

I had a job with upward mobility and a simpatico roommate trying to teach me to belly dance, the illustrious Mahara. I was in Vancouver's coveted Kitsilano neighborhood, where we shared two birds in a cage and two cats in our yard. There was nothing overtly wrong with my life, so maybe my tension was a symptom of the comparison game that occurs when a person compares what they remember from the past, with what they appear to have now. Perhaps my obsession involved a long ago love that ended sixteen years ago to be exact.

That single-minded adventurer had fled out west, to Edmonton I had heard, even though I imagined I saw him across busy Denman Street a few months earlier, while I sat in the early spring sunshine at an outdoor table of a coffee shop on my lunch break. Something about the roll of the man's gait caught my eye, stopped the breath I was inhaling, and I almost raised my hand to catch his eye. But that was silly. Edmonton was a world away from this charming city. I chuckled softly. How could anyone new compete with a phantom?

I needed an exorcist to rid me of a ghost.

At a trip to my physician regarding a stiff neck, she questioned the growing tension in my shoulders that I felt was from too many hours looking at a computer screen, and she asked what was on my mind. There was no choice; I admitted to a girlish obsession. She recommended heat packs and a psychiatrist, just to talk it over, as I would not respect the opinion of anyone else, and I agreed.

On the third session with the practical man, covered

under the umbrella of my medical plan, he agreed that I did not need medication or continued counseling. I understood archetypes and obsession. I was a sane consultant that gave counsel to others, yet held a blind spot for my own simple wounds, which was very common. Only my ego and my heart were bruised, and only time would heal.

My boss at the downtown office that employed me advised correctly that I would not meet anyone if I did not go out, nor would it hurt our business if he showed up at the Vancouver Chinatown Rotary lunch meeting with me, and my bouffant blonde hair, in tow. Getting attention when one is selling insurance is the first key to success. Not being Chinese, I doubted that I would meet anyone for lifetime compatibility—but why not go to lunch—practice is practice.

A wall of noise greeted us as the elevator doors parted and I smiled immediately. It was exhilarating to be part of this gregarious group. We found two empty seats on one arm of the u-shaped table setup, focused around a podium in front of a large, brightly embroidered blue and gold Rotary emblem. We settled in and my friend turned this way, and that, shaking hands, giving appropriate head nods of recognition.

There were a few women in the predominantly male crowd and they dressed in power suits for the office, in red or blue with large shoulder pads, as fashion dictated. My suit was fashionably body-fitting black, with a white cowl collar and cuffs that sported black polka dots. I wore my long blond hair puffed 80's large, but taken it down a bit, befitting our executive office. I admit it; I looked good.

The potent level of focus from the earnest men and women was impressive. They were at the lunch gathering to meet and greet, and combine social skills with commerce. Rotary International performs good works all over the world, every day, and this was a working and social lunch where bonds are forged and no one forgot that.

Business needs a full belly. Waiters lifted lids from metal serving pans that released the distinct aroma of Chinese sauces on chow mien, meats and noodles, hot and plentiful, while a kitchen helper deftly poured steaming soup into small bowls on a large tray—pick one up if you want one—and the aroma filled the crowded room.

At a silent signal, people instantly arose from one arm of the seating plan to form a long lineup for food that snaked in front of our table. Funny, how fast hunger hits our bellies when an enticing aroma wafts our way.

With the patience of Confucius, our table sat and pretended patience, watching the backs of the fortunate edging towards their enticing lunch and the businessmen turned to each other, to take advantage of the few minutes to exchange business cards and say their practiced few words of self promotion. I distracted myself, listened to the Chinese and English chatter around me, simultaneously loud and soothing. The sound was like an argument or a good time, hard to tell which. It sounded intense, like life.

Our conversation dried up as the line of blue suits and black suits, edged slowly towards the food table and my colleague and I glanced at each other. Were we going to be the absolute last ones to eat?

One man's gray suit caught my eye. It was not so much the weave of the fabric, which was a touch richer than those that passed before, or the color, a true dove gray, but a familiarity of how it lay on the back of the man that wore it, and stood three feet in front of my table, where I sat waiting my turn.

My throat tightened and my breath caught, and a

quiet gasp escaped me as I stared. I stared at the man's shoulders, the shape of his head, his hair—and his butt.

My boss noticed my fixed expression and glanced at the man, and then back at me, a question in his eyes.

"I think...I think..." I stammered, "I, I, think I know him..." My heart knocked. Should I stay sitting? Should I get up? Blood rushed to my face and neck and the rascal in me took over as I reached for one of my business cards in my handbag. I was on my feet and caught up to the man just as he reached the end of the room and stood fifth in line for lunch.

"I think I know you—Dax?" I queried, grinning by now, knowing full well who he was.

He turned, shock clearly written on his face from a familiar voice and a pet name from long ago, another place, another time. He leaned his back against the wall and slid slowly down to sit on the floor, his legs spread out before him.

Time stopped. Conversation stopped. This had not happened before at the luncheon. Ron was on the floor stunned, then quickly recuperated and arose handing his card to me, a blond woman no longer a stranger, and the woman was laughing.

I tried to be everyday, so nice to see you again, as I looked in his eyes, still blue, and filled with a thousand emotions. I glanced at his card and back to his face, his eyes, but there were too many questions, too many people staring, to start a conversation now. I held the card tightly as if it would get away, this lifeline to the past. It had been wild love before, and likely would always be again, but maybe he was involved elsewhere, even married. Maybe he thought I was.

Ron glanced at my card and back to me.

We could have stared all day, but there was propriety to consider, Chinese propriety, at that. I walked back to my seat, heart fluttering like a bird newly caged.

He turned back to the line-up for lunch.

My lunch-mate looked dismayed.

I must confess the afternoon at the office was not productive—my mind was somewhere else.

The astrological clock was right after all.

The planetary movements had indicated a time in my life, but did not force anything on me. The choice that I made within that timeframe, was where free will came in, and our engagement was official at the stroke of midnight, on New Year's Eve, sealed with a diamond ring proffered on bended knee on a rustic retreat on Hornby Island, and a mutual pledge to make love last a lifetime.

Before the next year was done, Aggie was with me again, now my mother in-law. At the wedding, she elbowed through the hopefuls in pretty dresses, their faces upturned, reaching, yelling, to catch my bouquet.

Fascinated by her energy, I studied her astrology chart, with strong "Mars in Taurus" pushing for her ultimate comforts. We have talked a scattered stream for over the last twenty years while I laughed and sympathized over the dramatically rich and colorful stories of her life.

With several planets in Leo, the Fire Sign of the lion, and a few in thrifty Virgo, and mothering Cancer, she is fast-moving sight to behold. With bold nerve and the energy to follow through, it was certain she would have all her someday dreams fulfilled.

Girls' Day Out

1991

Chapter 29

"Here's a place," Aggie called out. "We came here before, remember? Good coffee!"

She pushed through the glass doors of the restaurant in the mall, emptied of lunch customers, in the middle of the afternoon, and gave a nod to the waiter as she shoved her bags into an empty booth next to the one she wanted to sit in. Her pals followed her example with their shocking pink, red, or fuchsia plastic bags and boxes carefully imprinted with bold store advertising.

The women plopped into the next empty booth and scooted over to make room for all five.

Aggie's friend, Kelly, looked exhausted and heaved a loud sigh. "We look like starving troops recovering from war. This calls for coffee and a pastry."

Sharon glanced over the back of the seat to their overflowing purchases of sharp-eyed bargains. "It's a good thing we only do this once a year! I love it but my bank account does not!"

The other three women nodded in tired but happy unison and murmured contented noises when coffee and sweets arrived, with chatter following soon after.

Aggie primped her newly permed hair and asked,

"What's up with you, Gail? You're so quiet today."

Gail shifted her position, and lined up her spoon to sit exactly one inch from the edge of the table, the way she liked it. She took a deep breath. "My niece lost the baby I told you about. Then my sister told me it was an abortion. She was really upset that they told her a baby was coming in the first place."

"I had a child myself, when I was young," Gail continued, "and I was not married. I could not go to visit my grandmother's house, because the men might not understand, she told me. Grandma said her Irish mother told her there is an old-country saying: 'If a young girl is left alone, she will fall in love with the butcher-boy at the gate'. I'm not sure what I was supposed to get from that."

Aggie grinned, Kelly chuckled, and heads nodded. It seemed all the girls had private memories of being attracted to unacceptable boys.

"By wonderful coincidence, years later we did find each other, my son and I," Gail finished. "The agency loosened its rules just when I sent my last inquiry. We were lucky."

Kelly shifted in her seat, trying to settle her skinny body into the barely cushioned restaurant booth. She shook back her dark, shaggy hair and took a deep breath. "That was one in a million for you, Gail, getting reconnected. However, the abortion debate isn't new. Every culture has their remedies. Some work, some don't."

Sharon sat up straight and leaned her abundant elbows on the table—she had something to add. She raised her graying eyebrows and rolled her eyes a bit in parody, and then talked about when she was a kid and her aunts frankly discussed it all with no men around, trading remedies and drinking endless cups of strange medicinal tea.

They all nodded, but had no answers to the age-old question.

Kelly had just begun. "I saw something new on cable TV the other day. At a world panel, the moderator said that designer abortions offer choice now. Not the preferred sex? You simply abort. Bad timing? Same thing.

"That's for the rich, of course. For a poor woman, it's the old remedies, drink a toxic potion that might kill you, use dangerous implements, or expose it to the elements at birth."

All of the women were quiet for a few moments with their own feelings and memories.

Kelly continued the subject, leaning forward on the five bracelets up her arm to make her point, anger clear in her voice. "Women can abort baby girls in China, or India. They prefer boys, to keep the money in the family—and because a man makes more money to support his parents in their old age. Also, parents have more respect for boys, and if it's a girl, they have to provide dowry."

Aggie put in, "I read in the newspaper that Chinese men are looking for brides from other countries now. There aren't enough young girls in China, because of all that."

"Ha!" Gail chipped in, perked up in the company of friends, "that's nothing new! Don't get me started! One woman on my family tree ended up getting married to a man in Australia."

Aggie laughed and it relieved the tension, and loosed a string of raucous jokes.

"Yes," Kelly continued. "We are all immigrants aren't we?"

"But, did you know," Kelly persisted, "even in our

culture, today's parents select their children for health, too? For instance, you can have a procedure called amniocentesis, where parents can check whether a baby is likely to be born with Down's syndrome."

"Yes." Sharon volunteered. "I heard that after a number of babies, there is often a Down's child, as if the system between the parents misfires."

"That's right," Kelly continued. "Several Down's children can pop up in an isolated community, which could be genetic or some other unknown factor. There was a study done on the west coast where there is a large community of Dutch Reform. They don't believe in birth control so the last two children are invariably 'Downs'. Also interesting—the parents are usually over age 35. I know about it from some relatives out there."

Aggie was the oldest in this table of friends.

"There were no birth control pills in my early life," she said, "and no social assistance or such a thing as paid maternity leave. I had too many pregnancies to count. I think eleven for me, fourteen for my Aunt Jessie. Condoms cost money, so if you were having sex, you got pregnant. If a girl was late, she used a douche and cleaned herself. If you did it fast enough, it usually worked without a hitch. 'Lost it,' we would say, if we said anything at all, and that was that. We didn't really call it an abortion unless it went quite late, or the other remedies did not work and we had to sneak off to the backdoor of a person who could fix it.

"When Dr. McMillin confirmed I was pregnant with my last child, I didn't know what to do," Aggie said. "We had done those things in the old days, quite carelessly, but this one felt different.

"I can't afford it," I told him. "I have three boys, and Jim's money comes in, and goes out on booze. I almost cried, I was so unhappy.

"I wrung my hands like a schoolgirl. I remember that. My hands were twitching, I was so nervous. I had to hold them tightly together. He just listened, nodding his head."

" 'It's not up to me, Aggie, it's up to you,' " he said. " 'Go home and think about it. We have a couple of weeks to decide, but that's all.' "

The lines on Aggie face were showing as she frowned. "I was a nervous wreck trying to figure out the best thing to do."

"Didn't they have the pill by then?" Kelly asked.

"Well, that's just it. I realized that everyone was talking about the pill but I had been too busy to pay attention. Jim and I had not been together that much, if you know what I mean. I could have this one last child, boy or girl, and that would be it for me, guaranteed."

"What happened to your job?" Gail asked.

"When I couldn't be working in the pub. I had a part-time job at the post office so I kept that up as long as I could."

"That must have hurt financially."

Aggie's eyes clouded with introspection. "Oh, yes. When I got bigger, it was really hard to lug the boxes. You wouldn't believe how many heavy things there are to sort. I should have quit sooner. Of course, I wouldn't know what to do now without my girl."

"Where was your husband?" Gail sounded bewildered.

"He was out of town somewhere, on the road with the truck. Besides, he wasn't going to pay any of my mortgage!" Aggie was forthright. "Then he could have claimed some of the house, see. He paid his rent and that was that!"

"Oh, Aggie, don't ever change!"

"There were other ways we lost babies, too. We worked hard physically when I was young," Aggie commented. "A job could be a whole lot of sitting, but oh boy! After work, no one sat around. We were dancing, see, playing baseball, cleaning a house or chasing someone else's little kids around while they went to work. Once we had kids we carried our own! It seemed we were always in motion."

"In the times I didn't have a car, I stood at the side of the road with my thumb out all the time, with one of my kids on my hip, and holding another one by the hand. No matter what—you had to get around town to work, or shop, or see a doctor. We couldn't wait for a bus that came twice a day. We got up extra early and went to bed late."

"Now kids expect their parents to drive them places or provide a car! Everybody is so fat!"

"Very different times," Sharon agreed, with a faraway look in her eye. "Everyone watches television all the time instead of talking, or playing cards, communicating."

"Lots of miscarriages happened that way." Aggie revved up now, peering into the past and pulling out images. "Just lifting a child could do it. I lost one painting a bedroom! So much for those white shorts!"

They nodded to each other and Aggie continued.

"Someone else was standing behind you to take your job, see. There were always rumors, someone saying, 'Oh, I heard she was preggers,' or 'in the family way,' as we used to say, you know, 'knocked up.' When home remedies didn't work, there wasn't much choice except get an abortion. Doctors wouldn't do it, not usually, anyway, because it was against the law. They said tell the man to wear a condom or don't have sex. Good luck!"

"Yep, that's right." Gail agreed. "The big problem is that guys did not want to wear them. Probably still don't, even with their fancy designs. They say it doesn't feel the same—too bad, huh?"

"Amen to that," Sharon agreed. "Sex was supposed to be steamy—like in the movies, or else you were ruining it for the man. He has to let go of a girl to put on a condom, and bang! There goes the moment."

Aggie joined the knowing laughs and head nods.

Sharon had more to say. "'Wham, bam, thank-you Ma'am', remember that expression? Not like the old movies at all, with a man wooing a girl properly...and, the crazy rules!

"Women could work in a factory like a man, but could not go into a drugstore and ask for a condom. They looked at you as if you were a whore. Silly, really. Abortion, miscarriage, it was everywhere. Laws only made it more difficult for us. Laws made by men."

They fell silent. Aggie shifted in her seat to let the waiter pour coffee for his only customers in the middle of the afternoon.

The women raised their cups to salute the babies that did not make it into this lop-sided world.

Aggie chipped in, "That's right. Men had the power to make laws but didn't want to raise unwanted kids, and the orphanages were disgusting."

"It's hard to explain the difference to young people, now." Kelly had been quiet for a few minutes while she thought about it all, sipped her coffee, twisted the many rings on her fingers. "We were bad girls if we talked about 'it' or allowed a man near us. Now girls are incomplete if they aren't having sex. Girls don't act surprised anymore, pretending to let the man have his way with them, like we did, but I'll bet they still use the same places, cold back seats in cars or sneaking into a friend's house when their parents are out.

"My niece, Melissa, tells me that the young girls still want the same thing, a man and babies. They are in love with the romance of the idea and have regrets later when teething and diaper rash, and disappearing boyfriends, are too much reality."

Her face reddened, as if in a rush the room became too warm, and picked up the menu to use as a fan. "Hot flash. I don't get them much any more. It will pass."

Aggie chimed in with a twinkle in her eye, and a saucy grin, "It's good to be an adult and just wear our sexy nightgowns whenever we want!"

Gail's guffaw joined in.

"You have a couple of very sexy night things, I know! I must buy new nightgowns! Shock the old man into a heart attack and I can spend all his money when we shop next year."

The women laughed and nodded.

Aggie still had something on her mind. "There is a bigger problem than getting pregnant, AIDS, so I keep condoms in my bathroom. It's my responsibility to protect myself. But I'm on the pill now, too."

"On the pill? Isn't that dangerous?" Kelly was surprised. "I thought about it a few months ago to put off hot flashes, but my doctor was negative about it. I looked online but there is no clear answer."

Aggie shrugged. "I get checked regularly for cancer. That's all I worry about. I'm alive now—I want to enjoy myself. You never know how much time there is."

Then Gail grinned, changed the subject. "I read in a magazine that sex is like a three-act play: Foreplay, Intercourse, and Afterglow! Is that when you ask for the new shoes?"

"Hell, no!" Sharon spluttered. "You do that before the sex!"

When the laughing settled down, Aggie remarked, "I look around, though, and I see a lot of women that look like they're wearing pajamas all day. I can't get over it. Hardly anyone dresses up, except maybe on New Year's Eve. It's too bad, because there is so much choice now. I never go anywhere without nice shoes and earrings, and make sure my hair is permed and colored, the way I like it. I do it for me.

"We're dumb to miss out on all the fun. A woman just has to get out of the house and circulate, go to dances, stay active. The men are always willing, and then it's her responsibility to protect herself."

Kelly cut in, "That's right! Some women think older folk don't carry AIDS. It is urgent that people protect themselves because their immune system is often weak and they are having sex, even in their nineties, and they are becoming infected."

It was Sharon's turn. "I hear about it when I volunteer at the hospital. It makes a person think twice. Mostly, older women talk as if they do not believe that AIDS kills, or they think it is only among homosexual men. They are at huge risk!"

Aggie checked her watch and wound up the conversation; time was flying. "I pick and choose my partners," she concluded, "and yes, I have a steady boyfriend. He wants to marry me but after two husbands, and lots of boyfriends, I'm not ready to settle down."

"Hear, Hear!"

Aggie smiled at her friends. They were full of their opinions and so different from the leggy, former showgirls she palled around with in St. Petersburg, Florida. The southern belles would not be caught dead without their make-up, or talk like this in public, yet it seemed most women wanted the same thing at heart.

Waving, smiling, Aggie saluted good-bye after they all agreed to go negligee shopping on their next girl's day out.

Lunch at Davidson's

1993

Chapter 30

At 10 a.m., Aggie phoned in sick.

"Sorry, sorry, I know there will be a lot of tourists today but I'm sick from a shot the doctor gave me. I went to the doctor really early to get it over with and I could barely make it home. I've never reacted to a shot like this before, see. You know I'm hardly ever sick, I hope you understand. Please call someone else."

To her disbelief, Dan was pushing her, demanding that she come in.

"There is no one else, Aggie. Maybe it will pass. Come in anyway, you're only booked for lunch."

He hung up on her!

It was hot today, into August now, almost her birthday. Even with the air-conditioning on full-blast, she held down the button to open the driver's window hoping the rush of fresh air would clear her head.

Her mind was fuzzy, but busy. Maybe my stomach will get better soon, she reasoned, and maybe no one else will know.

Everyone knew, yet seemed to turn away when she entered, as if they had been talking about her before she came in.

"You look awful," her boss said, standing straight,

his normally pleasant face a mask, his brown eyes finding something else to look at. "Maybe you can work it off—you'd just be miserable at home."

Aggie would normally shake her head at that, but did not want to set the rocking sea in motion. The delicious food smells that usually made her hungry she tried not to think about now.

Except for one run to the employee's washroom, the cook staring at her hand over her mouth, she made it through the lunch crowd. Aggie was grateful when Dan took turns welcoming guests, delivering lunches to the tables and handling the cash when he was not seating more people.

"I think you need some country air," Chef said with a broad smile on her round face and a twinkle in her eye, lifting a fresh blue kitchen towel from the stack that always waited for her, and casually wiping her hands. "I had that shot last year, before our cruise, and was right as rain after a couple of hours. We'll catch you, if you fall!" She walked away laughing at her own joke.

Usually Chef was one of Aggie's favorite people in the world but Aggie stared at her, wondering if she was loco today. No one seemed to be listening to her!

She kept going, checking back to the tables, laying down the tabs and helping the waitress with the clearing as quickly as possible. Plates clanged together like ceramic bells out of tune and silverware crashed hitting the plastic bins, ready for the dishwasher.

The customers dispersed back to work or cottages, or continued on their merry way to summer afternoon pleasures on the lake if they were visitors. They came for the sailing, swimming, or simply lolling on the broad sunny beaches of Lake Simcoe, and often they checked with the staff for directions and information for their visit to the region.

She noticed Dan turned the door lock smartly today,

and posted the sign with the dinner hours on the window in one quick move.

Aggie made quick trip to kitchen with a few beer glasses left behind as the Chef was heading out the back door. A few moments later, Chef rushed back in, as if she forgot something.

Everyone seemed to be in an almighty hurry, Aggie observed, but that suited her just fine. All she wanted to do was go home and lie down, to stop the world from slipping and sliding.

"The staff's all going for a drive," the boss told Aggie with his head lowered like a bull ready for the arena, and a "you're coming, too!" look in his eye.

No one listened to her when she grumbled.

"Come on," Chef urged, "We'll look after you. Just a little drive to see my house. My husband's so proud of our new kitchen. It won't take long. It'll be fun!"

Before Aggie could seriously protest, she was hustled into the back seat of Chef's eight-seat van, and she was not happy.

She could barely look out the window, the passing scenery a blur of swirling green and tall trees zipping past like dizzying lights on a tilt-a-whirl.

Down a side road she was not familiar with, the van turned into a lane that passed through enormous black wrought iron gates and headed into spreading meadows, their foliage fading as if discouraged under midsummer's scorching sun.

When they pulled into a large parking area in front of a new mansion, Aggie wondered how it was she did not know this place, yet the cars out front were familiar. Yes, that was strange. Some belonged to staff at Davidson's, the people that hadn't worked the lunch. A van with a with distinctive paint job, musical scales with notes climbing the bars, belonged to someone she knew, and another to her girlfriend, Marge.

"Welcome to my house," Chef said, holding the van door open for Aggie to disembark the rough-sea voyage.

"Your house?" Aggie exclaimed. "What kind of job does your husband do?" She knew the chef's wages. Her paycheck could never afford this spread.

"He designed it. Welcome," she answered with a laugh, hand on Aggie's elbow gently guiding her up the broad stone front steps.

Aggie stood inside the over-sized wooden double-doors, a large winding stairway across the foyer beckoning her to the upper level.

Chef said, loudly, "This is all for you today, Aggie. We didn't think you'd want to miss it."

"Happy Birthday!!"

Laughter and good wishes poured from friends from every walk of life. Housewives, musicians, restaurant regulars, all leaning over the upstairs railing and urging her to climb up to join them on their way to the outside deck.

Holding Dan's hand for support, she climbed the stairs to join her friends and workmates, and Chef's tall and lanky spouse deftly turning kabobs on their oversized barbecue. He smiled at Aggie, then turned back to the grill and began brushing on more sauce. Aggie recognized the aroma of Chef's sauces—they were Chef's fame.

The surprise, and the tantalizing scent that teased Aggie's taste buds, was almost overwhelming, and tears sprang to her eyes.

She had more friends than she realized. All from working in one place for so long, and living in a small town she had grown to love.

From the bottom of her heart, Aggie thanked them.

It was an incredible lunch of the Chef's favorites, followed with a laugh-filled presentation of a couple of

Elvis presents to amuse and delight, and to add to her collection. They had collected money, too, and turned it into USD $120 to pay for her gas to Florida in October.

Never a heavy eater, Aggie picked a sampler size plate of her favorites from the buffet, settling for a bite of this and that, not wanting to aggravate her tummy, doing her best to honor the work that had gone into producing the meat, the salads, and the exquisite cake with an oversized letter "A" on top.

It was all a little overwhelming.

"What a day!" she thought, sitting back comfortably in the shade under a canopy trimmed with golden fringe, on a huge deck overlooking towering emerald trees and rolling hills, underneath the bluest sky of summer, with her dear friends around her.

Flying by, loaded with a fresh platter, Chef slowed down beside Aggie and whispered in her ear, "You know, we were always ready to catch you, if you fell."

"I know, I know," she responded a bit sheepishly, "I was so out of sorts."

A quick hug and Chef was off to replenish the food table.

Her dizziness almost gone, helped by the food, she thought, she still felt unsure how the car ride back to the restaurant would go, but she knew she had help if she needed it. Maybe 75 years old was a different story from 65, but nothing major had changed on what was a normal day after all.

This afternoon party is certainly different, she reminisced, smiling that they had actually tricked her.

In this quiet moment, her mind wandered to the future. It would be autumn soon at Davidson's and she would load the car to the top of the windows once more for the long drive to sunny Florida, before Ontario's cold and wicked surprises howled across

Lake Simcoe.

Luckily, the couple that rented her Barrie home lived in a trailer all summer, on the beachfront, and was looking for a secure place to pass the winter months. It was good to have someone trustworthy. It was her major investment, after all. Her children had chipped in to help buy it as an investment and their share had been returned to them.

Aggie was quite sure she knew where Chef would be, snug in this contemporary castle with a genteel country estate's view of snowfields covering lawns and picture perfect forests, or skiing the slopes with her handsome husband.

They probably had those noisy ski-doos, too.

"Oh well," Aggie thought, "they won't be disturbing anyone. This property goes on forever!"

Throw It All Away

Chapter 31

> B-B-Biloxi!
> Hey, hey, hey!
> That's what we're gonna do!
> Gamble all day!!

The continuous chant rose like a surging wave from the back of the bus through to the front as the smiling faces of the men and women topped with white hair, dark hair, blond-haired or no hair at all, swayed in time with the beat.

All skin shades represented. middle-aged and older, the passengers dressed in pink, powder blue, plaid, or wild prints and sang together, united, excited as they watched for the tall row of waving flags proclaiming proudly that they welcomed visitors to the state of Mississippi.

The driver relaxed into the road, sitting back in fifth gear in the middle lane and letting the crazies speed past her as if they wanted to be the first to die and win a prize—maybe the best seat in hell.

Contented, comfortable with the familiar wheel in front of her, the driver checked the rear view mirror, skimming the faces for repeat customers and enjoying their happy voices. Some took the trip month after month, whenever they were on the west coast of Florida, and never seemed to tire of the routine, relaxing, letting go in a luxury air-conditioned bus.

Maybe, she thought, that was the point exactly; they could count on it staying the same, which was more than one could say about most of what happens in a life.

Pickups in Tampa, St. Petersburg, and then a couple more stops heading north, they cruised up and around the generous curve of the Gulf of Mexico, feeding the tourist industry from the west side of Florida into Biloxi, Mississippi's mile of gambling glitz.

Once dropped off at the lavish Imperial Palace, the illustrious Grand, or something less grand, they checked in at their chosen hotel.

As "Bible Belt" restrictions disallowed gambling and drinking, once they were settled in they would make their way to brilliantly lit riverboats or embellished barges where these sins were legal off the shore of Mississippi.

Some chose the glitzy Beau Rivage, or maybe the allure of Treasure Bay Casino disguised as a pirate ship.

Sometimes, for a lark, they said, some passengers cruised the dimmer streets, guided by rough-made pamphlets handed out furtively for back alley gambling halls with cheaper drinks, saucy entertainment and no cover charge. Most of them gambled to their hearts content, losing all the money and more they had saved up to repeat this extravagance year after year.

There was an exception to the jolly mood, she noted, Aggie, a trim blond woman in the back section by the window, looked edgy today. She shifted in her seat, touched her fresh, stylish hair. The driver had seen her a few times before and usually she was the main cheerleader, a real joke-cracking rabble-rouser, but today her passenger cast dark glances at her seat companion, a gent who scowled as if in a torture chamber and rolled his eyes at the happy chanters.

Now that's a shame, the driver thought, flicking her eyes here and there, mirror to mirror, keeping tabs on the drivers speeding past her bus as if they were on a freaking raceway. "Idiot, Dumb Ass," she breathed to the reckless law benders not even noticing she spoke the catechism of the road softly but aloud. That pleasant woman was going to be stuck with that grumpy guy for two nights, the driver sympathized—been there, done that—not fun.

"This is a real mistake," echoed through Aggie's mind, her head slowly lolling on the back of the seat faking a nap.

She remembered her last trip up the coast with friends, and the trip before that, without a man along and having a whale of a time, but that did not help her feel better. My grandchildren are more fun, she figured. They know how to play! I should have brought one of them.

Aggie took inventory. Ben has no sense of humor today, whatsoever. He is tall, freshly showered and neatly dressed with a crease in his cotton pants, and that's it. For someone that was ten years younger, the deep lines in his face look like canyons in the morning sun.

He is all right in the clinches, Aggie considered, and didn't mind spending money. He even took it easy with the booze the first couple of weeks, knowing she didn't like heavy drinking, but that was over now.

The first slip up was the night he ordered more, and more drinks and got snippy, even rude. Last night he blew that mistake out of the water! Imagine! No other sign he was drunk until he passed out cold without a word of warning, smack onto the table at the Legion in front of her friends. Aggie had reeled back in shock.

Later came the puking, and the true confession that Ben was an alcoholic and no "cure" had worked.

He is not even happy when he is drunk, she assessed, so what is the point of it? Personality zero, now that the truth is out and another alcoholic in her life was no fun at all.

She had seen it all before and had no intention to let that problem back into her life again.

From the corner of her squinting eye, Aggie could see enough. His head lowered like an ill-tempered bull ready to charge, daring someone to cross him. He wanted to sit in a corner with her and not say anything to anyone, like she was his corralled cow.

Nit-picky "No" to this, and "No" to that, every time she suggested something.

Feeling twitchy, not comfortable in the sway of the bus as she usually was, she crossed her legs but her coral Capri pants felt snug in the wrong places. They had been a terrific price and looked great with her high-heeled wedge cork sandals, but she must remember to switch to something more comfortable on the trip back.

She looked out the window, finding harmony in a view she dearly loved, the ringed palm trees flicking past the hustling bus windows as if in motion picture frames. They curved up gracefully and opened green umbrellas of fronds gently waving, shading the bus and keeping the roads from melting into asphalt pools of blackish gray.

Aggie also saw the reflection of hung-over Ben, just like her second husband, when Jim used to drink. Alcohol turned him into a monster and she had feared for her life.

She felt that familiar anger growing, burning like a hot coal in her chest, a feeling she thought she had put behind her long ago. No, that would never happen again.

Facts are facts. If a person repeats the same thing over and over, they are stuck in that behavior for life waiting for something to set them off, unless they work especially hard to change. This guy is a liar, and liars are hopeless at change, they just make better excuses.

These trips were for letting off steam, Biloxi-style. It didn't matter what card she turned in a deck, or where a ball in a spinning wheel landed, or whether a machine lit up with running blue, yellow and red lights when she pulled a handle. The point of it all was just for fun, and she wanted some.

Aggie smiled benignly when he made a fuss about getting out of his seat to let her out. She was not going to get personal enough to edge her way out over top of him.

It only took two rows of seats before a woman in a boldly embroidered Mexican blouse reached out. "Aggie! Where were you?"

Aggie reveled in her friends, their jokes, the laughs, looking back now and then to see his sour face in his flopped-over head. He nodded off again, and his head bounced with the bus sway, looking like a bobble-headed imbecile with every bump on the highway.

Back in her seat an hour later, having climbed over the snoring lump in the seat beside her, Aggie was renewed. In creative reverie, she rehearsed her plan as her blue eyes flashed left and right, busy calculating how she would do it.

She thought about money first. The trip was totally paid in advance, room, food, a few drinks, and return bus fare. Some fools paid for luxury extras but she didn't need the "Ritz." The hotel she had chosen was clean and dependable, a good place to sleep, with a solid breakfast and a pool. It would be a quick walk to the casino on the gambling barges to play some slots and pull a few one-armed bandits.

When they arrived at the hotel, she would tell him straight out what she what she wanted. After one night to give him the cold shoulder, he would leave. He would protest, but be long gone before breakfast was over, taking his addiction with him.

Aggie envisioned his bags rolling away down the long, long, hallway, and herself leaning against the inside of the closed door with a satisfied grin.

She would sit by the pool in her new, pink, two-piece bathing suit and gab with her pals, careful to avoid the delicious but deadly rays of the mid-day sun.

In the late afternoon, after the senior's dance, as the sun dipped towards the tops of the swaying palms lining the shore, she would check local advertisements to see where her favorite bands or singers were playing, and pick the clubs with the best dance floor.

Sky blue sweater around her shoulders, matching the color of her eyes, her hand-bag secured in her armpit, she would be free to stride the balmy darkness with a couple of girlfriends, the soft brush of tropical evening caressing her face.

Leading her friends through moonlit seaside walkways, dotted with elegant black lampposts, confidence would shine as her skirt swished when she walked. All she need do was stand outside a club and listen for hot, sweet notes to lure her inside.

She knew most of the circuit groups well and they would call out when she entered, "Aggie!" "Aggie's here!" clang the cymbals, tap a tattoo on the drum, and blow a salute on the horn in the middle of whatever tune they were playing. Just as it had happened before, in Florida, and at home in Ontario, the next song would swing.

Completely relaxed, Aggie would take her time in the washroom to fluff her latest style haircut and perm, or refresh her lipstick, and tighten the straps on her red high-heeled dancing shoes.

She would still be dancing with the best guys in the place when most women had left, or were falling down drunk, giving up their good times, whether it was a dive or a luxury hotel.

At least she knew what she wanted, and how to get it.

The bus shifted and Aggie was jolted back to reality. Her "date" was still sleeping it off.

She wrinkled her nose in disgust. This man beside her chose to be above it all, the flat mirror side of drunk: too cool to participate in the party on the bus but snoring the day away, incapacitated without a drink in his hand. He was holier-than-thou, ready to throw it all away and he did not even know it.

"What happened to Ben," her daughter would ask when Aggie called her from home. "I thought you were getting along fine."

"It seems we weren't suited for each other after all." she would respond. "He drank, see."

A lazy smile pulled up the cheeks of Aggie's tanned face. Yes, she was going to look ahead, not look back.

The black and wildly green printed skirt would be the best choice to wear back to St. Petersburg on the bus. Nice and easy, not tight or tugging anywhere...and that new low-neck pastel sweater, and the soft-orange earrings, too.

Oh, yes! Things were really starting to look up. The ride back would be much more fun.

Fit for a Queen

Florida 2000

Chapter 32

The looming cement mixer ground around and around in a nauseating motion as Aggie's list of "things to do" revolved in her mind.

"Damn traffic!" Aggie exploded.

Her brakes groaned under her crushing stomp and her car stopped a mere six inches from the gyrating cement truck's bumper. She sucked in her breath and expelled it with a grunt.

Her lips churned in a mumble. "I hate being late."

"Don't worry about it, Aggie, who cares if we're a bit late?" Thunder sounded tense, worried, as his head swiveled back and forth, between her and the cement truck that filled the windshield.

Her agitation mounted. "But my cousin..." Aggie mumbled, her voice drifting away to a whisper.

Her rumination continued. "Must get the brakes checked."

Didn't answer the phone when it rang, just when I was leaving the house. An emergency?...whoever calls with an emergency?

I must pick up my cousin at the airport, all the way from Scotland.

The whole world is tilting. That doesn't matter. Check the brakes.

Without the breeze of the car in motion, the April morning sun scorched through the windshield and burned into Aggie's face. She lifted her right hand to her blazing cheek. It was hot, and her forehead too, and her head itched—maybe that was the new perm. The band on her skirt felt too tight and her new red blouse, with the frill down the front, stuck to her chest. She must get the air conditioning fixed, or sell the car.

Aggie drifted into a blissful vision of visiting a car lot and choosing a bright and shining new model, taking her time until the best one revealed itself. Instinct nudged her to alertness then and with great surprise, she realized the truck in front of her was so close it seemed to be backing up.

She yanked the steering wheel to the right, tapped the gas and bounced over roadside pebbles, with a ditch yawning before her that threatened to swallow the car. She tried to jam the brakes but her foot felt nothing, as if the waving world had melted from the heat.

"That's it!" Thunder reached his solid arm towards the dashboard and turned the ignition off, pulled out the keys and safely stashed them in his jacket pocket. He reached over and felt Aggie's blazing forehead—hot, too hot—no wonder she was acting crazy. She was sick, really sick.

He had to get out and flag someone down to get help. His head turned right, and left trying to look around them and figure how best to climb out of the car at this steep angle.

Motorists zoomed past with smug looks like they were glad to be in motion and not stuck in a ditch. They rubbernecked or pointed, except for one woman; she pumped her breaks while her tires screeched to a jolting jackrabbit halt. She called out to them, as irritated drivers behind her leaned on their blaring horns. "Wait, stay in the car!" She had to shout louder over the noise, "I will call an ambulance!"

Thunder nodded and raised his hand in gratitude as the kind woman pulled away into the frustrated traffic, and then turned his attention back to Aggie. She sat with her eyes firmly closed, trying to shake her head. He could not figure out just what was wrong. She sat doubled over and grabbed her stomach as if protecting it from a physical blow, and then vomit flew from her mouth. Helpless, he watched her, feeling inadequate and nauseous himself that he could not help her. All he could think of was to keep her from gagging if she started to do that.

"Missus!" "Missus!" With sweat dripping a track down the front of his uniform, the burly man from the ambulance service reached into the driver's window and smacked the woman's face lightly. There was no response.

The white-haired older man, in the passenger's seat, protested verbally and grabbed for his arm.

"Have to do this. Sorry." The attendant's educated gaze flew around the scene in assessment, calculating risk. Her window was open, no air conditioning running. It was very hot. The man with her was getting red, too. They had been there too long. If she passed out from the heat, that was one thing. There were worse problems than that. He smelled her breath for alcohol—none, just the acrid scent of sour breath and spiking fever. So many possibilities, from heart attack to appendix. No seat belt around her. Concussion was something else altogether.

"Could be head injury, or the Norwalk virus," the second ambulance attendant offered. He leaned out of the driver's window of the ambulance, as if making up his mind if he wanted to touch her or not.

The attendant by the car shot the driver a glare of disgust as he yanked the driver's car door open. "Get out here and help!" he growled.

The harried woman behind the nursing station flicked her tired eyes to the young and eager student nurse running up the hall towards her. The girl waved her hand merrily as if she was at a Fourth of July parade.

The woman glanced at her watch—three o'clock, so much for lunch today.

She stared down the student nurse interrupting her. "What do you mean she has no insurance? What is that in your hand?"

"I checked her wallet. She has the med-card for foreign seniors but no coverage for private. Dr. Freemont ordered isolation. She doesn't have private care."

"That's not our problem. Is there a bed?"

"Yes."

"Then get her in it. It's his problem now."

The air smelled funny. Aggie was cold, but her head was burning. She did not sleep with the air conditioning on because it ran up her electric bill. She was tired and just wanted to sleep, here in her black and quiet room. She bargained with herself. Just a few more minutes rest before she got up and flipped on the coffee maker. The blipping sounds annoyed her. Blip, blip, blip. That was not her coffee maker.

Someone touched her! Was Thunder here? Here in this cold?

Her eyes flew open.

A skinny man stood beside her bed, with his blond hair shaved off and dressed in white from his facemask to his shoes. Aggie blinked. Maybe he was a dream and he would go away.

He spoke loudly, as if she was deaf. "Good morning, Agnes. Intravenous bags hung on a rack, pulled close to her bedside, dripping into the needle in her arm.

"What...where..." She stopped when the man put his hand gently on her, and she stared at his hand on her arm.

"Don't fret. I'll tell the doctor you are awake. Stay put now. If you try to get up too soon you may faint."

A sudden alarm filled her mind; she did not want to be alone.

"I'll be right back."

He was gone.

That seemed to happen several times over that day, or the next, maybe. She was not sure.

Eventually she woke up, her mind clear, baffled but alert. She turned to the window, to a darkening sky, the sunset almost complete. She looked around the hospital room and heard the comforting hustle and bustle in the hallway, muffled voices and clinking trays. Her door swung open to the strange blue-white of hospital lighting. It stung her eyes.

"Well, the doctor ordered that you stay here for a few days until the tests come back. Norwalk flu is floating around, and it is highly contagious. That's why we all wear masks."

Aggie pulled back, raised her hand, trying to protest. "What? What..."

The aide hurried to calm her. "Sorry if that startled you."

Then his voice lowered and he spoke in a soothing manner, as if speaking to a child. "You are getting better. It is time to start eating again."

Had she become simple, too? She was not sure of anything.

"I'm hungry!" She realized this urgency and surprise had raised her voice. She looked at her arm, pleased the needle was gone, and hoisted up to lean on one elbow. Her arm wobbled but she was determined.

The attendant held up his hand in the "wait a minute" gesture and dug around in the drawer of her nightstand, like a dog digging up a bone. He stood up straight with a fistful of restaurant leaflets and beamed with triumph.

"That's right. No more intravenous! Of course, you are hungry! We don't cook here in the hospital any more, too expensive. If you give me your order, I'll have it delivered."

Aggie wondered if she was dreaming. "You mean, you will order whatever I want from the menu?"

"That's it! It saves the hospital lots of money when we feed you this way—much better than running a kitchen. The restaurant has special dishes for us." He handed the menu to Aggie to think about it, and he busied himself rearranging the sheets and making comforting small talk about nothing in particular.

Aggie flopped back on the pillow. Feeling feeble already and only awake for a few minutes, she shook her head, trying to clear her mind to ask anything at all, the skin on her face feeling tight, like a mask. Must concentrate, must order something, something. A low growl rolled up her belly like an angry dog in a big empty kennel. None of it made sense, but she was hungry. Eat meat. She raised the menu for a last look, pointed to a small steak and looked up for approval, wondering what the catch would be. It still sounded like a trick.

The nurse's aid, nodded. "Good choice, good choice."

He paused. His smile faded when he really looked at her unexpected menu choice of a steak. "It might be too early for this. I recommend you get a soup to start, maybe vegetable, to let your digestive system work up to a whole meal. Hmmm?"

Aggie agreed. "But I must have toast!"

"Of course, of course. Maybe you want to order veggies. Which do you like? Mashed potatoes and gravy would be a good start."

That sounded perfect.

The room felt wavy again. She wondered if her children knew where she was. "What's wrong with me?"

The thin man in the facemask turned away. "That's not for me to say. The nurse will be in to talk to you about that. They know you are awake now. The waiter will bring your order. Sleep if you can." He blinked his blue eyes in a friendly fashion and in a few steps he was gone, the door left slightly ajar.

Maybe Thunder could visit her now, and tease her and call her Lightning because she moved so fast. Thunder and Lightning—it always made her laugh.

She drifted off thinking it was lucky she was here because the hospital service was fit for a queen.

That was how it started, anyway.

She sat half the day in some hallway, in a stupid blue gown with the back gaping open, while they were trying to figure it out, dreaming up test after test. Pills, injections, X-rays that turned her body over, and over. Swallow this or that and then blow in a balloon.

Doctor McMillan said it was likely food poisoning and warned her that the U.S. is infamous for adding on useless tests—expensive, too.

"Their health system is nothing like Canada's," he warned her, when she phoned him. "They make their money by keeping you in there as long as possible for the daily charge, and for all the tests."

The American doctor just smiled like a know-it-all

when she told him that, and said nothing, as if Canadian doctors were somehow inferior, and he would not listen.

She wanted to smack him. Finally fed up—she got up, and walked out.

The stunning bill came, eventually.

"What was that all about?" That was the first thing Aggie asked Doctor McMillan, when she started to think it through. No one ever said that her insurance would not cover it, so she sat there day in, day out, test after test, and no one said anything to her.

Aggie threw it in the garbage.

Love Me Tender

2006

Chapter 33

So, who knew there were enough items of Elvis gimcrack to people a small planet? We stood agape, not certain if we were to comment on each piece separately or numbly smile, as we were doing.

"It's stunning, Mom," I murmured, as my eyes surveyed the collection of Elvis paraphernalia everywhere, and then to a figurine on a small stage down on one knee, his head bowed, in a jewel-encrusted white costume, right hand over his heart, singing earnestly into a tiny white microphone.

Aggie flicked it on. The spotlight was really a reading lamp, standing tall on the tidy stage, and the beam of light set the jewels dancing with color. Perfect to read a book in bed, or to turn the light off and slide into sleep pretending Elvis was crooning to you and you alone.

The guests that stayed in this room must be true Elvis fans or have learned to ignore their environment altogether.

"It is a wonder, Mom. How did the love of Elvis start for you?"

Aggie smiled and the look in her eyes held a thousand fond memories. "I heard a voice on the radio one day while I was driving to work, the sweetest voice, speaking directly to me. The man sang "Love me tender, love me true..." and it brought tears to my eyes."

She stopped walking around the room and turned to us, considering what she said, "Isn't that what we all want—true love?"

"Here, here!" I responded, a bit surprised at her seriousness but respecting her life experience. I thought to myself that someday we would really talk about life, about the old days, but today was not the day.

"Every year, Sharon and I, and some others girls too, would drive up to the Elvis festival in Collingwood to see the impersonators." Talking a mile a minute, her blue eyes danced, and a smile teased her lips.

"We would make our plans and go. It was the Elvis impersonators, you know. There was no way we could have gone to a real show. We planned and saved, collected pop bottles, anything for our get-away selfish time, tickets to Elvis."

She swept her arm in a broad circle. "Look what it started! Every one of these is a happy memory!"

"There...the poster of Elvis waving...that was when Rose, and Mary and I drove to the rehearsals. We couldn't afford the tickets but somehow we got in; distracted a guard's attention, or something. What a laugh!"

"Why stay at home and moan? I always hated that, see? Just like when the boys were young and I had no money but carfare. I took them on the streetcar to picnic on the beach of Lake Ontario. It was a long, hot ride but worth it. We could sit on a log, or just sit on the sand. When I had a car, we could get out of town, up to a cottage at Wasaga Beach. Lots of peanut butter sandwiches!"

Ron was just walking into the room at that moment and groaned, "That's right...lots of peanut butter sandwiches!" As number one son, he knew those days well.

He slowly looked around, "After last night's birthday party, you have even more. Thousands of Elvis...soon they will need their own house."

"Well, at eighty, nobody knows what to get me, so they just get me more." Aggie shrugged. "Elvis already has his own room. That's enough."

She stopped her walk around her guest room-picture gallery; pointing at a particular photograph of Davidson's Restaurant not long after it opened.

"The walkway was not redesigned then, as it is now," Aggie said.

Behind the building was just a patch of scrubby earth, where the herb and vegetable gardens would someday bloom in enriched soil. That allowed the restaurant cuisine to be truly organic. In two days, she would be back to work, walking, lifting, and carrying plates and trays, all with a smile, the same way in the same place for twenty-two years.

It was complicated, she told us, what her role really was at the restaurant. A friendly perfectionist, as far as the part-time summer girls were concerned.

"I've done every job there, except for chef. Nothing is as much fun as the old days when I was hostess and waitress, and a friend that knew how to swing a mortgage.

"Dan was the cook and when the business started it was spotty— seasonal back then. I did everything back in those days. Now there are two steady girls besides me in the summer, see, and a temporary girl on a busy weekend, on Saturday night, when the bookings stack up too high. All the girl's want to work at Davidson's now.

"I heard there was a lot of fun going on at the restaurant," I teased.

"Oh yes! We have a lot of laughs. Sometimes the work is hard, but it's all worth it."

There was a picture of the restaurant jammed on a Saturday night, many years ago, as it had been booked solid on this birthday, her 80th. She had not worked, of course.

She booked a huge table for friends and relatives that gathered from both Canadian shores and many places in between. Some came unannounced, surprised her and delighted her. Even her sister Bea had shown up, although she kept to herself sitting outside under the canopy and did not greet her nephews from across the continent.

An avalanche of gifts wrapped in colorful paper, a scarf, a napkin, or even shoved in a card, piled high on the bar, slowly opened later in the evening with a great fuss made over each, and admittedly, mostly Elvis icons.

A local band had played late into the night. Musicians from every genre joining in and all were her friends, paying tribute to their playmate as she danced her heart out on the floor long after the her family gave up and headed for their beds.

In a couple of weeks, when September arrived, the out-of-town restaurant aficionados would begin the trek to city homes. There would be a few more weeks of locals until the season slowed down to the resort-town-in-winter lull. After that, anyone who could escape to the south did so and the restaurant would be quiet for a few weeks. The owner went to South America, or somewhere else in the world, to be with friends, blocked by immigration from coming up to live in Canada.

Aggie would be gone by then, in her cozy home in Florida and the other part of her Elvis collection, and the trail of friends and boyfriends that eagerly awaited her return. She would rejuvenate the skating rink and afternoon dances, because there was no replacement for Aggie; no other generator that held such a dynamic spark, hard to catch, impossible to duplicate, but a vision to watch in her glittering skating costumes on the roller rink that she loved so much.

On the walls were pictures and our eyes followed where she looked. There was her first husband, Hank, and the first two boys when they were small. He called her a romantic, she said, the "World's Oldest Teenager," in love with love, as he had been in love with guns, hunting and intrigue.

Aggie rather liked the title. Hank did not dance, never had, day after day in the pool hall, smoke choking the air, where men full of intensity or bravado gathered in the undercurrents of crime, guns, and gangs. They had the skills to take each other's money back and forth, but flush or broke it seemed like a motionless existence.

She had searched for him there once or twice, amidst the cigarette stink and foul language, but she never heard the real story, she told us, and Hank was closed-lipped about it all.

She heard he had finally settled down and worked a real job to support his second family, and then Hank re-married, again, with wife number three, and she met the woman at our wedding in Vancouver. This wife liked Hank's style of driving around all day or fishing and hunting, bagging deer or small game and making endless deep pots of pasta sauce, but that was not Aggie's idea of a good time.

Aggie paused, thought about it for a moment. "Well, I guess I had enough of that in the hard times, when you didn't ask questions about the meat that ended up at your door."

Her face was firm. It was clear she did not even want to think about it any more and as Aggie preceded us down the stairs to the kitchen, I noticed her hand on the wooden stair rail looked thinner than before, still strong and capable but thin, with veins that showed. It was always a small shock to see signs of aging in her, as if she was naturally exempt.

She opened the fridge door to look inside to evaluate and then wrote a small list of basic items on the notepad. Then she checked the wall calendar.

August, her birthday month, was quickly closing and the autumnal cycle would spin again and the roaring Leo lion would become the expert Virgo packer. She would stuff her car with the jigsaw puzzle of items being transported to her home in Florida and keep track of what will come back to Ontario next spring.

"Soon it will be September," she remarked, as much to herself as to us.

Ron and I were quiet on the drive back to our B&B. We both knew Aggie was deeply into her own life and adventures and her generous nature was common knowledge, liberal with advice and a slice of homemade pie.

We knew Aggie understood value and knew how to stretch a dime into a dollar. Mostly, she knew how to entertain, how to have fun that came from the heart, not from the wallet.

Tomorrow we would drop in to say a quick goodbye

to Aggie, hug her close, but not crowd her, and say, "See you again," but who knows where, who knows when?

'Uh-oh'

2006

Chapter 34
Author's View

My inner voice said, "Uh-oh!" when Aggie's boyfriend confidently burst through the door of her mobile home in Florida. I had seen that sideways look in her eyes before.

Controlled politeness was not the response a guy would have hoped for, but he blithely moseyed into the living room area and plunked down in the lounge chair facing the TV, making himself at home, while she toiled in the steaming kitchen.

Ignorance is bliss, I supposed.

I could feel the irritation rushing through her as she raked the ancient peeler down the carrots with the determination of a gladiator. She chopped their bright orange bodies into bits with surgical precision and plopped them into a pot as the water boiled heartily, sending clouds of steam into the hot, small, and airless kitchen that won the battle with the air conditioning.

"Can I help with anything, Mom?" I volunteered, my armpits dripping sweat from the overheated small kitchen. Without making eye contact Aggie shook her head, no, she did not need help, and opened the oven door with a jerk.

She dipped a large spoon into the delicious smelling

juices surrounding the fattened bird, took a taste, nodded, used it to stir a pot of veggies and then thrust it back into the yawning turkey cavity to press down the dressing to ensure it remained moist.

She could do the cooking blindfolded—on tranquilizers. Cooking was her pride, her claim to fame among the retired American men and women in the park around her one bedroom turquoise winterized trailer, with sunroom and three TV's.

Aggie and Lilly in Florida

The oven door abruptly shut and Aggie looked pointedly into the front room, the passion in her eyes not diminished by holding her tongue. If they were able, her feelings would radiate zingers at the confident lump in the armchair lifting his second drink for a relaxed sip.

I knew her target and it was not her son, my husband Ron. Her children are almost perfect in her eyes; ergo it was her male companion.

What Aggie often told me seemed to be true. Older American men will gladly trade their sacred retirement income for the comfort of a home-cooked meal. Norman Rockwell would have admired the scene of the man sitting, rocking back and forth while the little woman dripped sweat like the bubbling pots, signaling he would soon have traditional Thanksgiving supper.

Aggie was bored with him; he was too old for her, younger in age, certainly, but his zip had faded. Habits and expectations had wormed into his ways and it was going on a year now.

She knew his rhythm, his next footfall, and the next

words he would say. She could predict how he slouched into a chair and groaned when he arose, and knew by heart the escalation of his snoring in the night. Perhaps she felt the choke chain of obligation tighten around her neck; it seemed so from the twitch and jerk of her shoulders.

It was tough to see her so agitated, with no solution to offer. Wisdom was to stand back, relax, and wait. As she was a big girl, with a plan of her own, I did what I could to help with the preparations as the only other woman in the place.

She did not have to say a word to me; we talk plainly to each other in private so I knew her ways—another guy was going down. Ron was oblivious and I was a bystander.

Her son also relaxed, noticed none of her actions nor would he catch subtle clues as the upcoming drama was bound to unfold, so I did not let on anything was amiss.

Ron was not a snoop—his mother's life would unfold in its regular order. The last thing he wanted was to "do something" about his mother's business. Besides, the smell was overwhelmingly good, and there would be homemade pie, a special treat for her eldest son.

Aggie and I wanted Ron to relax. Like his mother, he worked too hard and this was a well-earned holiday.

Relaxed was good, so it was easy for us women to play robot and do the job, make it nice, stir the gravy, wondering what the hell the point of the farce is, but doing it anyway—it's what women do. I set the trailer-sized dining room table and tried to distract her with chatter about this and that.

Aggie, the perfect host, coolly played her part all the way to dessert and beyond, while the unsuspecting man portrayed the ultimate dupe, patted his full stomach and praised the deserving meal.

Bedtime in a trailer is tricky. The owner and consort make their final bathroom visits and nod their way out the door to the comfort of the bedroom, then close their door to the rest of the home. By turning on their TV, they create their own cozy private world.

The snorer, my husband in this case, sleeps in the enclosed, heated sunroom at the side of the trailer by himself.

The daughter-in-law, me, that cannot sleep through snoring, takes the blow-up mattress on the living room floor. Extra-firm, velvet covered, with special fitted sheets and luxurious pillows, it is no penalty. The spacious room, the pastel décor, and the deep pile carpet are charming. A TV is close by, with the remote control securely enclosed in my fist.

The problem began when the late movie was over, the sleeping pill did not kick in, probably due to the evening's tension and sugary pie, and my current book was too boring to inspire concentration. Why an engaging book puts me to sleep, I cannot say. I only know how damned inconvenient it is, but this was only for one night; it was a speed-visit this time.

After about an hour of listening to crickets signaling mating calls, the real fun began.

Mom and her pal discussed something serious.

With no TV noise, Aggie must have thought I was asleep, or perhaps did not care how sound travels in a large tin can in the silence of night. That we could hear every night creature within two miles should have been a clue, but when one is impassioned, as she obviously was, minor details tend to slip by unnoticed.

Her voice started in petulant low tones, almost a gravelly rumble squeezed from Aggie's throat.

"Well, I saw you talking to her," she accused, lowly and harshly, "you slipped down the hall, and she met you by the stairs."

"No, no, it wasn't like that. She followed me. I was going to the toilet. She wanted to know all about Hal, from the Legion dance. You know—whether he works, or owns his own business, or if he owns that big house by the water, where he lives. That kind of stuff."

"That's not what it looked like to me!" Her hackles were definitely up now, and like a train conductor calling stations, she was concise, naming times he was unavailable, her voice quickening and then slowing as if plotting strategy, feeling out which tact would reach her goal fastest, I presumed.

He protested with sincerity and told his side of the story: explained his devotion to her. For over an hour, back and forth, back and forth, the argument rose and fell like slow ocean swells, but no matter what he replied, she always got her way.

Finally, he countered, "Oh, you know I wouldn't want to be with her—not when I have you!"

I knew that was a fatal error the second I heard it.

"No one HAS me!" Aggie flashed. "If you want her, you go get her. NOW!"

He broke down, and he cried, as I lay rock still and looked at the repeating patterns in the acoustic ceiling tiles to pass the time.

She kept it short. She told the bottom line. She had to be free to live her own life; it was her style, her flaw in the mating game. Yet, she was being kind. At ten years her junior, he was simply too old mentally.

Be definite, and be certain they have no illusions, take most of the blame and do not dawdle, have it finished in one go; there should be a manual like that given to all desirable dating women.

He begged while she murmured the same stubborn

mantra, including an increasingly determined, "GO!" Then all was silent except for the sound of a door closing and a car engine rumbling to life nearby.

I rolled over and pretended I was sleeping and sure enough, the connecting door opened. Aggie quietly padded past me to the washroom as I glanced at the clock, 3:30 a.m.

From the look on her face when his car first pulled up outside in the late afternoon, I knew a sword hung over the mantelpiece. I just never suspected that I would have to listen to the slaying.

Oh well. She would be much happier in the morning.

One Life

2007

Chapter 35

Aggie looked at her reflection in the floor-length mirror. Nothing discernable was changed.

Same girl, well not a girl anymore, that was for sure. Standing straight, dressed in young women's clothing, and stylish ruby-red raised platform boots, no one would look at her smart hair cut and bangles and think of her as aged.

Same girl, some would say, who knew her heart beat as strongly, passionately, as her daughter's or granddaughter's.

Who shoveled that quarter mile, winding driveway, buried in snow at the brand new house Lilly's boyfriend built? It wasn't that man shoveling—it was her, Aggie!

Lilly would not have made it up that insanely steep driveway. The boyfriend was down south somewhere, playing golf, and that was why she was here visiting in the first place.

That house was beautiful, though, looking over the rock face of the Canadian Shield and Georgian Bay, the road cut through tall, green, untouched forest, home of bear and cougar, and endless rock.

Lilly should be on title, she warned her daughter. All

the work Lilly put into that house, that property, from the blueprints to designing steel shutters to protect the cathedral ceiling windows from the fierce winter winds that funneled down the bay. It was a crime that man was so selfish.

However, today was not about how she felt about that man, or shoveling snow. It was about the lump in her breast. For the first time in her life, she doubted her courage.

She had seen others go through this, friends and customers that came into Davidson's, and women in her circle of friends in Florida, where her winter home stood waiting, if only she could get there.

It was not just for her that she had to be brave and get through this with flying colors. A lot of women looked up to her example of living free, independent, moving with the stamina of a forty year old, still working and almost eighty.

They admired the woman looking back from the mirror that ran through boyfriends until they no longer amused her, or were starting to take more than they gave.

Aggie kept her house in Barrie ship-shape, too. She amazed everyone. She crammed it all in. Every year she drove to and from Florida, where she played baseball, went to all the dances, and was the queen of the roller rink with her ex-show girl pals.

Now these pals would be watching her closely.

Now she had to be an example of how to do it with grace.

"Relax," Dr. McMillin had told her, as Aggie sat primly in his familiar office, rigid and silent. Her knees and feet together, her hands gripped each other in her lap and it seemed she was, really, not there at all.

It was too early for questions. Her head hurt from

thinking about what he had just said, so she listened, like in a dream, or a movie, emotionally numbed.

She caught her breath, and inhaled deeply.

"Come on, Aggie, we've been through a lot together in, what, fifty years?" Dr. McMillin had tried to sound calm, but she could hear a lump filling his throat, as this was her, Aggie, not a semi-stranger he saw twice a year. "We're partners, right? Right?"

She had nodded her head in automatic response, hearing the echo of words. Some place deep inside her chest felt shattered, yet her heart pounded, the centre of her being counting out her days. She wanted to freeze the moment to stop it, or pretend it never happened. She was strangely mute, her usual flood of questions turned rigid like stone boulders, impossible to move from her throat.

She had to tell her daughter and, once spoken, the words proved the truth of the unchangeable fact in the conversation with Dr. McMillin. The news would spread like wildfire throughout the family, the restaurant, and the network of town gossips.

"Where's Aggie today?"

"She left for Florida."

"No, she's not going, didn't you hear, she has cancer, Big "C", CANCER."'

"Well, she's almost eighty–can't get away Scot-free."

Some old biddies would purse their lips self-righteously, heads tilted together, pass the word through the town, at the dances, or bingos, sitting in the restaurants over multiple cups of tea or coffee: Aggie was not sprinkled with pixie dust after all.

Many eyes would fill with tears, "Oh no! Not Aggie!"

Not their icon! Not their indefatigable girl in shining armor—their modern goddess defying aging and death.

Ironically, her breasts were her claim to fame originally, until the phenomenon of her stamina blew everyone away, and Aggie did not want that boulder to start rolling downhill. Yet, here it was, and like everything else in life, it would gather its own momentum.

"What do we do?" she asked her doctor, filling the void of empty air that had elongated to a point of tension.

"It will require surgery," her doctor answered softly, "possible removal. I am sorry, but it is too soon to tell. We will know more when we get in there."

"When will that be?"

"A few days."

"A few days!?" she squeaked, sitting up straight, eyes wider now. "But I'm leaving for Florida in a week. I need to plan things."

"Sorry, Aggie. Nothing is more important than this. People have to understand—so do you. There will probably be a treatment schedule after that."

She lowered her head thinking, trying to sort through the unbelievable information.

She looked up suddenly, looking her doctor in the eyes. "I want you there with me, in the operating room. If they take my breast I want another one put on right away."

It seemed her trusted old friend could not help himself. He had to smile a little at that.

"Well, it might not work that way, right away, Aggie, but the surgeon will take care of you and so will I. I will be there, with you, no matter what."

He paused, and gave her his no-nonsense serious look. "But, you know, my dear, that's it for the hormones. You need to stop them now. If all goes well you will be on prevention medication, but no hormones."

"Oh, God. Will I get a period? Almost 80 years old with a period?"

"That's hard to say at the moment. There are not a lot of precedents. We'll have to wait and see." He rose from his seat, walked around the desk and gave her a warm man hug, finishing with a pat on the back, for courage, it seemed.

Reaching her car, opening the door to the blast of heat collected from autumn's last scorch of sun and humidity, she knew what she would do—grab life and hold on, take nothing for granted, and not trust anyone but Dr. McMillin. In that, life was business as usual.

Foot touching accelerator, foot touching brake, with no overt attention. See it, do it.

She did what was necessary, as in all of her life.

Nothing had changed, except there was no music in her head. A numbing silence poured into a chasm of the unknown. Plans were ridiculous, regrets meaningless, the thought of not existing unfathomable, blank, numb.

Disoriented, streets did not feel familiar but somehow precious, like in the spring when she got on the highways heading back to Ontario—sad to leave Florida, happy to see her family.

Busy thoughts, a long list of things to do, popped into her head and instantaneously vaporized in the no-space of her mind. She drove straight home.

Yes, Dr. McMillin told her she must stop taking hormones immediately and that was a staggering thought, considering the low level of life-enjoyment she saw in older women around her.

With few exceptions, like a plug pulled at the end of a woman's menstrual years, their interest in an active life seemed to seep away. The women sat like lumps of dough, leaning on tables for support to rise from a chair, and shaking their heads if some guy asked them to dance, as if it was all too much effort.

Her cupboard full of vitamins and her excellent diet

now had to carry her carefully designed extended youth. Maybe she could go back on hormones later, but intuition informed her not to ask her doctor about that now.

Aggie moved towards the kitchen, as if something required her attention, looked at her tidy counter, the neatly folded dishtowels. "Nothing to do here," she mumbled.

Heading pensively to the bedroom, she felt a bit woozy, suddenly exhausted, and without removing her jacket, she lay on the bed and looked at the ceiling.

How could she bear not going to Florida? A winter in Ontario was unthinkable. There may be radiation after the surgery, he told her, or breast replacement. What a horror of a thought that was. Her daughter-in-law had waited almost two years for that, and the recovery was no picnic. How could they make anything look like her?

Oh, oh, but that was a stupid thought; she would be alive. Yes, yes, that was it.

Hormones or no hormones, breast or no breast, with this one life to live, she would spend half of it in her beloved Florida, where nature should have put her in the first place.

Aggie thought she should tell someone, all of her life she had gabbed on the phone, ignored television, lived to communicate, told her story, shared her news, but, not tonight. She did not have the heart for it.

Tomorrow she would ride that rock—that lump—and not crushed by it. As always, she would need to be active, to set an example and be courageous for her daughters and granddaughters, and thereby for herself.

Lovin' USA

2008

Chapter 36
Author's View

Ron and I flew from Vancouver to Toronto, carefree like jubilant children escaped from school, happy to set out on our odyssey of simply being together for twenty-two days.

We spent our first night in a nice hotel near the Toronto airport with a divinely comfortable bed. Snuggled securely in the mound of pillows, entwined in a lover's embrace, it seemed an even better idea to stay nested for an extra hour in the morning.

Aggie met us at the hotel in the morning, ready for travel in smart blue cotton pants and high-heeled boots, plus a late October jacket.

In Aggie's car, our home for a few days, the trunk and backseat were pre-jammed with necessities for her six-month Florida season. A bedside table, a colorful lamp, unmatched suitcases and various sharp objects, squeezed together in the trunk and back seat, with barely enough room for the third person, me. I was not driving so it made sense logically, except for the squishing of my lanky body.

The station wagon was not a good candidate to contain our luggage too, but nonetheless, a shuffle of this box, and that lamp, and "Bob's your uncle", we were in. Slightly behind schedule, we headed for Hamilton, on our way to the U.S. border.

My cousin, and his lovely wife, had arranged to meet us for coffee at a convenient café on the way and this made my heart happy. It had been a long time since we visited them last. My cousin was the closest thing to a brother I had in my youth and his wife is dear to my heart. We are the last in our family, of our generation, and the keepers of our carefree childhood memories.

Hugs and smiles, coffee and chatter kept us busy for over an hour. It could have taken forever and would have been all right with me.

We pulled away from the gas station with good-byes and cheers, heading straight for the U.S. border crossing, not knowing that Aggie marched to the tune of her own drummer's schedule, but we caught on fast. She had learned to ignore her children a long, long time ago.

We drove across the industrial top of the United States, through crowded cities with sky piercing towers, and into countryside. We followed the highway signs to take us from Windsor to Pennsylvania, making time by zooming past the jammed parking lots of mega-malls.

Finally, after passing quaint, historically rich houses in Gettysburg, guidebook in my hand, flashlight held to map in total darkness, we sought a suitable place to sleep. I spotted a sign for the recommended guidebook choice and a skirmish ensued: a debate of cost over comfort, but, nonetheless, we were here now, and the day had been long. An unlit sign at the side of the road pointed up a laneway bordered with a thick evergreen hedge. We had found our chosen motel.

The chorus rang out. "Turn here!" "Turn right again! Now left!—there's the driveway!"

After a night in a decent bed, and a hearty breakfast, we were all eager to hit the road on our first full day.

The area seemed to carry a weight of its own, poignantly laden with history, as the U.S. election could possibly vote in the country's first black president in a couple of days. Once again, the philosophy of the battle at Gettysburg, the epicenter of the Civil War, or the War of Northern Aggression as southerners say, challenged America, this time at the election booth.

A discussion brewed gently until I commented, to no one in particular, about the president-elect. "They forget he's half-white, too, and who cares, anyway? He has eyes, ears, a heart, and walks on two legs. Looks like a man to me."

Aggie took the opportunity to vent her grudge about the black punks living close to her mobile home park that liked to race around at night, radios blaring. "They rev their engines, pedal to the metal, in case someone doesn't think they're dangerous."

I continued regardless, "When I was young in Toronto it was the Italians doing that." At least everyone in the car got a laugh, as I am married to the son of one of those Italian men, Aggie's first husband, Hank.

"First, the museum," I reminded.

Aggie sat stoically in the car playing music tapes for the two hours Ron and I speed-walked through the fascinating, and sometimes horrifying, Gettysburg Museum. The museum of history's truths and brutalities held no allure for Aggie, for her time was ticking on and we were doing nothing to further that.

Like most wars it was a cruel conundrum—everyone suffers in war. There is no universal truth except compassion, I mused; right and wrong equals war.

Filled with early photographs of fashionable women with liveried servants, paintings and memorabilia of romanticized war and slavery, the museum quickly moved from "Gone with the Wind," to graphic and horrifying. I held Ron's hand tightly as we passed displays of people buying and selling other people, and the actual treatment and equipment of torture of these people. I felt faint, nauseated, and I had to leave the area for the sanctuary of the gift shop.

Fussing through the colorful brochures, souvenir books, maps and trinkets that pay the bills of the museum, I bought gifts for the males on my list who seemed eternally fascinated by any war at arm's length, and a t-shirt for me, that I would likely never wear. I spent the money to help support exhibits that told the truth.

My daughter's souvenir was easy: a shot-glass with "Gettysburg" and a Confederate soldier decoration. My son, an amateur historian with a strange emotional tie to that era, would love his book of battles and maps. For my other son, the spiritual peacenik, I would not even mention we had been there.

Aggie sat enthroned in the car, behind the wheel, ready to hit the road the moment we emerged. If her errant children had not gotten the idea that this was going to be a three-day sprint, not a five-day tour, we were at least growing suspicious.

Heading out of the small town, and passing the actual Gettysburg battlefield, now ordinary but left unplanted, a hallowed ground with no extraordinary marker, I sat quietly in the back seat and said an inward prayer for soldiers everywhere, to the peace goddess, whoever she is—she has to be female.

The usual election hullabaloo was indeed in full

swing.

McCain—Obama, McCain—Obama. The opposed party's election signs peppered lawns along the small highways on which we ventured further south. It seemed the road peeled out in an endless stream through fabulous rich communities and desperately poor ones, where unemployed youths lolled on porches to watch cars cruise on by. Hip-hop music blared from boom boxes and young men did not turn to look at the steady traffic.

Opposing views sprang up. I maintained it was hard to scorn someone for not working when there were no available jobs, and in addition, if there were jobs no one would hire these youths to fill them.

Aggie scoffed. "They don't know how to work."

Obviously, some subjects were best to leave unexplored.

By that time another female voice, nicknamed Martha, had invaded the car and the newly installed GPS direction finder's schoolmarm orders conflicted with common sense, sometimes advising the longest road to anywhere.

Ron, as usual, remained introspective.

Aggie felt thrown off her annual route.

Silences were awkward, broken only by Martha.

While the passengers were reasonable, Martha was strident!

We zipped through Washington in a downpour with no time or ambition to see the sights, relieved to have it behind us, but the great culinary quest, was fading like the wisps of early morning dreams. One last hope stirred, surely something that was attainable—seafood from Chesapeake Bay, until Fate's idea of mockery struck.

Idolized Chesapeake Bay dissolved in an end-of-

October deluge. The chill and grey downpour pounded the car roof, lasted the whole day, and came accompanied by the windshield wiper's slap, slap, trying to beat it back.

It felt exactly like British Columbia, and refused to quit until the last southerly bridge to the mainland looped them back onto the shore, finally.

Nestled there, almost under the bridge in falling darkness, brightly lit windows peeked through the gloom and an extremely large sign beside the riverside restaurant advertised fresh catch right out of the bay.

"Look, look! Stop the car!" I cried out. There was a blackened catfish waiting for me—I knew it.

We pulled abruptly into the small, dark restaurant parking area, and sat blinking in the quiet stillness, our minds numbed by the windshield wipers and swish, swish of wet tires on a slick road.

We flexed our fingers, ostensibly lifeless, and a realization hit us all at the same time—we needed the washroom—fast.

Unfolding stiff arms and legs, stifling moans, we climbed out, almost staggering, grabbed our carry-alls, locked the doors and ran towards the best meal yet.

The next day's journey offered patchy sunshine, and to everyone's relief none of us was fond of listening to hollering, preaching, pounding, American radio stations. On the straight-like-an-arrow U.S. highways, we broke up Martha's lack of charm and continual reminders to stay on the same road for hours on end, with comedy tapes. A bit of human hilarity always works well on a road trip and Bill Cosby reset our minds with a good laugh.

The comedy tapes were interspersed with news broadcasts and Aggie's collection of music CD's. Big Band, Old Favorites, soft music, and dance music, many of those sent by her son for Christmas and birthdays, ate up the hours.

Lunch in Charleston, South Carolina, was elegantly perfect, calling for peeling off a couple of layers of blankets and traveler's jackets, and as the sun cracked through the gloom, a stroll through gift shops and outrageously priced antiques, made us visibly relax. We had landed back on a smiling planet Earth.

On our leg-stretching walk around the picturesque shops, we paused to lean on the wrought iron, and stone, sea wall that looked as steadfast and permanent as the sea itself. Ron's camera appeared and we took sweet photos at the glistening water's edge, relaxed faces in the soft breeze. Mesmerized by floating pleasure boats, and loving the slosh of working vessels, we felt at home at last in the warm wetness of the South.

Still, the clock had been ticking and there were miles to burn through and it was time to hit the road.

After turning down low-cost, low-end cabins that resembled shacks straight out of Beverly Hillbilly's, we eventually bedded into the cold, damp sheets of another night's questionable rest. Thrown in for the price was an imperfect breakfast.

Eager to leave, we hit the road early, ready to pound through the miles, closer to our goal.

"Hey, let's stop for a coffee." Aggie suggested.

"Or lunch?" My voice from the backseat threw out the offer as I turned off the cell phone call from my friend in Toronto. It was Bev's nickel. If she wanted to pay, I was glad to talk to her; I would not turn down good company.

A huge sign heralded a shopping and food plaza, good for a quick meal. We pulled off the road and crossed a glassed-in, elevated walkway from the parking lot to reach it.

We checked out the assorted restaurants inside, all fast food but slightly above the usual pit stop fare. It was good to stretch the legs, have a coffee somewhere that was not a moving vehicle, and smile at the slogans on naughty nightshirts.

After our choice of light meal, our trio dallied over trinkets and shoes, but all were carbon copies of items in cheap malls everywhere, so we exited back through the walkway. We looked for Aggie's blue car in the parking lot. We couldn't see it. We went to the spot where the car should be and looked at the empty space. It was gone.

We stared in disbelief, looked at each other, looked around as desperation flooded our faces.

"That's all my summer stuff," Aggie called out, and croaked on "stuff."

Ron's breath caught in his throat as we stood staring at where the car should be and he groaned, "It's been stolen!"

I instinctively felt for my small travel wallet, passport, ID, driver's license and money, my biggest concerns. My cell phone was hooked on the waistband of my pants, with my shirt pulled down over it. Good, they were safe and I would surely notice if anyone made a grab, but everything else was in the car that had been stacked to the rooftop with luggage, clothing, blankets, and half a year's supplies for Florida.

There we were, stranded in the middle of nowhere with no vehicle and nothing but the clothes on our back.

My heart pounded as we walked back to the exit door and I put my hand protectively on Aggie's arm in lame comfort and faint hope. "Is there another parking area?"

"But, I know this is it!" Aggie's frantic eyes were

rounded and flitting from face to face as her cheeks lined with worry.

We looked back and forth at each other, from face to face, hoping for resolution, something obvious we all had missed.

"Our car's been stolen," Aggie said weakly to people coming out of the exit. Some stopped, surprised and sympathetic, but unable to help.

"We have to ask somebody. There must be a management office."

A woman was coming in the door, maybe she knew, and I boldly asked, "Is there another entrance?"

The stout woman in too many sweaters looked us up and down and shrugged. "I always come in this door!" she drawled, then shook her head a couple of times and continued in her hurry to wherever she was going, her belief in tourist stupidity confirmed yet again. We were definitely in the South now.

My head flew around to face Ron and I raised my eyebrows. I was croaking, my eyes squinting at the word—"Police?"

He looked at his mother as she turned bright red with agitation, which was not a good sign.

"I guess it's the police," Ron muttered, punching 9-1-1 and waiting for a connection. An operator answered after an interminable number of beeps and listened patiently to our problem. "Just a moment, sir. I'll connect you."

It was a very long moment, but at last, a police officer came on the line.

"Our car's been stolen," Ron said matter-of-factly.

"Where are you?"

"We don't really know. We're in some kind of highway stop that has a glass walkway over the highway."

"Well," he paused, "We get a lot of calls from that

mall, actually."

Ron looked like his heart fell in his chest and pounded and thrashed like an angry bear trying to escape from a trap while his mother looked faint and my eyes must have reflected my breath-holding graveness.

"First of all," the officer continued, "I need to know if you have checked both parking lots, east and west."

"Both? East? West?" Ron turned around and pointed across the highway, showing Aggie.

"Yes, Sir. There are parking lots in each direction and folks often get confused which one they actually came in. It happens all the time."

"East? West?" Aggie echoed, but Ron was already moving and she followed, running. I hurried behind her as fast as I could, like a flustered duckling trying to catch up to her flock.

We went back through the walkway, past the restaurant, and through another walkway. Aggie thrust the door open and there was her beloved late model Taurus, sitting locked up tight as we left it, waiting for its occupants to return. It felt like finding the "Treasure of the Sierra Madre."

We took a good look at the construction of the travel mall. It was perched over the center of the north-south highway, with entrances off both sides of it, the eastern side for people travelling south and the western side for people going north. The two parking lots looked identical down to the last detail and there were no signs to indicate whether it was the east or west entrance. We had went in one entrance and exited by another. Yes, it could be real confusing for tourists.

Understandably subdued, we headed for Georgia.

Savannah, Georgia's romantic turn-of-the-century architecture, in the heart of the city, demanded appreciation and a stroll. The buildings with white or red brick finishes charmed with black wrought-iron scrollwork on balconies and porches. The windows, most of those bracketed with black or white shutters, were reminiscent of Europe, and every balcony held planters bursting with deep rusty colors of autumn shrubbery, or sat dormant ready for the vivid colors of spring.

The same style of black wrought iron continued on the gates and fences surrounding civic parks with curving walkways beckoning, dwarfed by enormous, deep green, spreading trees. We drove around, looked, and left—we did not tarry.

The warmed air called to Aggie like a homing pigeon, and her right foot was planted firmly on the accelerator with the determination of a conquering hero ready to breach the beaches of Normandy.

Finding Normal

2008

Chapter 37
Author's View

Entering Florida boosted our morale. Finally, we could take a couple of days to view some of the beaches of the Eastern seaboard and dine in the local restaurants recommended by my cousins, and rest. What a glorious word that was to contemplate, rest.

After being satisfied by a seafood dinner and then locating the condominium complex, came a round of hunt-for-the-manager. It was dark, after hours now, and they were not rude, but also not amused.

Once in our suite, eager to watch the water in the moonlight, I stepped out the condo's double-doors to the long, sixth-floor balcony. White steel storm shutters blocked my precious view, but the latch was within reach.

Stretching, grunting at the winter stiffness of the latch, the first gust of wind-eddies tossed my silver-blond hair in swirls, a rough nest around my head, and as soon as the lock released, the incredible weight of heavy steel began to slide irrevocably off the track with a tremendous clatter and knocked me to my knees.

The waterfall of steel kept coming and the weight of it dragged yards of thunderous storm shutters flying off the track. Stunned as the tremendous burden smashed into my arms I called out Ron's name—but it was one request too many for the day.

Gale force winds whipping around his head, Ron's frustrated stare burned a dangerous look towards me, the force searing my mind.

He turned away, grabbed the closest object to stand on and balanced his solid frame precariously on the slippery surface of a white plastic chair shoved against the sixth floor balcony rail.

I gasped in horror at what I caused, my widened eyes flying from Ron's stubborn grimace, to the cement surround of the oval swimming pool far below. My words of anguish tore away into the night, towards the moon reaching full, casting a shimmering pathway on the writhing Atlantic Ocean.

The flimsy chair swayed as Ron reached and pulled at the salt-crusted metal and he slid unsteadily in his stocking feet with his temper on display. He yanked with all his might, his body half over the railing as surreal thoughts raced through my imagination.

Daring fate, so far below—how ugly with his wife and mother here if he fell—how dreadful! I felt vomit rise in my throat with my anxiety and guilt for the release of the latch, in my desire to connect with the sea.

Shudders coursed through my body uncontrollably. I managed to say, "I've never been so afraid for you."

A power to defeat me surged from Ron's steely gaze and he retorted with a sneer, "I don't give a damn!"

Clutching pride, I spun on my heel and left him to it.

My petite mother-in-law stood stock-still beside the eating bar in the condo kitchen, watching, blinking. Her short and perfectly permed hair, her festive blouse and high-heeled sandals fit for a beach party, seemed out of place in the unfolding drama.

I jibed as I passed her, "Not all marriages last, you know. It's been eighteen years!" as if that was a long, long time to last in a relationship with her son.

Eighteen years was as long as any relationship my mother-in-law had managed—longer than anyone in either family had stretched out a marriage, come to think of it. Most of Aggie's had lasted a few years tops, I thought with a toss of my head, and instant regret choked me. I had not intended to be mean. She pushed us to drive on and on, past all reserves of emotion and energy that compacted a five or six-day journey into three days, and she was in the line of fire.

Aggie went to her bedroom on the garden side of the condo and firmly closed the door, as if to say "that's your problem, deal with it."

It is just as well, I thought. Aggie works hard to carve out a life that allows maximum freedom from other people's moods. She had her own problems, and as her daughter-in-law, I knew Aggie was not interested in the squabbles of married relatives.

My emotions flipped like a dolphin doing tricks, and I pondered. Aggie believes in freedom, Elvis, and squeezing every drop of enjoyment she can finagle, from life. A slim, engaging and appealingly dressed eighty-two, that still enjoys sex, she is a goddess in that society, and her only goal is to sprint for St. Petersburg a few miles per hour faster than traffic laws allow.

Once again, Aggie's tremendous fight for what she must have created its own luck, an exotic energy circle that Aggie carries with her, daring the world to throw a circumstance she cannot overcome. We had the "May the force be with you" Aggie, right here in the car, and it was Aggie's car.

She makes the tough decisions, down to the last penny or the last few minutes of time, and could command an army. We would leave in the morning.

After a guilt-ridden phone call to my cousins, and a conference with the condo manager, I sank into two generous pillows and pulled the handcrafted, blue quilt over my legs. The delicate floral decorations throughout the large condo soothed, comforted, and welcomed, like the artist that placed those, the superb wife of my favorite cousin.

I would say no more. I gave in entirely to avoid a wedge between myself and my mother-in-law and worried about my husband, instead.

When I heard the door to the balcony slam shut, I heaved a sigh of relief—Ron was inside. I breathed in and let the breath out slowly, and I took stock. I had my own relationship to deal with. It was too late to take back the impulse on the balcony in the moonlight, or Ron's frustration, born in the fatigue of days of driving and the impossible task of trying to find something decent or natural to eat at the highway truck stops. For Ron, they were smelly pits of unwashed humans rushing for somewhere else and cheap, greasy, excuses for food. It was no wonder Aggie usually took her own food in a cooler.

The bedroom door began to open and I was surprised as Ron entered, thinking the effects of the ruckus might stretch longer, torturously into the next day, or the next. Maybe he just had to get that famous line out—"I don't give a damn!"

"Why did you touch the shutters?" he asked quietly, his face and stance more relaxed now and his blue eyes seeming more concerned for my welfare than in making a point.

"To see the water—and the moonlight," I responded with a helpless shrug, "It's what I do."

"Look," he said, perching on the bed and edging his arm around my shoulder, "I will help you as much as I can, just don't go over my limit. Don't interfere and don't be so afraid."

That went over my limit. "If I ever climb on a plastic chair, on the sixth floor balcony, with socks on, I hope you'll be afraid for me!" But, the maelstrom had passed.

There was only the two of us and his determined mother, whom we both loved, and one more day to go. By tomorrow sunset, we would be on the west coast of Florida in a bungalow on the beach, just the two of us. At least, that is what the rental website assured us.

All forgiven, all forgotten the next morning, a quick breakfast and coffee consumed, finally hard driving through Florida's turnpikes across the bulk of the state, we called out the mile markers, like children on a school bus, "Tampa 40 miles! Tampa 25 miles!"

We stopped only once, pulling off to follow a secondary highway, looking for a store. Aggie wanted a couple of items fresh from a cooler, cream and bread, and passed on her advice. "Don't forget to check the date on the package. These off the road places like to get what they can, you know. Always check the prices that they ring up. You have to watch them, see."

While Aggie picked her purchases from the shelves, I ambled through the two aisles, curious about the pleasant smell of grill-roasted meat coming from the other side of the compact store and stand-up food counter.

Two tall young black men, likely still in their teens from the look of their hip, head-to-toe black baggy clothing, looked everywhere but at me. I felt like a ghost of "Christmas past," barely marking my passage.

Curiosity ruled me, as usual, and I nodded a friendly greeting and headed towards the enticing aromas and noises of metal pans. A menu board hung above a pass-through into the kitchen and just reading the board made me hungry. I wished it were still lunchtime, but there was only cleaning up going on.

The young men were not openly hostile, but wary, as if an alien was nudging them and they were not sure whether to deploy a frozen face or leave. Dressed almost identical, hats on backwards, they faded quickly from my peripheral vision, edging smoothly to stand behind the stacks until I left the area and a younger brother smiled back.

The boy took a keen interest in our little group of three strangers and headed towards the small checkout counter near the entrance.

Curiosity resolved, I headed there, too.

The cashier had the air of a bank teller about her: an organized woman in her thirties, alert and polite, fingers flying on the keyboard of a paper-fed calculator. Her expression pleasant, slightly guarded, slightly amused, she added up our few purchases as the young boy leaned over with his elbow on the counter and watched her hand intently.

My attention drifted, looking out the window as I waited. There were only flat fields in view, acres and acres picked clean in preparation for their chilly season. It is hard for a Northerner to call that "winter" but the fields know the time to rest.

I nodded goodbye, with a smile for the boy.

Backing out of the driveway, it was a shock when the store door flew open and the young boy ran pell-mell towards the car, and it took a moment to realize he waved a plastic bag in his hand.

"Stop!" I shouted, but Aggie slammed the car into first gear and gunned the gas.

"STOP!!" I shouted louder. I reached from the back seat and latched my hand firmly to Aggie's shoulder.

Aggie hit the brakes while I rolled down my window.

"You forgot your bag!" the small boy called to me,

his face creased with concern. I bought something separately, a bag of biscuits for nighttime snacking to ease the path to dreamtime, and had forgotten all about it.

I reached for those out the back window. "Oh, thank you, dear! Very sweet!"

He stood smiling and then slowly stepped back as the car swung around to leave.

I called to him, "I will remember you!"

His smile, from ear to ear, was my high spot of the day.

Like school kids, we sprinted for home before dark.

On October 31st, we pulled into St. Pete's as night fell, just in time for the Hallowe'en dance, and Aggie disembarked right on time.

We piled her essential bags and baggage on the lawn of her Florida mobile home, then hustled into the sunroom, while Aggie chattered joyously through it all. She was absolutely bursting with the excitement of meeting friends, old and new, at tonight's party.

"Don't worry about the rest." She was almost giggling with glee. "I'll get someone to help me later!"

Her voice trilled with excitement as she grabbed a suitcase out of the pile inside and plowed through it for something to wear to the party.

"I'm not sure what I'll wear. I can throw together a pirate costume, there is a nice red, low-cut blouse in my closet, that will do nicely, and I have an eye-patch! Hope I can find it." Naturally, being the belle of the ball wherever she is, her boyfriend options would quickly line up.

"Keep the car." Aggie chirped, waving us away like sending kids out to play. "Keep it for a couple of days. No use paying for another one if I'm not using it. There is the Hallowe'en party tonight and a dinner tomorrow.

Lots of leftovers. I have to get the gasman in for hookups, and then the telephone—I'll see you later in the week."

She had never said Hallowe'en was her goal, but the power of Aggie ensured it happen. Chalk it up to the secret of her success; first get what you want, and then be magnanimous. That last part most people forget once in the driver's seat. Aggie never forgot.

"And," she said, talking faster, "there is a beach party coming up, and baseball starts soon and they need me—their star player!"

The thing is, she explained, that time flew so fast at her age, faster every year, and it seemed she had just arrived and had to leave again!

Lilly and Aggie on Florida Beach

Time did fly by at the seaside beach cottage that held every attraction as advertised. Liberally decorated with oceanic bric-a-brac: Captain's wheel clock, sextant, and seashell salt and pepper, they were a constant reminder of our Florida location. We stood at the sliding patio doors in the living area that opened to miles of soft and sandy Gulf of Mexico beach, spreading as far as the eye could see in either direction.

The calm aqua water lapped the unobstructed shore straight ahead above the sparsely occupied golden sand. Circling white gulls traced lazy patterns on air currents or swiftly dived into the white-tipped surf for tasty prey. Pelicans swooped down to the shallow water in their own quest for food.

The phrases, "Isn't this amazing?" rotated with, "What a nice place," in our conversations.

Warm lazy days blended tranquilly into cool evenings with the vision of the ball of fire sinking slowly below the western horizon. The eternal sight wiped the mind clean with awe.

A large television was a bore with regurgitations of sound bites and endless flashing pictures of the American populace voting in a new idea. This stirring show of possibility for their national psyche, breaking new cultural ground, equalized the noisy game shows, and violent or sappy movies—just like home.

The feminine Moon was now full, and I realized I missed Aggie, the vigorous physicality of her presence, and who knew when we would see her again. In a couple of days, we would be heading south to Key West to continue our holiday. Just the two of us, no pets, no jobs, easy to watch green-blue waves breaking by seaside restaurants and sharing treats from stand-up counters, remembering why we stay together.

An urge to call Aggie, to apologize for interfering in her lemming instinct, settled into me. She had become strong because she had to obey those instincts to survive, and now it was second nature and very useful as the clock ticked her years away, faster and faster.

"I wonder what Mom's doing...," I ventured.

While reaching for the phone—the phone rang. The inter-communication still worked.

"How are you?"

"What have you been doing?"

Simultaneously, we rushed into unnecessary apologies. Aggie had relaxed away from the itchy-scratchy got-to-get-there panic, into her magnanimous parent spirit once she was with her pals, feet firmly planted on her beloved Florida soil and sand between her toes.

Gas, air conditioning, plumbing inspections booked, seasonal cleaning done, her setup for the winter season had been accomplished. Now she wanted to treat us with wonderful fresh oysters, at her favorite waterfront restaurant.

"Pick me up at noon," Aggie said enthusiastically.

She dressed as she always did; smart, colorful, coordinated and the restaurant owner greeted her as an old friend and twenty-year patron. Menus in hand, he led us to the best table, by the large window on the riverside. Although Ron would not touch the tasty creatures, Aggie and I dug them out, slurped, chewed, and swallowed, with gusty sips of white wine.

Lunch is the beginning of playtime for the elderly, Aggie explained to us. Driving Florida streets and busy freeways is safer in the sober sunshine. They hold dances in the afternoon or roller-skate with high-top boots in the arenas peopled with energetic teenagers in the evening hours.

For special nighttime events, the senior with the best night vision is the designated driver. They travel in full cars, or leave the darkness for the careless denizens of the night. "There truly is safety is numbers," Aggie said.

Dropping her at the afternoon dance felt like turning back the clock. The bar/dance club could have been the set for a Bogey movie, dim lights, bar seats full of hopeful men, ceiling fans shaped like palm fronds lazily moving air. Groups of two or three women, plus a few bored couples, occupied small tables while large speakers relayed dance music of sentimental favorites mixed with a little rock'n'roll.

In a black blouse and slightly flared black skirt, cinched at her waist with a blood red belt, and perfect make-up to enhance her features, she walked in like a 1950's movie star and the room was hers. With her intense focus and high-heeled strap shoes, she needed nothing more. Delicate earrings matched the lipstick shade on her smiling mouth, yet there was no artifice, only the skill of the seasoned sophisticate, a socialite entering a Parisian salon.

No wonder the men awaited her return—to liven things up! It was obvious some local and Snow Bird women suddenly looked disheartened, as if wishing they had paid more attention to grooming. Aggie was back and they looked dumpy in uncared for hair. Their men's heads swiveled away from the women's pastel pants, stretched over bottoms that signaled the women (and many of the men) abhorred the word diet. The men looked at Aggie, instead.

To hear her tell it, most of the retiree women in the group never bothered to cook, whereas she could quickly throw a dinner or a pie together. Pastry was her thing. Any fruit could go in a pie—and a man just loved a pie. A man could sweet-talk her into a quick haircut, if he was willing to lift a paintbrush, or a hammer when required.

Her friends greeted her with hugs, enthusiastic "Hi Aggie!" and "Hey! Aggie's back!" They could count on her to stir things up and within a few minutes, she twirled on the dance floor in a quick waltz, her black skirt billowing around her, her head back, her smile wide, entrusting herself to the skill of her partner.

I perched on a bar stool and chatted, hanging around to enjoy the show. It was not a magic trick. The eighty-two year old woman did look like a teenager on the dance floor.

Only I knew that now, today, she was looking for someone, a man she had seen sitting by himself at the end of last season. He was a good-looking man, who had looked around casually, observing the crowd, looked at her, then had danced with a woman, really danced, not just an awkward two-step to keep the ladies happy. Aggie had thought about him all winter, like a schoolgirl, but, no, he was not here.

She raised her eyebrows to me and smiled. I grinned because I knew—the hunt was on.

It was time for her kids to go away, mission accomplished.

BBQ Spaghetti

2008

Chapter 38
Author's View

Still, Aggie explained on the phone, she felt they could not leave without a homemade spaghetti dinner on their last day, before they moved on south for the Florida Keys. That, theoretically, would have been a good move, except it had taken longer than expected for her to hook up the gas, and clean up from tiny wildlife invading her cupboards, and the only means to cook was on the barbecue.

Back for the promised meal, crowded against each other beside the side door of the mobile home, Ron and I nodded in bewildered agreement at whatever she said.

Flushed from rushing back and forth between the patio barbecue and the kitchen, blond curls bobbing, a teeny frilly apron protecting her blouse and mid-calf pants, Aggie stirred the thick red sauce with bits of "mystery meat," as Ron called it, in two small pots over the flames.

We stood, stunned, watching the flames make the tomato sauce splutter, hoping the lava burps would miss our clothing. We hung back cautiously—Aggie was in motion, turning from us back to the barbecue, and turning back again to flash a satisfied smile.

Her hand reached out to adjust the flame as she hurriedly explained, her lively eyes darting from one pot to the other. "The gas man was supposed to come at 9 a.m. so I waited and got busy around here. He didn't come and I had to go to Nadine's, just around the corner, so I left a note to say where I was. He didn't see it and told George, next door, (you know he's such a nice man for one of those, you know, that don't join up with the ladies). Anyway, he said he'd be back at four and that was too late to start. So, I came out here!"

We dutifully followed as she stepped up into the trailer and wound her way down the narrow shotgun hallway, through the living room and into the tiny, perfect, freshly painted black and white kitchen, where puffing clouds of steam arose to the ceiling.

We marched behind her like automatons, but before we got very far we had to press ourselves to the wall as she zipped past us towards the back door once more, and her other pots on the barbeque.

Ron and I shot glances at each other, not knowing whether to stand, sit, run after her or try to help. We tried acting casual, as if this was the normal way to do things, then gave up entirely and squeezed through the limited space into seats behind the dining room table, to safely await the next clue.

A triumphant exclamation trailed back along the corridor with the pungent spaghetti sauce aroma as she headed towards us again, continuing her last thought. "Then the gas man showed up half an hour ago, so I've got it half of the sauce on the stove and half here!"

We looked at each other. Yeah, we knew that now.

Cupboard doors slammed. Water boiled madly. It sent up copious clouds of steam threatening the paste-on border trim encircling the room with its festive

Mexican-styled salt and pepper sets.

"I wonder where I put the pasta," came drifting from the kitchen. "I hope the bugs didn't get into the box."

Ron focused on his mother like a pointer dog spotting prey. I knew he inwardly cringed at the idea of years-old pasta, maybe or maybe not recently infested with small things that crawled during the hot Florida summer, while Aggie was in Ontario.

Out of the hot mist, Aggie's voice rang triumphant. "Here's some pasta and no bugs! Pour the wine, kids, and I'll cook this right up!"

Instantly, Ron arose from his chair, the charging bull look in his eye. "How far is the nearest store?"

"Well, if you want to go," Aggie responded, absent-mindedly shaking the box, her blue eyes round. She looked from the boiling water in the pot, to the pasta, and shrugged—miming that there seemed to be enough for them all.

"There's a 7-11 a block away," she offered as an option, her perfectly drawn on eyebrows furrowed with puzzlement.

Aggie set the box back on the counter with a shrug and reached for her spoon to stir the bubbling sauce.

Ron had the car keys in his hand when he shrugged his jacket on and pushed open the door from the sunroom to the driveway.

Without a backward glance that could evoke a critical comment, Ron left without Martha, and I did not want to interfere, not again, not so soon, on our last night in St. Pete's, and held in a groan trying to escape from my throat. No. Not a Ron-hunt-for-perfection. I wished I could just put my head down on the table's pretty, red cloth and weep.

I glanced furtively at the clock, as it ticked away minute after minute, knowing Ron was tired and hungry, but the 7-11 would never be good enough for him, so the pasta search was on. The tiny, winding streets of the trailer park were a maze that often led to nowhere, circling back on themselves, and looked identical in the dark. He could be anywhere.

The crust hardened on the garlic bread as it cooled on the plate, its biting aroma fading. The salad lost its crunch and shine. The rich tomato sauce in the bowl thickened, darkened, and grew a hardened skin like ice on a pond, trapping the bits of beef.

Conversation spun erratically along, but our female voices carried a worried strain as the clock ticked past fifteen minutes, and then thirty minutes. Old memories, good ones, filled the room with Christmas' past as each woman tried her best to reassure the other that their souls were still in sync. Eventually, at 45 minutes, ignoring the current crises grew impossible. Our eyes darted furtively to our watches as we fought our private anxiety. The park Aggie lived in was well kept, but bordered rougher neighborhoods and the darkened park was a maze, difficult to navigate if you didn't know it well.

I gave in. "I wonder if he has Martha?" Martha, the GPS that had guided them to the park. Martha, that mono-toned integral part of the female trio of voices that had clashed now and then, on the long, long drive from Toronto to the west coast of Florida, sat silent on the coffee table.

"Oh damn! It's here," I cried, holding up the useless GPS unit.

The emotional floodgate exploded.

Alarm flashed through Aggie's eyes. "The streets around here are so confusing—people get lost all the time!" Up she jumped, cheeks flaming, grabbed her car keys, and reached for her coat. "I'll get in my car and search!"

"Oh, no!" I took control. "Then there's two of you lost in the dark!"

I quickly assessed. His cell phone was not on the table, good. Ron must have it with him. Holding up my hand to haul Aggie back from the door if necessary, I grabbed my own cell phone and dialed Ron's cell number on my call list with my thumb.

Relief flooded as he answered. Biting back several possible sardonic greetings, I simply said, "So, you didn't go to 7-ll."

"I went to the Safeway," he replied, "I'm back at the park and I've been driving around and around but these places all look alike."

"Where are you," I asked, then realized he would not be able to read the unlit street signs at night. It was a retirement park with empty streets deserted in the dark.

I changed tactics. "What are you looking at out your front window?" My mind whirled with all the possible kitschy lawn ornaments in the popular community.

"It's a laundry," he said. Energy drained from his voice as he spoke.

I turned my head. "Mom, do you know where the laundry is?" I asked, hoping for a specific answer.

"Well, there are two of them..."

I handed Aggie the phone and let the flood of relief flow through me. I would let them work it out from here.

Slowly exhaling, reaching for a chair behind me, I settled into it. My head weaved tiredly back and forth. My heart rate had calmed its rapid pace as I watched Marvelous Aggie's animated face and curly blonde hair bounce in excitement while jamming her arms into her coat, chattering constantly. Her sea-blue peddle-pusher pants, and petite pastel pink bedroom slippers with the high heels, were somehow perfect for a South Florida, early November night.

"Everyone gets lost out there. Wonder why he didn't go to 7-11? It's only spaghetti! We'll be right back!"

Happy for the call to action, Aggie was gone.

Living Legend: One More Time

August 9, 2011

Chapter 39

"Eighty-five, I can't believe it!"
"I can't believe it!"
The words echoed through the customers sitting at the tables, and rang in her ears until Aggie doubted it herself. She thought of racing to the hectic kitchen to check her driver's license, but that was silly. There was no time to take it all in, not now.

The restaurant filled up fast—deuces and fours—while larger parties passed their time in the lineup. Waiting to be seated they turned towards the large dining room, taking in the ambiance designed with deep blue tablecloths dressed with burnished silverware, all aligned in perfect order, and illuminated by flickering candles.

The clientele leaned in, drawn forward by whiffs of slow-roasted pork with apples, kissed with cinnamon and southern spices, that teased from the ovens. If they preferred, they could choose fresh fish, caught that day, and now sizzling on the grill. All options arrived to the tables with ceremony and accompanied by local organic vegetables and herbs.

The same local apples wafted their heavenly aroma from pies that sat waiting, begging the clientele to leave room for a slice.

Some groups had booked reservations, but others simply came when word spread it was Aggie's birthday. Some were regulars who aged along with Aggie during the twenty-odd years she had been winding herself into their hearts. The difference was they had added canes, walkers, and dressed like their grandparents in long hanging skirts in colors of ten years ago and pants too big for their disappeared bottoms. The younger crowd simply stared, with the imperative of youth, finding it hard to grasp. Sixty years old seemed ancient to them, and eighty-five was beyond comprehension.

Aggie was, and always would be, blond. Her hair, recently cut and styled in the current mode, topped perfectly arched eyebrows, delicately applied cheek glow and freshened lipstick. She wasn't trying to look young. It simply never occurred to her to stop enjoying the richness of light makeup choices, or the enticement of new combinations.

The two, thirty-something, female dinner servers were grinning and catching her eye, nodding at the forming lineup. Like, hey! Look at that!

They were ready to take advantage of the birthday bonanza of happy big spenders. Fresh and crisp, they wore smartly designed royal blue uniform blouses with a slim black, patent leather belt, and long black skirts, slit in the side for evening. Their black patent leather shoes had slight heels, and the effect was elegant, as was the restaurant they represented.

Today, because it was her birthday, one more time, and a special one at that, Aggie had shopped her favorite haunts for sales of quality garments. Her magic timing brought the perfect thing to hand, almost as soon as she reached out, and the featherweight black dress had flowed from the hanger as sweetly as it now flowed close around her body.

The slightly stretchy, no-wrinkle fabric, touched just below her kneecap, and the V-neck showed just as much cleavage as she desired to do, when reaching down across tables. It was a size 6, or 8; she had not checked closely. It looked right when she held it up to her in the store, and fit beautifully now that it was on her body. Crowning her look were long silver earrings, and her shoes were high-heeled turquoise leather with a touch of silver on the strap across the top.

The gorgeous shoes had originally cost $59.00. Then half off, then half off that, and the final cost was $15.00. The dress price had been cut to $9.00, and the slim black belt $5.99. So much elegance for $30.00! She didn't have the heart to tell her customers. Most of them would not be caught dead prowling the sale racks, yet envied her outfits. It was a mystery to Aggie.

Earlier, she called her daughter-in-law, to tell her all about it, and Janice said the prices were so good that it should be called "Aggie-nomics," instead of economics.

Dan and Aggie, hustled back and forth between the door and helping other servers on the floor. The house was filling already.

When Aggie took one patron's order, the woman asked her what all the fuss was about tonight, so Aggie told her, "It's my 85th birthday," and the customer gasped.

"Oh my God!" Her voice was loud enough to raise the roof. "How do you keep your figure?"

There was no time to explain. Aggie thought if the woman watched her work, it should tell her everything she needed to know. She took her order and went to the next table.

It was a poor night for the dishwasher to be late.

She had to chuckle though, running another gift of flowers into the steaming kitchen, looking for something to put them in. It didn't matter how many years you were in business, if someone didn't do their part then the boss would do it for you and tell you about it later.

Dan stacked plates.

His tailored blazer long forgotten, his white shirt sleeves rolled haphazardly to the elbow, he leaned as far from the steamy plates as possible to save his best dress slacks. His face glowed, reddened by heat from quick marching between the kitchen and the door but also from happiness. Ha! What a night!

The other two girls on the floor good-naturedly handled the bulk of the tables, but became confused with all the questions. Their eyes sought hers for confirmation, and Aggie nodded a go-ahead.

"Yes, she is eighty-five," is all they really knew, "and yes, she has been here 26 years," and "yes, she's really nice—smart, too!"

Aggie wanted so much to stop and talk. These customers returned year after year, and some were now good friends. She had been to their weddings and heard their stories of divorce as they sat at the bar commiserating after hours, waiting for her to close up the place.

She had told them about her first husband, Hank, telling the judge in court, "The boys couldn't have a better mother." Then she had ladled out her parental wisdom to help them with their own marriage woes, or children's escapades.

She saw familiar faces from the nights when she and Dan tried to shovel food into grieving patrons to sop up the alcohol they had consumed all over town. They came to Davidson's for sympathy and coffee so they could drive home safely. The roads were dark in this beach area, as soon as one got past the strip.

"They all felt safer now, that's for sure," Aggie often

said. Nice shops had built up around them, and now that Dan was on the town council, they felt they had a voice in the community.

"Eighty-five! What's your secret?" some woman asked, leaning forward over her second dessert, earnestly listening for an answer. Aggie wanted to say—"Don't eat that second piece of pie"—but she did not have the heart for that advice tonight. She must move quickly; it was expected. If she knew one thing to avoid, it was the mood of a crowd without service.

"You are my inspiration to live," one frail woman said from a wheelchair, a delicate floral shawl wrapping her shoulders, and a thankful look flooding her eyes rimmed with dark circles. The woman strained to see her through a film over those eyes, as she placed a bone-whitened thin hand on to Aggie's arm in a surprisingly firm grasp to hold her there, as if Aggie would not dare break the flow between them.

Aggie could not recall a single conversation with the woman, as if her own words could ever be that important. It seemed such a silly thing for the woman to say. She did not know how to respond and stood still a shard of a second, looking into the woman's disturbing eyes, opened her mouth to speak but closed it again while her gaze flew around the room, to the next necessary task.

Nodding with forced sympathy, she muttered, "Oh, now, you just have to keep going, you know." She twisted her hand briskly to slip free of the woman's grasp. There was no time to be ensnared; she had enough of that. Aggie was working. Eighty-five years old, all right, but still working and there was a packed house. No time for talk. She stuck the $12 dollars the woman handed her into her bra, picked up the finished plate and whacked a few crumbs onto the floor with the cloth napkin, avoiding the woman's old black dress.

The patrons were having a party for Aggie, in their eyes so she nodded, and with a pirouette, she was gone.

Even with the smallest section on the floor (just so she would have the tips that a host missed out on), and trying to co-host the door with Dan, she had to get a move on. Smile and keep going back and forth, put down and pick up, table to table, the room packed now—Dan could deal with any newcomers—and across the floor she glided through this extraordinary occasion.

She had no time now to inspect the bright ribbons decorating the gifts and bouquets. She scurried the continuing flow of gorgeous bundles to the kitchen, to toss to the bus boy who had decided to show up, and now helped Aggie look around frantically for more empty counter space to stash the gifts, and for empty containers to get the flowers into water.

"Who is this from? Wow, they're beautiful," the youth exclaimed, and pulled the scarlet blossoms closer to bury his nose deeply into the loose, wide blossoms.

Aggie gulped, hoping the donor names were on the cards because she would never remember.

They flung open all the lower cupboard doors again in search of flower-holding vessels.

"Get down and look under, at the very back," she urged. "I think I remember something else under there."

A muffled grunt of triumph echoed back to her. "I found three more!"

She ran back to her customers. She smiled until her cheeks ached.

A part of Aggie's mind remained aware of red-faced and grinning Dan, scurrying from the kitchen to the line-up that reached outside now, winding down the russet-toned, inlaid stone walkway curving around the large front window. With the door held wide open, welcoming on this balmy August night, he almost hid his angst sorting the reservations from the drop-ins, trying diplomatically to shuffle them to the small tables in the bar without hurting anyone's feelings. The air-conditioning unit struggled to cope with warm lakeside air.

Aggie refocused, her hands busy as always, and it crossed her mind as the lineup trimmed down, that "busy hands" is the real secret to success.

Misty-eyed regular customers simply had to kiss her on the way out, whether in her section or not. One woman pressed something in her hand and when Aggie looked, it was a $20.00 bill for an extra tip. The familiar face leaned in to murmur, nodding towards Dan, "You know, he's so lucky to have you."

Aggie nodded her thanks. The thing was, Aggie knew she was lucky to have Dan, too. She had watched him grow from a young man with a dream, and the beginnings of an organic garden, to a successful and respected business owner. He was her boss, her friend, her comrade-in-arms.

No one seemed to want to leave tonight. Some musician friends were regulars of the restaurant after-closing parties, many being Aggie's birthdays. Tonight there was no room for drums, or a small keyboard, though a lone guitarist strummed softly and, after they ate, faithful patrons sat around in the bar area with the unoccupied musicians, or stood outside under a canopy enjoying the warm August evening. They all came to tell Aggie that she had no idea how she influenced their lives. A living example, someone said, and another person called her a living legend. She heard that a lot lately and it baffled her, but she was happy if she helped anyone on a path to healthier living or gave them hope in some small way.

A bit dazed by the blatant admiration, she nodded, smiled, picked up finished dinner plates, handed out the dessert menu and efficiently moved on.

She felt too bossy sometimes, like a busybody, as she doled out Aggie wisdom and titles for books about healthy diet, vitamins specific for anti-aging, exercises to stay limber, and her breast cancer recovery and determination to regain her health. Many of her audience chose to sit around and turn into dumplings, but if they asked, she told them the truth and they returned for Aggie's smile and advice like lemmings drawn to the sea.

It was a team effort. They also returned for Dan's local organic food and recipes, his kind words late at night when no one else would listen, or the occasional ride home if they had too much to drink and he cordially relieved them of their car keys.

Tonight, both Aggie and Dan were too busy to do more than nod their heads, smile, and keep going.

The buzz in the large room grew louder. No matter how quickly the tables turned over, the line did not diminish and the boss ran now, snapping open a fresh blue cloth as soon as anyone would vacate a table and relocate to the crowded bar, lured by a free glass of wine.

Aggie ran behind him with silverware and menus, as another cascade of laughter trilled through the room and if she dared to stop a moment, someone grabbed her hand, kissed it, and another round of "Happy Birthday to You," threatened to raise the roof.

The cook's laughter rang from the kitchen, caught up in the spirit, echoing the diners, and his hefty baritone voice boomed through the boisterous crowd, "What a place to work!"

Inside Story

2011

Chapter 40

"The story," a police officer will often say, "is different for everyone. If all witnesses give the same statement with the same details, it would be a planned story."

Lilly kept that in mind as she pushed back the errant lock of blond hair that blocked her view of the guest list, and tucked it behind her ear. She was coming to understand that the seating at her daughter Cindy's wedding presented an issue. It was tricky when factions were meeting for the first time in many years.

Her head leaned back on the tall chair, wondering if it really mattered who saw what, or said what, and felt whatever, back in the old days. The only certainty was that each version of the old family stories would be as seen from the speaker's emotional point of view.

True, she had been on the see-saw of those emotions for a long time, but now she hoped that the reception remain civil, for the bride and groom's sake, even though everybody thought they had the inside story.

Her mother was not on the same page as herself. A Grandmother of the Bride should look, what, stately?

Dignified? After hours of shopping, her mother had held out a burgundy prom dress with bare shoulders, the skirt sweeping the floor, and an open-weave matching shawl.

Lilly's eyes had been wide open, staring. "This is a young girl's shop, Mom. Why are we going in here?" The dress showed so much, and maybe that was the point.

"It's a perfect color for late summer. Burgundy is perfect and I like it. It isn't red or anything, a nice autumn color, a perfect choice for me."

There really was too much to do, but Lilly could still hear the tension in her mom's voice when she had told her that Dad was going to be there, too.

"If your father is going, by god, I'll choose what I want. If I'm forced to be around him, I'm going to bring a real man and wear the dress of my choice. A dress I want to wear. That's what counts."

So that was the inside story. Lilly understood now that Aggie had a score to settle.

Lilly's father, her mother's second husband, Jim, had sobered up and finally stayed sober for a long time now, after making Aggie's life hell for twenty years.

During most of that time, her mother dragged him from clinic to clinic looking for the magic bullet for sobriety and, "By all that's holy," Aggie had said holding the burgundy dress high, "I'm determined to look good."

Her mother only saw it one way and Lilly knew that.

In the end, as always, Mom got her way.

Getting busy now, clearing up the kitchen, checking the laundry cycle, and opening a book that she had to read to prepare for a class she was teaching tomorrow, Lilly realized the point was to stop torturing herself because, in the end, it was not her decision to make. That was obvious, so she reminded herself to stop frowning.

Lilly was maturing now, despite the cornflower blue eyes shining in her freckled face that belied the fact that she was the bride's mother, and had a few fine lines to prove it. She was not a girl, but her clear skin shone with youthfulness, probably from the good genes handed to her at birth, and her use of high-quality facial products that she could never talk her mother into trying.

On the wedding day, Lilly was joyful, torn between staring at her daughter, the bride, with satisfaction, and being the charming host trying to double-guess who was comfortable and fed, and who still needed assistance, some of the many duties of mother-of-the-bride.

Laughing to Lilly, at the reception, one busy-body old man said, "You know your Mom—Aggie has to look like a teenager!" echoing just what her daughter had been afraid of with that strapless dress. Lilly wondered if he had too much to drink to say such a thing or if he simply had no social graces. Her mother would never have been so crude, no matter what her opinion. Some people did not know the meaning of manners.

Although the rude man's statement did not strike Lilly as amusing, it was true that the youthful attitude in their family came from her Mom. Her father had aged as most people do from lack of activity, and a spouse that needed extra care. He did his best, she supposed.

He had been sober for many years, but once violence is committed, it carries unforgettable, unforgivable, ugliness. She understood that from her own relationships, but Lilly had no desire to open her memory bank today; the whole issue was behind her. There would be no more drunken men—bottom line.

She had hoped, against hope, that her parents' rocky relationship could remain smooth for just one night.

Irony struck and Lilly marveled. It was remarkable how life could smack you in the face with a wet fish when things are going smoothly.

Comfortable at the reception, Lilly's father laughed about the past and shared stories with the bride's neighbor, who now happened to live in the same small town in which Cindy lived. Ironically, the older man had been a neighbor to Aggie, her ex, and the kids, when Lilly was a small child, when all the ugliness happened on Langside, and he had seen it all.

Lilly and Cindy both noticed and exchanged quizzical looks when the bald man and her paunchy father sat together, not getting any younger, and punched each other in the arm old-man style, barely touching, when they laughed with their heads together and made good-old-days jokes about the drunk years.

Then they slapped the table with glee at the thought of the police breaking up fights as Aggie's "ex" broke up the house.

After racing to the police station to get help, little girl Lilly had sat in the front seat of the cruiser with her wee black cat in her lap while the police dragged her hollering father into another car, in handcuffs, not for the first time...and now the two old geezers sat there and laughed about it. Lilly just wanted to forget.

Aggie steamed at the bad-mannered display. She had heard that Jim usually acted like a recluse, holed up in his house as his religious sisters and silent mother had, and now with his ailing wife. Today he sat there in the brilliant sunshine making light of their years of suffering under his drunk or hung-over dual personality and his reign of terror and violence, laughing with his old neighbor.

Lilly saw it all in the furious look in her mother's eyes and wondered if there would ever be an end to the hostilities. She sighed. Can't people put down the knives for a day? Set aside grievances, vendettas, and celebrate? Apparently not, but must they take every advantage to jab the knife in, again and again?

Her brothers, in from the west for the wedding, glowered at her Dad, and her mother did too. None of them would ever sweep the domination by violence under the carpet; it would never be funny to Aggie.

Lilly's own daughters, including the bride, looked baffled by that display and it was confusing to try to explain the scene. Mostly, she was glad she had been too young to remember much, and Lilly focused on happier sights. She told everyone to put it aside for the sake of the bride and groom. Some listened—some did not.

The bride and bridesmaid's dresses were beautiful, the groomsmen fresh from the barber, and the weather behaved—what a blessing that was—and spirits were high. Even the groom's little children were there, thrilled to have the bride that had lived with them for several years, now to be their official Mom.

It was Aggie's triumphant party, too, and Lilly watched her mother's face, full of joy and pride in the children she raised. One brother had come from Calgary and another from Edmonton. All of her brothers were educated now and into successful lives.

They understood her mother's angst and did not talk to Jim, for fear of punching him out, but they wanted her to have a good time. They stared daggers and let go of it for a day.

Aggie seemed to put it all behind her later in the

evening. At least it sure looked like that when Lilly saw her mother grooving with full vigor on the dance floor. Her mother loosened up with each passing hour and put a couple of generations to shame.

Lilly often thought to write an article entitled, "Why my Rebel Mother is a Hero."

"Oh, I wish you would do that!" her sister-in-law, Janice, in Vancouver concurred when she shared the thought on the phone.

The scale of her mother's behavior would always be tipping back and forth in society's eyes. It is hard to be unique, Lilly thought, and there is always someone quick to judge, according to his or her moral code or life experience.

Simply by being divorced and independent, easy on the eyes and successful, some viewed Lilly with suspicion, as they had viewed her mother before her. They did not know about the years of black under her eyes from lack of sleep and excessive study to get where she was today, and she was not inclined to explain.

The wedding day emotions passed, and a couple of weeks later it was Aggie's birthday, a special one, and Lilly suspected it was her Mom's last summer of working. As always, Aggie kept quiet about it, not wanting to let on that her metabolism was slowing down since cancer, and the banning of her hormone treatment. Nevertheless, she still performed miracles compared to most people of her generation, living the life she invented for herself. She had freedom in all ways, dressed with dignity in town and wore a bikini at the pool. She liked it, her boyfriends liked it, and she did not much care about other opinions.

When the wedding photos came back, Aggie looked

wonderful because, somehow, she understood that the burgundy netting on her dress would pool around her shoulders and create the illusion of a halo of color that flattered her skin. Lilly would never understand how—it had all seemed random when Mom chose it—but her mother had an instinct for that.

"You do look like Aggie, born good-looking, and have her energy," her sister-in-law suggested. "It must be the "Super Woman" genes passed down the line from your mother."

Lilly scoffed, and then agreed later when she looked closely at the wedding pictures. The growing genetic line of mothers and daughters had all looked good that day. She was contented with that.

Making Sense of it All

2011

Chapter 41

Mel visited his Mom, and talked on the phone to his son Christopher, in Edmonton, with a tone of wonder in his voice. "Grandma's out hanging clothes on a line. Her dryer is sitting unused, in the basement."

"It's a nice day," Aggie said.

Aggie settled comfortably on the couch, the old, fading afghan around her legs. She rarely had time to do that. It had been a wild week, starting with her birthday. She had some thinking to do.

The problem had come the following night, out with the boyfriend and her daughter, Lilly, when the private part of her birthday celebration had been a disaster.

She was probably tired, Aggie admitted, but he just did not listen to what she wanted, for her own special birthday. He wanted to do things his way, to surprise her, so they were not booked into the restaurant she had asked for—the one she wanted. It was some place she didn't even like.

Lilly wanted it, the guy wanted it, but Aggie did not want someone else's surprise. She was too old to have her life be about what someone else wanted.

It was, simply, not the gift Aggie had pictured and she had hinted, too, but her boyfriend had not cared enough to listen. She could not figure him out. If he could not afford it, she would never have hinted. What remained if the one she was with did not see her, and did not listen? Might as well be talking to the wall.

Aggie even pointed out the real gem earrings she was wearing, the ones her son in Vancouver bought for her. Ron always bought real gems, she had insisted at the end of that miserable evening, looking at the fakes her boyfriend had given her and she almost threw them at him.

So, she shut up tight. If he had been smart, he would have known that was a bad sign.

"What's for dinner?" he always asked, and "When will you be home from work?" He wanted her to be there all the time, and cook for him, but still wanted her to go to work.

"I'm 85 years old!" She said to a friend who was willing to listen. "Most men would have wanted me to quit. Then he'd give me hell when I got home."

" 'You're so late,' he'd say, complaining, as if I was running around after work. It's late at night and I've worked a full shift on my feet in a restaurant, and then driven home."

Aggie could not tolerate cooking every day. The man was twelve years younger, and waited for her to cook, because a lot of women don't cook, and he loved her meals. What a fuss he made, pouting like a child if she wanted to go out with her girlfriends for dinner.

It was different in Florida, where she did not have a job, but expecting that service here in Ontario was dreaming.

The thing was, he had a perfect setup, with a house in New York State that had a gorgeous pool, as well as a Florida home. She had already been there several times and Lilly had been there, too, and he was good at the handy stuff.

"Both of his own houses are perfectly kept," Aggie said aloud. "What could he care about my money from my summer job?"

She walked a few steps to the sink, plunked down her mug and ran the water for a few seconds to rinse it. Enough energy spent for now, she headed back to listen to the whoosh of her blue couch cushions squished by her body plunking down.

She did not feel the slightest guilt about the scene two nights ago. When she came home, she was so fed up she went right to her room and firmly shut the door without answering his complaints.

He had rambled around, moving this and that, a plate clunked on the counter and then he came up to her door and tenuously called out "Aggie, Aggie, are you awake?"

She did not answer his stupid question and pretended to be asleep when he tenuously opened the door and said her name. She kept her eyes closed in case he had enough nerve to touch her, and mumbled, "Uh, uh, uh," as if he was waking her up.

She rolled over and went to sleep. It was too late for him to be in her life anymore.

In the morning, he was gone, and so was all of his stuff.

He called her the next day with an apologetic tone, but before he could get started, Aggie said, "Dave, you did the best thing. You're just too controlling for me."

Maybe, we're too much alike, flashed through her mind as she spoke to him. We are two self-sufficient people that do what we want to do, when we want to do it.

Aggie had listed several more reasons for ending it and then she told the man, "It's too late."

"I need to have time for myself. Let's leave it at that and not be calling it off and on."

Dave had answered in a rush, "Is there a chance for me?"

Aggie then launched into a speech about how she always did her best, the best for her children, and her grandchildren, and "No," was her answer.

She explained quickly and efficiently that she definitely did not want his control, and "No," she was not looking for anyone to split her focus.

She had no intention to look for someone else at this time. She did not want to be tied-down to anyone. That was the point.

She admitted to herself, with a note of justified cause, that she did rub it in about someone else getting diamonds for her, for her birthday, her special 85th birthday. It was her dear friend, Mary. In some ways, she said, it was the best birthday and worst birthday, ever.

"I just don't care if a man has his own house, or if he can dance, anymore." She told her friend a week later.

"I can't be pushed because my daughter thinks he's the right one for me. She seemed to like him more than I did."

"Maybe she likes the idea of you taking it easier," her friend ventured.

"Well, maybe, but it wasn't going to happen with him. He liked it just the way it was."

"I'm not going to look for a new boyfriend. No one really wants to look after anyone else when it comes right down to it, and if someone does look after me, the price is too high! They expect too much!"

Aggie paused, like she was making a decision on the spot. "I'm going to sell my place in Barrie. It's too big for me."

"The thing is," she explained, "I don't want to do it all again. I don't really care what men want."

"You really want to sell the house?" The friend was surprised at that, the abruptness of it all. "Do you want to think about that a bit?"

"No. It's right," Aggie answered, "I can get good money for this big house now, and buy a small home on the beach at Wasaga, or maybe on Lake Simcoe."

Her friend opined that Aggie had seemed to be very happy when she lived in the beach area, before the bigger house in Barrie.

She agreed. "It was a good life. The profit from the Barrie house will make me enough to take it easy, if I watch my money."

"Not too hard for you...watching your money," her friend agreed.

Aggie snorted, yes, she was surely good at that.

"I just won't settle for half of what I want in a relationship. I'm fine on my own."

She knew couples that had found the perfect person for them, such as her other friend named Mary, in Florida. Mary arrived there broke and unhappy, pulled by the belief that dreams could come true, met the man she would marry and then wanted him so bad. Lucky for her, it wasn't long before he felt that way, too.

"He has a lovely home." Aggie said, "They just put in a new eight thousand dollar pool in the yard, and he insists, 'It's not just mine—it's yours, too.' "

She paused. "That's what I thought I had in Dave," she said, pensively. "He wasn't a bad dancer, either. Not great, but not bad."

Another successful couple, Aggie told her, is her girlfriend who is fifty-nine. She met a man who is seventy-five now and really, rich, and they are very happy together.

"It can happen," Aggie said, "and I can't stay where I

am unhappy, or supposed to be something I am not.

"But, you know," she continued, over the sounds of her rustling her newspaper, folding it up to dump it, "what I really don't understand is how some women make themselves old before their time. They stick with something that isn't working. I think fear does them in. What's there to be afraid about?"

"I have a friend that won't drive her car on the highway. If you don't keep doing something, you'll forget how. I make myself drive down to Toronto every week. I make my friend drive her car to my home, and then we go out from here. They don't have physical problems, you know, they just lost their nerve," Aggie said.

She added, sagely, before she hung up, "You can't bother making sense of it all. You live every day as it comes."

Briskly she climbed the stairs to the guest room—the Elvis Room—the room with the largest closet in the house, and hauled out her suitcases.

Now life made sense. She was free.

She started to pack for Florida.

Everything I Am

2012

Chapter 42
Author's View

Finally, finally, Dan returned my call.

Dan, Aggie's boss for over 25 years, has been Deputy Mayor of Innisfil, Ontario, since November 2010. With a popular restaurant to run, "Davidson's", and political responsibilities, it makes him a hard man to catch.

Writing Aggie's biography, it was my understanding that Dan and Aggie share a close relationship, and my task was to find the flipside of her, the on-the-job working woman seen through the eyes of her boss. In her home, highly organized Aggie's command of her kitchen is well known.

When Dan phoned me, he called Aggie his mentor.

He talked fast while I scribbled down my notes and said freely, "Everything I am, I learned from her. Aggie had input on the whole thing."

"The standards of the business throughout the restaurant are hers," Dan said. "At work, she dresses like a lady and sets a high caliber with her own personal rules. No cursing. Never say, 'not my job.' Show up, or have a legitimate reason why not.

"Aggie always has her eye on the prize," Dan said. "Her mind is like her speech, ten times faster than everyone else's. This motivation for life, this race for time, comes with a great curiosity. If she needs to know, she is not afraid to ask 'what's up?'

"Instead of dwelling in the past, she is more likely to say 'I plan on...,' whatever is next for her. She refuses to accept the past as anyone's excuse for bad behavior."

Dan paused, as if formulating the best words to frame the picture of Aggie. "She does not have time for anger. She would rather do something about a problem, or create something new—like throw a surprise birthday party."

Like the birthday party that all the staff planned, with great food, good drinks, and then the pile of presents. Of course, he could not open Aggie's first. She said he had to open it last, so he figured it was slippers, maybe..."But," Dan added, "with Aggie, you never know."

Dan chortled at the memory.

Aggie, Dan and Partiers

"When I got to her gift, as soon as I loosened the paper, the top popped off. Stuffed tightly inside were blown up condoms of every color that flew all over the room. We laughed so hard and somehow I ended up in her lap, my white socks waving in the air. Of course, someone snapped the picture. It was times like that, that are unforgettable. They make the hard times easier to take."

When he stopped laughing, Dan grew serious.

"There have been good times and tough times. One year, I had no time off. I had not taken a holiday in several years and I needed a break. Aggie was very generous. She told me to go to her place in Florida and do nothing. The chef can handle it at the restaurant, she said, and it worked. Her Florida home is close to my parent's place and I could visit my dad at my leisure. Aggie was at the helm. I did not need to worry."

Dan paused, as if caught up in a memory. "It was a tough time for me during my dad's cancer years, especially in 1997, when I was in Mexico for the winter. I could always call Aggie."

He related another difficult time through the challenges in the early 90's, from the reaction of some people towards his sexual orientation. "We had graffiti spring up on our walls overnight," Dan said, "and our signs had been damaged. Aggie took it in stride. She was there for me, like extended family. I could tell her anything. There was never a problem with my being gay because Aggie has always been ahead of her time."

"Her thinking patterns are forward, open to diversity. That security gave me the courage to follow my yen for politics and the year I became Deputy Mayor, 2010, Aggie would not go home until all the votes were tallied."

"I'm staying until you get in," she said, and she did.

"She looks at sexuality that way," Dan said. "It is a non-issue for her."

Education will help you along, Dan now says, to anyone who objects to his orientation. His customers and friends had no problem, and gradually the town caught up with the times and learned that hiding is out, and Deputy Mayor Dan is in.

Dan was certain; Aggie heralds change in society.

When she reads about a new subject, her first question is, why? Why and how does it work? She attacked the vitamin issue that way. Now she is a living example of the benefits of adding those to her diet.

"Aggie loves her dancing!" Dan laughed. "She says dancing is exercise plus fun! She skates at the roller rinks in Florida and exercise is one of the major keys to keeping her young. Just ask her!"

"Whenever she is away, the restaurant customers want to know when she is coming back. They are interested. They have followed her life, her example, because she is always one beat ahead of everyone else.

Customers pepper her with questions about vitamins, medications, anti-aging, and she gives them hope, makes them feel all is right with the world."

"Now when the restaurant closes in the winter, Aggie is in Florida and I am usually somewhere south."

Dan laughed. "I was in the Amazon last year and tasted everything. I ate crunchy roasted bugs and brought some home to the staff and told them they were nuts!"

As his laughter boomed through the phone, it all became clear: how Dan and Aggie were so suited to work together. They each had the curiosity and spirit of a joker, with no-nonsense goals.

Buying Paradise

July 2012

Chapter 43
Author's View

"You did what?"

Aggie chuckled. "I bought a house, where I always wanted to be, Wasaga Beach. Did you did see the photos I asked Lilly to send you?"

"Yes," I answered her right away. "I like it, too. You sure do work fast."

The three-bedroom beach home showing on my computer screen was impressive. Aggie's keen insight into real estate amazed me. The clean and cared-for house was located on a wide street, and in a seniors section of the relatively new housing development, and winterized. The three-bedroom, roomy home, sat very close to the beach, but not on it, with restaurants and shopping a short walk away.

Spacious inside and outside, a wide deck off the kitchen spread across the back of her home, and beside the deck was a large metal shed for storage. Behind her, and beside her, grew a tall row of stately trees.

Neighbors were not within spitting distance, a common problem in newer developments. Roads were good and the house had its own driveway with a decorative lamp on a standard.

The sandy beach was very close by, but she was not

on it, usually a good thing as sometimes there are problems with young male, summertime yahoos. This section of long Wasaga Beach held nothing to interest them: no bars, no pubs, no junk food, no water sports, only a fine beach for walking.

Most people would scan the real estate market for days, or weeks, to confirm their instinct before making an offer—not Aggie. She had a calculator built into her brain that understand value and knew it would be gone in a flash if she did not act quickly.

The price was right—and one look had sold the deal.

"I'll be flying to see Vincey first, then on to Mel in Edmonton. I should be at your place about July 2. I'll stay a couple of nights and catch the plane home."

"Mom!" I protested, "We're supposed to be checking facts and getting your input on your book. We can't do all of that in two days. Ron will want to show you around, too."

"Oh, yes." Aggie thought about it. "I'll take the train down from Edmonton sooner."

"Save some energy for us," Janice teased her.

"Oh, don't worry about that, dear."

They both laughed. Aggie always had more energy than all her children combined.

"A passenger can get off the train at Abbottsford. There's a train stop there," the railway representative assured Ron.

It sounded like a good idea: no need to drive from Maple Ridge to the downtown Vancouver station in morning rush hour, then turn around and drive back home—a couple of hours, minimum. Getting to the nearby town of Abbottsford for seven a.m. was early enough.

It was a fine day when we headed out to pick her up.

Warmer than most days had been this rain-gorged spring, and while eastern Canada baked in the heat, the Vancouver area did contented sun dances. Weather had not disrupted crops yet and, in fact, they were record heights and even our own gardens needed machetes to trim back the jungle.

My attention flicked from a homemade map to the computer-generated map, but still, all that filled my vision were fields. "I don't see a station."

Ron checked right and left. "I don't either."

"There's a road I'm looking for. Oh, wait, TURN LEFT! Oh, jeeze, we missed it."

After backtracking, we passed endless green fields and long white greenhouses filled with the bright red tomatoes that would soon appear on local tables everywhere in the region. Alas, no train station sign appeared, instead a small road sign indicated a turn over a bumpy railway track.

Where the first reality had been prosperous, the modern technology of mass farming, this place had forgotten roads that had not seen a repair, and stones kicked back against our bumper. Trying to dodge deep ruts for a short distance, looking at a large farmhouse and smaller basic houses scattered here and there with fencing falling down, we saw a startling transition from one side of the tracks to another.

"I guess this was a homestead area," I ventured. "We haven't been off the main roads for a long time." It was quiet so early in the morning, eerie in a way with fog still curled in the fields, and we felt invasive with no one stirring, as if we were trespassing.

Ron was heading straight for a farmhouse when I said, excitedly, "We passed the tracks! We have to stay near them—turn left, now!"

"Is that a road?" Ron was rightfully confused. What asphalt there was, pitted with yawning potholes, threatened to engulf our car. He swerved right, and then left, until the car rode a thin ridge between road and ditch.

"We need to follow it—it's all there is," I said. "It hugs the railway tracks."

Although it seemed impossible, there was no barrier, only their car next to the tracks and an oncoming and speeding train would surely rock our car with its draft.

Reason took hold of me. The track must be unguarded like this through countless miles of open farmland, unusual only to the citified occupants of our car.

"Keep going...," I urged, as we bumped along a short way, and there it was, just one pole with a sign slightly bigger than a street sign, ABBOTSFORD. "That's it, up the little rise to your left. Oh my god, there is someone there. It's Mom! Stop, stop!"

The brakes slammed on.

A big grateful smile lit up Aggie's face and we all hugged, greeted, took a photo to remember the odd experience and bundled into the car, laughing.

While I had visions of western movies, where the great train grinded to a halt to let the perky little lady, Katherine Hepburn, climb down with her baggage, here there was not even a hint of a building—just a patch of asphalt beside the tracks and a pole with a town name on it.

Aggie told them the porter had looked at her, and said, "I hate to leave you here. Do you have a cell phone?"

She confidently told him, "No, no, don't worry, I have a phone and my son said he would come."

Then she told us that concerned faces had looked back at her from the windows and waved goodbye, so she lifted her hand to assure them everything was just fine as the huge train heaved forward and moved on down the tracks.

"The berth was too expensive," she insisted when we asked how she spent the night. "I sat for the entire twenty-four hours in my double seat: good thing I had it to myself."

"I took my own food, so my meals were alright. At night, I folded up this jacket and put it under my head for a pillow. Cute, isn't it—I really love this shade of turquoise."

"Yes," I responded, "I dearly love turquoise, too." I was already shaking my head at my mother-in-law's pluck and I seemed to do that a lot around her, I noticed.

"I hope you were warm enough?"

Aggie shrugged.

"Was there anyone else sleeping in the seats?" I was curious why someone would choose to travel by the slower railway. Perhaps the incredible mountain views was the reason, and perhaps convenience if the airport was hard to access, and maybe the lower price.

"Oh sure, a woman in the seat across from me did the same thing, but she came prepared with a small blanket and pillow. Guess she's done it before."

"Did anyone offer you a blanket, or anything?"

"Their little pillows are too expensive for one night," Aggie declared. "Then I would have to lug it around after that and my suitcase is jammed now."

"They asked me if I wanted anything to drink and I told them, 'Never mind, I'll get a coffee at the station.' Some station," she laughed.

It made good sense from her stalwart point of view, but I could not see myself on that train, "Not for me," I replied, "but maybe on the Orient Express."

Mom talked continuously and was too excited to listen to anyone, her words quickly bursting like bubbles from a glass of champagne, and her children drank them in.

Aggie had come, talked our ears off, and thoroughly enjoyed herself.

We had a surprise for her, too.

While on a cruise a few months before that, I spied a framed picture in the art gallery of Elvis holding a microphone in one hand and singing his heart out. Half bent over, his wide black pants were swinging around his legs as they both rotated. His black hair flopped onto his forehead, and his other arm outstretched as if to embrace his audience.

The black and white photo, nicely framed, had a life-size Betty Boop cartoon beside him, with her classic, startled big eyes, and lips forming o-o-o!

It went up for auction, I bid and won—and Aggie's hoots of laughter when she saw it, was worth it all.

It would be one more item for her incredible Elvis collection and accompaniment for the Betty Boop auto floor mats, personalized with "AGGIE", that we sent to her the year before.

We girls shopped at Sears in Langley, for girly bras with lace where it counted while Ron looked at electronics, and once we were all satisfied, with less money in our wallets, he dropped us at our home and scoured Maple Ridge for the best, fresh, local fruit.

At night, we gabbed girl talk. We spoke of life, history, health and money, and the inevitable subject for women, which is always—children.

"I understood the word joy when the doctor said it was a girl," Aggie said.

I laughed. "Yes, I guess having three boys first would

do that!"

Graciously, Aggie made strawberry pie with berries fresh from local fields, in high excitement, the way she does everything.

On a cool, but spectacular sunny day that showed our city off to the very best, we toured Vancouver and once again, as in years passed, we relaxed on the leisurely drive through the ancient forest of Stanley Park and around the modern flowerbeds bursting with startling color.

Our pleased and peaceful trio dined at the Tea House as the sun settled into the west, and we were, each of us, completely satisfied.

The day before she left, succumbing to heavy hinting, the type you do before the begging starts, Aggie's busy hands flew into action. Tart pans and ingredients haphazardly strewn on the counter, measurements by memory, she baked her son's favorite butter tarts with crispy, flaky crust that tortured us with the scent of baking brown sugar.

The tarts melted in our mouths soon after, crumbling into tasty flakes in the two bites it took rabid devotees hovering over the pans, hot from the oven, to wolf them down like children.

Carefully, Ron counted out the remainder as a hopeful guarantee they would last for a few days.

Amazingly, Aggie flew through the chapters of "Someday House, The Passions of Aggie O'Hara." She speed-reads two newspapers front to back, to stay informed about the local real estate market, some politics, interesting medical and general health reporting, and of course, bargains.

She altered a date or a name, or told fresh anecdotes, but gave the gold seal to the rest. It was a good commendation to our sparse hours on the phone, when I scribbled like mad to capture her moods and memories, her sometimes happy or angry words, words where a note of pain remained.

Aggie being a "grab her as she flies by" kind of person, I had to often act quickly as the recorder of this remarkable woman's song.

We said goodnight on the last day with a tinge of regret, packed her suitcase with care to make sure Elvis and Betty Boop arrived in one piece, and by eight in the morning, she was gone, leaving behind a house filled with echoes.

Ron and I shared an exhausted stupor all weekend after her departure, eyes wide in wonderment—all that in four days. It felt like a closure but was really another chapter in her adventures.

Head bowed over my keyboard, I was glad when Aggie called a week later, full of her comings and goings in her busy life.

"I've been moving loads from Barrie to Wasaga Beach, then I saw a stove in the paper and it sounded like a bargain, if it was true. The old man was so taken with me for some reason, because of my age, I guess, he said, 'Never mind, dear, you just take it away. I would have paid money to haul it, otherwise.' I couldn't believe it—he wouldn't take my money!"

She was so amazed about it all, she told me again.

"He even asked a couple of local guys hanging around to load in on my trailer, so I could take it home. I thought for a minute that there must be something wrong with it, but he had just lost his wife, see, and maybe I reminded him about her. Anyway, he wouldn't take my money and it's the best stove I ever had!"

The next week, I asked Aggie if she had seen Lilly lately. I wondered if she was incredibly busy, as she usually was, following the gene pattern of her always-occupied mother.

"She's been so wonderful. She was here last night and we used the barbecue. She's so busy with teaching and her new courses, always going after more education. I don't know how she has time to sleep!"

As Aggie told me about her full days, I smiled to myself.

She sounded happy, occupied, struggling to find time to accomplish all she wanted to do someday—in her lingo, business as usual. After all, she is only eighty-six and not working at a job for the first time in her life, besides doing everything else.

Mind you, she was talking about being a greeter at Wal-Mart, and what a great fit that would be—she would never run out of words!

Salute From Janice

August 2012

Chapter 44

Walking the perimeter of my summer garden, with my black cat, Sebastian, who thought he was a dog and followed at my heels, I pondered the bold steps my mother-in-law took without a backward glance.

I set my coffee cup down for a moment, beside the stone, garden Buddha with his serene smile, and sat beside him on the small porch of the former child's playhouse, now a spirit house.

Here in my peaceful oasis of green foliage, with yellow wands of blossom and blazing orange lilies in full bloom, the gently waving flowers, bushes and trees, rendered a splendid reward for waiting for them year after year. Maybe in August I could return the favor and find time to hack the weeds.

I carefully carried a bonus in my left hand, a single chocolate left over from the trip to the pier on the shore of Vancouver, by the Five Sails Convention Centre, and I took a tiny bite that coated my taste buds with heaven. That way I could make it last for at least ten minutes, and then I licked the rest off my palm.

Soon, I vowed, the garden would thrive in the new summer heat, completely tamed and watered, and yes, someday there would be a space of time to do that, but not today.

This is the day to conclude the story of my mother-in-law, a salute to the incredible Aggie O'Hara, but between us, there will never be an ending.

Made in the USA
Charleston, SC
14 July 2013